HARQUA HALA LETTERS

The story of Arizona's forgotten 1920's Smithsonian Institution Observatory

By Pieter Burggraaf

Cultural Resources Series

Monograph No. 9

Published by the Arizona State Office of the

Bureau of Land Management
3707 N. 7th. Street
Phoenix, Arizona 85014

May 1996

Contents

List of Photographs

Preface

I have lived in Arizona, in three separate moves, for over thirty years. I was first exposed to Arizona's nature and history in Florence, where I lived as a youngster. I am also an amateur astronomer; my brother-in-law introduced me to the wonders of the night sky when I was a teenager. My interests in Arizona and astronomy fit together nicely with the events that have led to writing this book.

One night, I don't remember the date, while observing the sky out in the desert of the Harquahala Valley west of Phoenix, my observing companion, Mike Toye, casually mentioned that Gary Weisner, a local independent geologist, had told him there was an old observatory on nearby Harquahala Mountain.[1] My first vision was of an abandoned building with a classic white dome that once held a telescope.

I didn't think much more of the site until one day in the summer of 1990, while my wife and I were returning from a trip to Laughlin, Nevada, driving through the Harquahala Valley, I thought I saw a glint of something on top of Harquahala Mountain. I began asking questions.

My first inquiry went to Dr. John McGraw at the University of Arizona's Steward Observatory in Tucson. By letter McGraw told me, "The Harquahala astronomical site was used by the Smithsonian Astrophysical Observatory many years ago, principally as a solar observatory. I'm afraid I know very little about this site, though I have seen pictures of it in books."

McGraw referred my inquiry to Dan Brocious, the public information manager at Fred Lawrence Whipple Observatory, the modern site of the Smithsonian Astrophysical Observatory, south of Tucson. In turn, Brocious referred me to the book *Lighthouse of the Skies*,[2] a comprehensive history of the Smithsonian's efforts to measure the so-called solar constant;[3] here there were the pictures of the "observatory" on Harquahala Mountain, a building quite different from my first vision. The book, however, provided only a few details about this site. I was determined to go there myself.

Gary Weisner told me of the few times he had been to the site and suggested that I call the Bureau of Land Management (BLM) for more information. I dreaded making this call because I thought the BLM was a police department that kept people off government land. I was very wrong; the BLM is doing a good job of managing our "public" land.

---

[1] Today, the adopted spelling is "Harquahala" (one word), the convention used here in the Preface. Back in the 1920s, the accepted spelling was "Harqua Hala" (two words), the convention used in all other chapters.

[2] Bessie Zaban Jones, *Lighthouse of the Skies*, The Smithsonian Astrophysical Observatory: Background and History 1846-1955, Smithsonian Institution, Washington, D.C., 1965.

[3] Discussed in Chapter 1, the solar constant is a measure of the amount of heat the sun sends to the earth

At the BLM's Phoenix District Deer Valley office, Jack Ragsdale put me in touch with Rich Hanson, supervisory outdoor recreation planner of the Lower Gila Resource Area. While Hanson cautioned me that access to the site was via a difficult four-wheel road, he encouraged me to go and faxed a map to me. I was on my way.

Early one Saturday in November 1990, Mike Toye and I left Phoenix for the summit of Harquahala Mountain. It took us two hours to drive to the base of the mountain and then over an hour to go ten miles to the mile-high summit. Only in the last mile or so could we see the odd building prominently placed at the summit of this barren, mile high peak, so typical of the many mountains in the Sonoran Desert.

Up close, the narrow two-story structure was odder still. It was completely covered with corrugated steel, except for a door with bars on the south side. It certainly didn't look like an observatory, instead more like an old barn. Two concrete water tanks, sagging gutters, an empty secondary foundation, the remains of wooden attachments and the building itself gave Mike and me the impression that wind, rain and snow had taken their toll.

A BLM sign at the site identifies this building as a 1920s field station for the Smithsonian Astrophysical Observatory.

That day, in November 1990, was a relatively nice Arizona day, yet at the top of the mountain the wind was miserable. I could only imagine how difficult living on this mountain had been for those who operated the field station. I was determined to find out more about this site.

Back in Phoenix I made an appointment with Cheryl Blanchard, archaeologist, at the BLM. In the late 1970s the BLM stabilized the building on Harquahala Mountain and had it placed on the National Register of Historic Places. To support this effort they had gathered what records they could find and documented the stabilization work with photographs. Blanchard let me sit down in a conference room and pour through the BLM files. In these files I first saw a few period letters and photographs obtained from the Smithsonian Archives. I was beginning to find the level of detail I was looking for about the beginnings of the Harquahala site.

My next inquiry went to the Smithsonian Archives in Washington, DC. They didn't reply for a month, but it was well worth the wait and the real turning point in what was by then a legitimate research project. Archivist William Deiss sent me additional period letters about the Harquahala site, including an unpublished compilation of letters from one observer to his family, and copies of dozens of period photographs. Deiss advised, "There is additional material here, and I think that you should consider coming here to look at it. This material may be too voluminous to photocopy."

What kept me going was the fact that few in Arizona seemed to know about the Harquahala observatory. The few that did, had no idea what it had been used for. I felt I had an opportunity to contribute to written history; my first effort was an essay, written in the fall of 1991 and published in the 1993 spring issue of *The Journal of*

Arizona History. In addition, I presented the essay orally with slides at the 1993 Arizona History Convention in Bullhead City.

In the spring of 1992 I got a call from Jane Pike, an archaeologist at the BLM. Pike was putting together a brochure about the Harquahala site and wanted to look through my records for anything that might help. During our first meeting I casually mentioned that I thought there was more information at the Smithsonian Archives that could lead to a book, but proper evaluation of this material would involve a trip to Washington. To my surprise, Pike mentioned that possibly the BLM would sponsor such a trip. Before I knew it, I signed on with the BLM as a volunteer research assistant. Early in August 1992 I flew to Washington and the Smithsonian Archives, and spent the better part of a week combing through records related to Harquahala Mountain and the Smithsonian Astrophysical Observatory's efforts to measure the solar constant.

Deiss' comment about voluminous records was very accurate. With the help of Susan "Libby" Glenn, I found an almost complete set of letters written between the observers on Harquahala Mountain and administrators at the Smithsonian. I also saw firsthand the sizable collection of remarkable photographs that documented life on Harquahala between 1920 and 1925.

Most of the letters to and from Harquahala were lengthy, five and even seven typewritten pages. A typical letter began with a summary of the scientific work on the mountain during the preceding week, particularly about the tedium of keeping the delicate instruments working. Other than for a scientist in the field of spectrometry, most of what the letters discussed regarding the observatory's instruments and work might as well be Greek.

However, what is very interesting in these letters from Harquahala Mountain is the incredible detail they provide about living on this remote mountain. In almost every letter, after the technical business at hand was discussed, the writer would give a glimpse of the social situation in Wenden, the mental and physical burdens involved with living in such isolation, the insects crawling on the wall of the simple building, and countless other details.

I collated copies of the letters and then read them all – March 7, 1916 through November 24, 1925 – over 1300 pages in 535 letters. They read like a diary, detailing the history of the Harquahala site against the background of the Smithsonian's solar constant research program. I felt as if I was there, back in the 1920s, reading and writing the letters myself. To me it was fascinating reading about science in the early 1900s and Arizona in the 1920s. I felt that if I could condense the letters into book form, others would also find it interesting.

In a nutshell, this is how I have come to put together the pages that follow. My intent is to tell of the lives of the observers on Harquahala Mountain back in the 1920s. While this is not the scientific story of the solar constant measurement effort, which is well documented in *Lighthouse of the Skies*, I have included enough about the scientific work to give the reader a rudimentary understanding of it.

What follows is mainly a compilation of the letters from the observers. While each letter was usually promptly answered by administrators in Washington, I have used the latter only where necessary to keep the story moving. In addition, especially in the early chapters, I have brought in letters from others that significantly add to the story.

To have simply compiled the letters as originally written would have resulted in a tome you would not be inclined to pick up. Instead, I have cut each letter significantly. However, what I have included from each letter is word for word, including some misspelling and dated English usage; I have only had to edit in a few places for clarity. In addition, while the normal procedure is to insert an ellipsis when omitting sections, I decided early in the writing process not to use such marks as they would cover each page. I have also tried to capture the atmosphere of the writing process by presenting typed letters in a typewriter-style font and handwritten letters in script font; further, I have given each letter writer a script font that is as close as possible to the writer's style (and persona).

Pieter Burggraaf
Phoenix, Arizona
March 31, 1995

Introduction

Harqua Hala Letters is a unique story of the lives of about a dozen people associated with making observations of the sun's radiant energy every clear day possible for a period of over five years in the early 1920s. Harqua Hala is an isolated mountain peak in the southern Arizona desert about half way between Wickenburg and Quartzsite, south of U.S. Highway 60. The nearest small hamlet, with a population of some forty souls at the time, was Wenden about fifteen miles distant. This factual story, that reads like a novel, is told by the author through the personal letters written under the most primitive conditions. The reader will get to know and like, or dislike, each one of them personally, and will share their problems and concerns.

One cannot but admire the scientific zeal of the man who spent little actual time on the peak as compared to the others, but was the driving force that inspired the others to endure the hardships and discomforts to get a job done. He was Charles G. Abbot, director of the Astrophysical Observatory, and later, secretary of the Smithsonian Institution of Washington, D.C. His mission was to try to verify the constancy of the energy emitted from the sun, a program his predecessor at the Smithsonian, S. P. Langley, began in 1881. He dealt decisively with the personal problems, the discontent, and even the questioning of the validity of his basic program at the Harqua Hala site by his observers.

The only access to the top of the mountain in those days was a five mile trail up the northwest slope. Radio had not yet been developed, so communication with Wenden was done by heliograph (mirrors) and Morse code. This was time consuming and very unsatisfactory. The one character that provides continuity on the peak was an old prospector by the name of Bill Ellison who lived by a spring, a mile and a half from the top. He had filed several mining claims around the peak; but he readily granted the Institution surface rights to use the land. He, with his burros, was the supply link to the outside world, and often brought the later residents vegetables from his garden or a piece of freshly killed venison for dinner.

It is interesting again to experience the advent of radio broadcasts during the observer's last years on the peak. Attempts to establish communication by way of wireless telephone were never successful. Finally a telephone wire was strung between the peak and Wenden so that daily values of the solar "constant" could be sent to H.H. Clayton, a climatologist and private weather forecaster, for use in short range weather forecasting.

In the Epilogue, the author masterfully puts this project in its perspective. After the abandonment of the Harqua Hala site, determinations of the solar constant by Smithsonian personnel continued for another thirty years at several other sites. The

U.S. Weather Bureau was vitally interested in this question, and as early as 1947, several years before termination of the Smithsonian observations, sponsored another observational approach to measure this constant; first from studies of the reflected light of our sun from the planets Uranus and Neptune, which eliminated the uncertainties of the earth's atmosphere, and as a byproduct, a study of the constancy of solar type stars in general. Much of this work was also done in Arizona, at Lowell Observatory. This 28-year study showed there was no more than two-tenths of one percent variation. With the advent of artificial earth satellites, observation of the sun's radiation outside the atmosphere became a routine procedure. These observations for the past eighteen years, covering more than one full sun spot cycle, show a variation of no more than one-tenth of one percent.

It is a great tribute to these hardy Smithsonian observers who struggled with temperamental, primitive equipment and rugged living conditions on high windy mountain peaks to lay the ground work for what is now an easy routine observation. The effect of this small solar variation on terrestrial weather is still being debated in scientific journals.

Henry L. Giclas
Lowell Observatory
Flagstaff, Arizona
June 14, 1995

Chapter 1

The Legacy

Hired about October 1, 1920, Frederick A. "Keg" Greeley immediately boarded a train west to Wenden, Arizona. He was the new assistant for the Smithsonian Institution Astrophysical Observatory (APO) field station on Mount Harqua Hala, a few miles east of Wenden. Certainly Keg Greeley had some idea about the work ahead of him: His younger brother Paul E. "Peg" Greeley was doing similar work at an APO field station on Mount Montezuma in Chile. And Keg was a cousin to Dr. Charles Greeley Abbot, director of the APO and assistant secretary of the Smithsonian Institution. At the time, the task underway in Arizona and Chile was on the forefront of climatological research.

Harqua Hala Observatory
October 20, 1920

Dear Mother,

    This is the place and you will notice there is smoke coming out of the chimney. We had a windy rain storm up here yesterday, mostly wind for most of the rain fell below us. It was very cold so we had to keep a fire all day and today too. This morning the bushes were plastered with ice and when the sun came out it was a beautiful sight. Wenden and the desert were still covered with clouds and that was beautiful too especially when the sun peeped over Harqua Hala and began to shine on them.

Much love to you both,
Keg

Greeley's first letter to his mother and father in Pelham, New Hampshire, didn't tell of the incredible remoteness of this desert mountain or of the stark facilities at the Harqua Hala field station. Nor in his first weeks there could Greeley foretell how arduous living on this mountain, or how tedious the scientific task, would become.

The extraordinary story of this remote Smithsonian field station began with the scientific vision of Dr. Samuel Pierpont Langley, director of the Allegheny Observatory at Western University of Pennsylvania.[1] He served as observatory director and professor of physics from 1867 to 1887. Langley believed changes in the sun caused "vicissitudes in terrestrial climates." He wanted to measure such solar changes, their causes, their periodicities and effects on earth. His vision was that scientists might eventually "foretell climatic events in a way to be of great value to mankind." He likened this ability to that of Joseph, the ancient prophet in Genesis, who predicted that seven years of famine would follow seven years of plenty.[2]

Scientists dubbed the measure that Langley sought "the solar constant." Of it Langley said, "If the observation of the amount of heat the sun sends the earth is among the most important and difficult in astronomical physics, it may also be termed the fundamental problem of meteorology, nearly all of whose phenomena would become predictable if we knew both the original quantity and kind of this heat; how it affects the constituents of the atmosphere on its passage earthward; how much of it reaches the soil; how, through the aid of the atmosphere, it maintains the surface temperature of this planet; and how in diminished quantity and altered kind it is returned to outer space."[3]

Pursuing his vision, in 1881 Langley led an expedition from Pennsylvania to Lone Pine, California and Mount Whitney – the highest peak in the Sierra Nevada mountains. He wanted a mountain site because he believed that solar-constant measurement accuracy depended on reducing absorption of the sun's energy by the earth's atmosphere. After his expedition, Langley published the value he determined for the solar constant, yet, at the turn of the 20th century, scientists still debated the various published values.[4]

Langley left Allegheny Observatory in 1887 to become the third secretary of the Smithsonian Institution in Washington, D.C. There, in 1902, he established the APO. Part of the APO's charter was to continue solar constant measurements.

Charles Abbot picked up Langley's vision of a useful solar constant, eventually pursing this knowledge more passionately than his mentor. Abbot was born in Wilton, New Hampshire, in 1872, attended high school there and Phillips Academy in

---

[1] Western University is now the University of Pittsburgh.

[2] Charles Greeley Abbot, *The Sun and the Welfare of Man*, Smithsonian Scientific Series, Vol. 2, 1934, p. 4.

[3] *Ibid.*, pp. 10-11.

[4] Langley's solar constant was 3 cal/cm²/min. In 1901 solar constant values ranged from Pouillet's 1.76 cal/cm²/min to Angstrom's 4.0 cal/cm²/min.

Andover, Massachusetts, for one year before entering Massachusetts Institute of Technology where he earned academic honors in physics. In 1895, after completing his first year of graduate study, he began working for the Smithsonian APO. Abbot quickly established himself as Langley's protégé and, in 1906, became APO director just before Langley retired.[5]

When Langley retired, the Smithsonian board elected Dr. Charles Doolittle Walcott the fourth secretary of the institution; although a preeminent paleontologist, Walcott continued to support the APO's effort to determine the solar constant.

From 1902 to 1905 APO observers made many solar-constant measurements at the Smithsonian. Interestingly, by 1904 this work led to the premature conclusion that the sun was a variable star – a star with dramatically changing physical properties.

Another conclusion during this period was that Washington, D.C. was not a good observing location. Writing in later years Abbot said, "Dr. Langley recollected the wonderfully clear sky of the California mountains and knew that nothing satisfactory could be done within the bounds of a smoky and dusty sea-level city." The search was on for better a location.[6]

In 1905 Abbot accepted the invitation of astronomer George Ellery Hale to use the grounds of the Carnegie Institution's solar observatory that Hale had established in 1904 on Mount Wilson, northeast of Los Angeles.[7] On Mount Wilson, Abbot made solar-constant measurements in summer and autumn from 1905 to 1920, except 1907.[8] He compared these data with other measurements made at Mount Whitney in 1909-10, at Bassour, Algeria, 50 miles south of Algiers in 1911-12, and from a Weather Bureau balloon launched from Omaha, Nebraska, in 1914.

Slowly, Abbot received recognition from the scientific community for the Smithsonian's solar-constant work, and the Smithsonian regents endorsed continued study.

---

[5] Despite his passion for solar constant research, today Langley is better known for his pilotless airplane that flew in 1896, seven years before the Wright brothers.

[6] Abbot, *The Sun*, p. 20.

[7] Hale built his now renowned 100-inch telescope on Mt. Wilson in 1918.

[8] Publication of the non-periodic APO annals kept him in Washington.

1331 Connecticut Avenue
Washington, D.C.

March 17, 1916

Dear Secretary Walcott:

Dr. Abbot's researches have shown that atmospheric conditions profoundly affect the amount of heat received from the sun and it is important that the solar constant for each day should be determined as accurately as possible so that the relation between the amount of solar energy reaching the outer limits of the atmosphere should be ascertained and compared with the amount of heat actually received by the earth's surface. The connection between solar variations and changes going on in the earth's atmosphere are so well worthy of investigation as to warrant, I think, the proposed allotments. I quite approve of your recommendation to allot $5000 a year for three years from the Hodgkins Fund for the establishment and expenses of the proposed station in South America for that period.

Yours sincerely,

Alexander Graham Bell [9]

Describing his need for a good, permanent observing location that he proposed for South America, Abbot recalled in his 1934 book, *The Sun and The Welfare of Man*, "We desired to establish a solar-radiation station at which measurements could be made daily, as far as possible, at all seasons. It was known that great interruptions of continuity would occur in the winter months at Mount Wilson."[10]

Even from May through November when APO observers used the expeditionary station on Mount Wilson, the average of good observing days was only eighteen per month. Abbot recalled, "Mount Wilson atmospheric conditions had proved unsuitable, and seemed steadily deteriorating for these exacting purposes, as Los Angeles and neighboring towns expanded. Every day, towards mid-forenoon, the sea breeze rises there, and brings a haze over the mountains which is aggravated by the smoke and dust of the business of this immense population lying between the mountains and the Pacific."[11]

---

[9] Then seventy-five years old, Bell was a regent of the Smithsonian until his death in 1922.

[10] Abbot, *The Sun* . . . , p. 62.

[11] *Ibid., p.68.*

Actually, Abbot believed he needed two stations, at widely different locations in the most cloudless regions of the world, to confirm observed fluctuations in the solar-constant and to ensure that observations could be made virtually every day. With the original set of solar-constant measuring equipment still at Mount Wilson, he had another "outfit of apparatus" built at the Smithsonian by Andrew Kramer, the APO's instrument maker. This equipment was ready in April 1917, just when the United States entered World War I. The uncertainties of the world situation deterred Abbot from his first-choice site in South America. Instead, he tentatively selected Mount Hump, North Carolina. There, APO observers made solar-constant measurements from June 1917 to March 1918, but the results were unsatisfactory because of the high humidity in southeastern United States.

Finally, in June of 1918, Abbot had the Mount Hump outfit transferred to Chile. He said, "By the excellent advice of Dr. Walter Knoche, formerly in charge of the meteorological service of Chile, we chose the region of the Chilean city of Calama as the most favorable, one not likely to be involved in the operations of war."[12]

The first year of observing at Calama proved this site to be the best yet; seventy-five percent of days there were suitable for observing. Increasingly, the data gathered appeared to support an ability to forecast weather. Several meteorologists were studying the effects of solar radiation variations on the world's weather. Most notably, American meteorologist Henry Helm Clayton, working for the Argentinean Weather Bureau, was using reported observations, made daily at Calama and telegraphed to him, for officially forecasting the weather of Argentina. At the time, Clayton reported, "For nearly a year numerical and graphical analyses have been made of the solar variations and of the variations of temperature at twenty selected stations well distributed over Argentina, Chile and Brazil. This analysis shows that each variation in solar radiation has been followed by similar variation of temperature in South America, with a few exceptions which may easily have resulted from errors in the measurements of solar radiation. The results of these researchers have led me to believe that the existing abnormal changes which we call weather have their origin chiefly, if not entirely, in the variation of solar radiation."[13]

In the fall of 1919, Abbot continued to pursue approval and funding for a second station, one to replace the temporary use of Mount Wilson. In a written proposal to Smithsonian Secretary Walcott, he explained, "Though suspected since 1903 and proved since 1913, the variations of the sun are not yet adequately measured. The variations of the sun are of two kinds, first, those which run their course over a period of several years, often in attendance on the periodicity of sunspots, and, second, those which run their course in a few days or weeks. The study of these latter is the object

[12] *Ibid., p. 62.*
[13] From a published paper referred to in Abbot's October 8, 1919, proposal to Walcott for an additional field station; the journal of publication is unknown.

for which the observatory is desired. The range of the variations of the sun frequently reaches three or even five percent within a single fortnight. The maximum range hitherto observed since the year 1902 is twelve percent. Knowledge of the matter sufficiently complete for general forecasting requires better data. Daily observations of the radiation of the sun must be secured at sufficient stations to get good mean values for each individual day. For we must assure ourselves that these data are accurate to a small fraction of 1 percent. There is no hope of this without more observatories. The station in South America will be continued. A station in Egypt is proposed, also one in Australia, but these are as yet uncertain."

SMITHSONIAN INSTITUTION
Washington, U.S.A.

October 8, 1919

Dear Doctor Walcott:

I enclose herewith a copy of a proposal in regard to a new observing station as a branch of the Astrophysical Observatory, to be located near Bagdad, California, for the purpose of studying the variations of the sun and their effects on the weather. As I wrote you some time ago, the Weather Bureau has been making some reconnaissances in the general neighborhood, including the states of Nevada, California and Arizona, and it seems definitely established that such a station should be situated on an isolated mountain within a hundred miles of Bagdad, California, which is by all means the most cloudless region in the United States.

The Weather Bureau will probably undertake detailed observations of the cloudiness for a period of a year or more at several of the most promising stations, so that by the time a year has elapsed we shall be in a position to know where to choose our place.

It seems to me that if possible an effort should be made to induce Congress to appropriate $25,000 to be made available July 1, 1920, in order that the site might be procured, the road to it arranged, building erected and necessary equipment purchased, with a view to occupying the site in 1921. It will not be necessary to use a staff of more than three persons in order to carry on the work and to be in position to furnish telegraphic reports

daily of the variations of the sun for such purposes of
forecasting or otherwise as the Weather Bureau and others interested may desire. This may be done, I am sure at
the cost of $8000 a year.

Very truly yours,

C. G. Abbot
Assistant Secretary

Despite Abbot's intentions to expand the APO's solar-constant program, the Smithsonian did not have available funds. Until 1920, much of the support had been coming
from a bequest to the Smithsonian from Thomas Hodgkins,[14] but this fund could not
support expansion of the program. Abbot's only recourse was a direct request to Congress supported by some lobbying from the scientific community.

The University of Chicago
Yerkes Observatory
Williams Bay, Wis.

October 14, 1919

Honorable Charles D. Walcott
Secretary of the Smithsonian

My dear Dr. Walcott:
        I am very glad to learn that a plan has been proposed
for the establishment of a station at the cloudless point
of Bagdad, California, for continuing the invaluable
researches of the Smithsonian Astrophysical Observatory
on the changes in the radiation of the sun. In my opinion
there is not a more important study being made in astronomical science, reckoned by its possible benefit to the
human race.
        If the committee having charge of the mining inter-
ests of the country was approached for a small
appropriation to study methods by which variations of
from five to ten per cent in the production of coal could
be brought about, it cannot be imagined that there would
be any hesitation in making the necessary appropriations

---

[14] A reclusive English eccentric resident in the United States who supported the study of the influence of the atmosphere on the well-being of
humanity

and initiating the researches at the earliest possible
moment. The argument is only stronger when we consider
that the sunshine is free for all, shining alike on the
just and the unjust, that it cannot be exploited for the
benefit of any particular group of promoters. This very
fact that such researches cannot be capitalized for the
benefit of special interests makes it a reason why the
support of Congress, the guardian of the interests of the
whole people, must be asked.

Very truly yours,

Edwin B. Frost
Director of Yerkes Observatory

The Smithsonian's solar constant program received other endorsements, including one
from George Hale at Mount Wilson and from William Wallace Campbell, director of
Lick Observatory. However, even with the compassionate appeal from Frost, Abbot's
request for a $25,000 Congressional appropriation failed.

Chapter 2

Finding a Mountain

Although the funds needed to expand the APO solar constant program were not in sight, Abbot confidently continued his search for a location in the United States to replace the unsuitable Mount Wilson. He informed Charles Frederick Marvin, chief of the United States Weather Bureau, that the desired qualities were cloudlessness, uniformity of sky, elevation above the surrounding country to avoid the dust of the plains, and an isolated but accessible and habitable mountain site.

Marvin ordered a special research effort to find such a site. At first, Edgar H. Fletcher, assistant observer at the weather bureau office in Phoenix, Arizona, made two journeys to prospect for suitable mountains. After surveying the deserts of the Southwest, Fletcher recommended Table Top Mountain twenty-five miles south and Montezuma Peak fifteen miles northwest of Maricopa, Arizona; Black Peak near Ajo, Arizona; two peaks in the Mohawk Mountains between Gila Bend and Yuma, Arizona; the Chocolate Mountains thirty miles north of Yuma; San Jacinto Peak near Idyllwild, California; the Calico Mountains ten miles north of Daggett, California; Old Dads Mountain fifteen miles northeast of Bagdad, California; Sugar-Loaf Peaks in the San Bernardino Mountains near Barnwell, California; Kessler Peak five miles north of Cima, California; Crescent Peak twenty-five miles northeast of Cima near Crescent, Nevada; and Mount Harqua Hala seventy miles northwest of Phoenix near Wenden.

From this preliminary list, Marvin recommended the mountains near Cima,[15] Bagdad[16] and Wenden for further evaluation; he thought these sites were the most accessible. Marvin contracted local residents to make daily observations of the amount and kinds of clouds, direction and velocity of the wind, and the visibility at seven and nine o'clock in the morning, noon, and three and five o'clock in the afternoon. These special observers began recording data in December, 1919, with the objective of continuing for one year.[17]

---

[15] Between Barstow, Calif. and Las Vegas, Nev.
[16] Between Barstow and Needles, Calif.
[17] C.G. Abbot, "Values of the Solar Constant, 1920-1923," *Monthly Weather Review*, February 1922, p. 71.

With the site selection process underway, Abbot also found the much needed financing, at least enough to get started; John Augustus Roebling of Bernardsville, New Jersey, came to the rescue. He was a son in the Roebling bridge-building family[18] and chief heir to the fortune earned by the Roebling Iron Works of Trenton, New Jersey. After a brief period with the family firm, Roebling devoted himself and his inheritance to his own private chemical research and to worthwhile efforts of others. Hoping for a modest gift of $5000, Abbot first met with Roebling at the Plaza Hotel in New York City on May 15, 1920. To his surprise he came away with $8000 and later, on June 3rd, received $3000 more.

With Roebling's financial support and approval, Abbot first moved the station in Calama, Chile, to a more remote location, "about 2500 feet higher and about six miles away," in the Chilean mountains near Montezuma.[19] Although the observing conditions in Calama were acceptable, at times drifting smoke from a mine at nearby Chuqui, and from the residents of Calama burning their trash, interfered with observing the sun. Abbot planned to use the remaining funds to establish his new field station in the United States and to help keep both stations running.

Anxious, in hindsight perhaps prematurely so, to begin the second permanent field station by June 1920, Abbot believed data collected at Cima, Bagdad and Wenden were showing that Mount Harqua Hala near Wenden was going to be the winning site. Reportedly, on almost 60 percent of the days at Wenden the sky did not exceed 10 percent cloudy in the morning hours. Considering information from Fletcher's field reports, and other weather bureau data that showed Yuma and Needles, California, had slightly better skies, Abbot also favored the Wenden location because "the prevalence of dwarfed vegetation in the desert and upon Mount Harqua Hala would tend to keep down dust." In addition, the mile-high altitude of this mountain was 3700 feet above the surrounding countryside.[20]

Abbot first inspected the Harqua Hala site the summer of 1920, stopping in Wenden on his way by train from Washington, D.C., to Mt. Wilson.

Wenden, Arizona
June 24, 1920

Dear Dr. Walcott,
I reached here Monday afternoon June 21 at about four o'clock. The people here are very friendly and interested in the projected observatory on the mountain. I went up there on

---

[18] Builders of the Brooklyn Bridge.
[19] The new Chilean station was in operation by August 3, 1920; Abbot suggested naming the field station "Roebling," but the station director later selected the regional name "Montezuma."
[20] Abbot, "Values ...," p. 72.

Tuesday with Richard Bunker, a late soldier, whose mother is renting me a room. There are not more than thirty houses in Wenden and three general stores. The Bunkers, who keep one store, are putting up a concrete hotel of about twenty-five rooms. The contractor, Mr. Turner, will bid on my job.[21]

The mountain is a good way from Wenden, but can be reached by auto in about an hour or less. The trail is an excellent one, five miles long. There is a fine spring half way up. We walked up in three hours.[22] The top is quite flat with many rocks, but much green stuff growing though no trees. I'm very favorably impressed by it as an observatory site.

Please inquire immediately of the proper bureau, or even the state government of Arizona if necessary, and get definite authorization reserving to us the right to use permanently for observing purposes any ground lying within 300 feet of the summit point of the great Harqua Hala Mountain, where is now placed a wooden pyramid, and where heliograph stations have hitherto been located from time to time by the Government.[23] I think it very necessary to get this authorization definitely and especially, for all of these mountains are being prospected continually for gold and copper, and someone might wish to locate one on our very spot just to hold us up for money.

I have drawn up sketches and specifications and Mr. Turner and a Mr. Banks will offer bids tomorrow. I hope to go on to Mt. Wilson before the end of the week.

It has run to 105° in the shade every day here, but does not seem more than ordinarily hot. One drinks gallons of water. I could have observed every day so far although they all say it is

---

[21] In 1995, the "concrete hotel," which had most recently been a bar, was for sale. Standing in front of the building, with keen eyesight or binoculars, you can see the old APO field station about fifteen miles away on top of Mount Harqua Hala.

[22] Today, the trail to the top of the mountain and the old observatory building are within the Harquahala Wilderness Area, beautiful, but vicious desert. This trail ascends over 3200 feet in approximately six miles. Although marked with cairns, at times it is difficult to follow. It should be attempted only by experienced desert hikers.

[23] During settlement of the West, soldiers would flash Morse code messages from mountain tops.

fixing to rain. The sky is perfectly blue right up to the sun.
Mountains stand out as if cut in brass. I believe this will prove a
great place for the work.

                                   Very truly yours,
                                   C. G. Abbott

Abbot stayed in Wenden for a week, hiking twice to the proposed mountain-top site. Before leaving on June 28th, he agreed to a contract for construction with Thomas Banks and Frank Lucas.[24]

                              Wenden, Arizona
                              June 28th, 1920
          We hereby propose to furnish necessary sand, water, rock
          and adobe, to pack from Wenden to the summit of Mount
          Harqua Hala, necessary building materials, and to erect
          in a workmanlike and substantial manner on the site
          agreed upon a building as per plans submitted by C.G. Ab-
          bot acting on behalf of the Smithsonian Institution of
          Washington, said building to be made ready for occupancy
          on or before September 15th, 1920. In compensation the
          said Smithsonian Institution shall pay for said packing
          and said erection of the building, two thousand nine
          hundred dollars.
                              Signed,
                              TM Banks & Frank Lucas

In addition to the construction contract, J.E. Matteson, a Wenden merchant, agreed to obtain the necessary construction materials from Phoenix for an additional $800.

   Also, before leaving Wenden, Abbot obtained authorization to use the summit of the mountain from a reclusive miner who held mining claims on Harqua Hala.

                         Right of occupancy
Permit to build, maintain, occupy, and operate an observatory building,
for the purpose of astronomical investigation.
      Said building being situated on the New State No. 1 mining
claim owned and in possession by the undersigned William B. Ellison

---

[24] 1991: The contractor's son, Westley Banks of Oregon, has the original contract.

of Wenden Yuma Co. Arizona. Grantor of this permit to C.G. Abbot of Washington D.C. agent or agent in fact for the Smithsonian Institute, Washington D.C.

In granting this permit the undersigned William B. Ellison waives all and singular any responsibility from damage or injury to said building or to the occupants, contents, instruments, pots, pans, crocks or broken crocks, or any property whatsoever that the Smithsonian Institute or its agents may have there.

William B. Ellison[25]

Plans were that Abbot's field station director in Chile, Alfred Finley Moore, would transfer back to the United States and direct the new field station on Mount Harqua Hala. With family in southern California, Moore looked forward to the new station which Abbot described to him.

> Pasedena, Calif.
> June 28, 1920
>
> Dear Alfred:
>
> I am just in from Wenden, Arizona. I contracted for a building of adobe as mud of the best quality lies within a quarter of a mile of the summit. I build on level ground thus: that is a cellar half underground, the other half banked up to top of cellar. Dwelling house above of four rooms. Cellar ten feet by thirty feet, dwelling house ten feet by forty feet inside. Instruments all in the cellar.
>
> There is a miner about one and a half miles beyond the observatory who has animals and garden and is a good sort. There is no water within one and a half miles,[26] but with eavestroughs and a 500 gallon tank we shall get some water from rains. I think I may engage a young ex-soldier at Wenden as camp rustler and assistant. I expect to be there myself from September to January.
>
> Yours truly,
> C. G. Abbot

---

[25] Initially, Abbot established a verbal agreement with Ellison. This document, in Ellison's handwriting, is dated January 17, 1921.

[26] Harqua Hala is derived from *Aha qua hala,* Mohave Indian for "water there is, high up" – R.G. Willson, "Arizona Days," *Arizona Magazine,* Jan. 5, 1969. Although dry today, you can still find the site of this spring on the trail.

From California, where he, his wife Lillian and APO assistant Loyal Blaine Aldrich were conducting the APO's last summer of solar constant observing on Mt. Wilson, Abbot oversaw the construction of the Harqua Hala field station and laid plans for moving in, in September. Much of his communication with the Smithsonian was to Harry W. Dorsey, chief clerk.

Mt. Wilson
August 10, 1920

Dear Mr. Dorsey,

I enclose a bill for $750 on account from Matteson at Wenden. He has furnished all of his $800 contract except the galvanized iron for the ceiling as okayed by Banks & Lucas who are the builders. Please have the $750 sent at once as he needs the money.

The boy Bunker who expected to come on the mountain to be camp rustler and assistant has gotten a better job. I offered the place to a boy in Ohio, but he also is engaged otherwise. Paul Greeley's father asked me if we would like to get his older son for a similar job to Paul's, and said he was more studious and likely more suitable than Paul who according to Moore is doing splendidly in S. America. Could we not get a boy on the APO rolls who would grow up into a director of the station eventually? Of course the Civil Service is almost a hopeless bar to doing so, but I wish you would make a try. I don't care what roll he comes on, messenger, computer, cook, physicist or jack, just so he is honest, interested, companionable, a country boy, and really got stuff in him that will make him fit to live with on a mountain twenty miles from anywhere.

We could pay up to $100 a month basic salary to start with. We must have him in Arizona by October 1 or very soon after. If you think there is no hope through the Civil Service, we can go after Greeley or some other that we know about, with Roebling's money. But I would much prefer to get one on the

APO. I hesitate to go after that St. Louis Weather Bureau assistant that sent in his request, or any such person, because it's indispensable that whoever we get shall be some good to us as a companion, an interested wholehearted chap, with good horse sense and willingness to do anything that will help along. Indeed he ought to keep his mouth shut, unlike pigs, when he eats. That is almost as essential as a college education.

Yours truly,
C. G. Abbot

On August 17, 1920, Abbot received word that the field station on Mount Harqua Hala was completed, well ahead of schedule.

Mount Wilson
September 2, 1920

Dear Mr. Dorsey,

A week ago Monday I went down leaving at 2 p.m. and got back at 11 a.m. on Wednesday, having in the intervening 45 hours visited our station on the Harqua Hala and taken there the picture I enclose, besides doing errands and getting my hair cut in Pasedena.

Now we are beginning to pack up for Arizona. Probably we shall be there by Sept. 20. After that mail once a week will be more than we can expect and telegrams will take their course with the mail. Aldrich will probably stay a couple of weeks.

I telegraphed to Greeley of Pelham asking if his older son is available. No answer yet.

Yours truly,
C. G. Abbot

Chapter 3

Moving In

Accompanied by APO assistant Loyal Aldrich, Abbot returned to Wenden about September 20, 1920. They brought the solar-constant observing instruments from Mount Wilson. Since his last letter to Harry Dorsey at the Smithsonian, Abbot had hired his cousin Keg Greeley as the field station assistant or, as Abbot called the job, camp rustler.

Abbot's wife Lillian, who had been with him on Mount Wilson throughout the summer of 1920 experimenting with solar cooking, did not travel to Harqua Hala. In a letter to Walcott Abbot explained, "There is so much necessary to do for the work on Mount Harqua Hala that I did not feel I could spare the time to equip a domestic establishment that would pass muster with a woman." Instead, Mrs. Abbot stayed several weeks sketching scenes on Mount Wilson and then moved to a little apartment in Pasadena, California where Abbot planned to meet her in January before returning to Washington.

Packing the observing equipment and living supplies up the tortuous trail, on the northwestern slope, to the summit of Harqua Hala proved more difficult than Abbot and the local hands from Wenden expected. On September 30th he wrote Dorsey, "Our equipment is all up today and in fine shape and nearly all ready to use. It has been a hard dangerous job but fortunately there were no accidents, though one close escape. The work takes much out of the animals and is a nerve racking job for the men. We hope to observe tomorrow." In a postscript, Abbot added, "It is not likely we can correspond inside one month. I may be able to telegraph and receive telegrams after a little."

Aldrich stayed on Harqua Hala long enough to help get the field station up and running, leaving after Keg Greeley arrived the first week in October. The plan was to have Aldrich return to this station in January, replacing Abbot and filling in as station director until Alfred Moore completed his transfer from Chile, after taking four months of accrued vacation.

Busy setting up the observing routine and making the instruments work correctly, establishing a heliographic link to the Bunker's hotel in Wenden for ordering supplies and relaying telegrams to and from Washington, and training Greeley, Abbot simply did not have time to write to the Smithsonian until late in October. By then, in a letter to Secretary Walcott, he first revealed the bittersweet nature of field station work and some difficulties peculiar to Harqua Hala.

Harqua Hala Mt.
October 25, 1920

Dear Dr. Walcott,

This station is proving quite as favorable for the solar work as hoped. We have observed nearly every day this far in October. The sky keeps good all day and all night most of the time.

Naturally there is a lot to do besides the observing. I get up at sunrise and keep busy til bedtime and still the work looms up before me. We haven't even yet put the kitchen to rights but cook any way at all, on chairs and boxes. Our wood pile at least is getting on and it's very necessary. I have grown into quite a cook. Make lots of nice things to eat.

It takes from two to four hours a week to heliograph to Wenden to order stuff and send messages occasionally to The Smithsonian. We need four things badly. (1) Wireless telephone, $1600 (2) Two thousand gallon water tank underground, probably $1000 (3) A road, probably $25,000 (4) After the road a Ford Truck, probably $1000.

It is very isolated here. We never go down and last mail up was October 16th. We don't even know who won the World Series in baseball.

Very truly yours,
C. G. Abbot

Abbot's letters to the Smithsonian always praised his field station staffers. After only a month in Arizona, he wrote to Secretary Walcott, "The more I work at Harqua Hala, the more impressed I am by the enormous amount of splendid work Mr. Moore and his assistants have done in South America." Abbot also was impressed with his camp rustler.

> H. H. Wenden, Ariz.
> October 25, 1920
>
> Dear Mr. Dorsey,
>
> Greeley is getting better every day. He already observes with the pyrheliometer about as well as I can and takes hold of plotting observations and reading off from plots in great shape. He is perfection as a companion in this isolated place. Eats without noise, interested in the work, ready to do anything, cuts up a fine woodpile, makes biscuits, washes dishes, and in short does everything I ask with enthusiasm and doesn't jar on me at all. His education ended with graduation from Nashua High School. His experience as a farmer, a painter, a soldier has made him willing and able to tackle anything in camp life. His disposition is so suited to the work and life here that I should be in dismay to think of getting a new green hand. I do not know, as matters stand now whether the Commission wants that application filled and will hold it until further word from you.
>
> Yours truly,
> G. C. Abbot

It was obvious that Abbot valued assistants with "an ability to live pleasantly with others so on an isolated desert mountain they would not be sticks in the family." The right individuals were so rare, and Greeley so exemplary, that Dorsey finally convinced the Commission – The Civil Service Commission – to waive its required examination because "angels seldom came under its jurisdiction." (In later years, G. Edward Pendary, science editor of the Literary Digest, called the APO field observers "heroic sentinels of science.")[27]

---

[27] Bessie Zaban Jones, *Lighthouse of the Skies*, The Smithsonian Astrophysical Observatory: Background and History 1846-1955, Smithsonian Institution, Washington, D.C., 1965, p. 328.

William Ellison's presence on Harqua Hala and his willingness to serve as Abbot's supply link to Wenden and water were also immediately apparent. Abbot, Greeley and Ellison quickly built a friendship on this desolate mountain.

Harqua Hala Observatory
October 20, 1920

Dear Mother,

Last Sunday afternoon Chas and I hiked down to Mr. Ellison's our nearest neighbor, one and a half miles. He has been here in the mountains all alone for twelve years and works several copper claims here making a very good living.[28] He has three burros and brings us all our water and provisions. He owns a garden about forty feet square, a copper mine in itself, so treated us to a watermelon. That surely hit the spot. He also gave us some onions and carrots and oyster plant. Made some stew out of the latter and you couldn't tell the flavor from real oysters.

Chas and I did a three weeks' washing Monday morning and took a bath to boot. Put my winter undies on this morning. The army pants are just the thing for this place. It is terribly hard on shoes here and have worn out my old ones so expect another pair of work shoes when Mr. Ellison comes back from Wenden.

Much love to you both,
Keg

Abbot paid Ellison to replenish the observatory's water tank and to bring up supplies and mail delivered by Wenden merchants to the bottom of the mountain. Water was to be a continuing problem: when it rained the eavestroughs could collect some water from the roof of the observatory. But the observers could not count on frequent rain, so several times a week Ellison hauled water from a spring at his camp. Establishing a routine for living, Abbot and Greeley rationed about thirty gallons of water a week for drinking, cooking, bathing, dish washing, laundry and processing photographic plates.

As Keg's mother could read in his newsy, unscheduled letters, the observers did all their own housekeeping, instrument and building maintenance, and doctoring.

---

[28] Later Greeley wrote, "Mr. Ellison doesn't make very much at mining. He has a few gold bearing ledges. Before we inhabited the mountain he used to grind out ore with the burros and get enough gold dust to live comfortably on. Now he lives on what we give him for packing our provisions. Like all prospectors he is waiting to sell to some company who will operate on a larger scale."

Harqua Hala
November 9, 1920

Dear Mother,

Expect company next Saturday, a Mr. Adams from the Mt. Wilson Observatory. He is going to stay a few days so I am banking on sending this letter down when he goes. You needn't feel a bit worried if you don't hear from me regularly for the traffic from here to Wenden is decidedly irregular and I am afraid it is going to be more so as Mr. Ellison goes down where it is warmer every year about the last of November and doesn't come back till sometime in February. He is going to fill our 500 gallon water tank before he goes so all we will need are provisions and we can take them up the trail ourselves. Mr. Bunker brings them to the foot of the trail for us. He is the fellow we have the light signal code with. We communicate quite a bit that way. Chas sends and receives all his telegrams thru him so we are not so far away from the rest of the world at that.

Today was Tuesday, but it seemed more like Sunday for the sky was so we couldn't observe and we didn't do a thing all day. It is the first day I have really loafed. We were both sick this morning. Something we ate last night I guess. Chas lays it to some ginger bread he made. After breakfast we took some physic and went to bed again. I got up about ten and took a bath and he followed suit. We had an appetizing dinner of weak tea and toasted bread then took a walk and explored some of the surrounding mines near by. Feel decidedly better tonight. Good enough to finish my computing and write this letter.

Love
Keg

The need for improved communications and access to the top of Mount Harqua Hala remained at the top of Abbot's list. Anticipating another chance to convince Congress of the necessary appropriations, he surveyed a route for the road through a canyon down the more gradual northeastern slope.

Harqua Hala
November 20, 1920

Dear Mother,

Dr. Chas, Mr. Ellison and I took a ten mile tramp yesterday. Observed in the morning and got started about 10:30. Got back about five with hats off and tongues hanging out. Today we needed crutches we were so lame. The object of our exploration was to find a suitable place to build a road from the desert to the observatory. From here to Mr. Ellison's it is rather a rolling country so a road can easily be constructed by digging along the sides of the hills. Below Mr. Ellison's for about a mile down the canyon it is a difficult proposition. Never saw such a jumbled up mess in my life. It is one massive ledge on both sides with rocks and boulders from the size of a water bucket to a baby grand piano and on up to the size of a good sized cottage. It is just about as easy to get lost among the boulders as the mountains themselves. Chas says the road is a possibility providing Congress will appropriate the money.

Just got through talking to Wenden and got some news. Chas got a telegram from the Secretary and has to go to Washington tomorrow morning to appear before the Appropriations Committee of the House of Representatives and give a hearing on the proposed road I was just telling you about so I have to hold the fort for at least ten days. I am thinking it's going to be a lonesome job.

Love to you and Dad,
Keg

Forever optimistic, Abbot was more positive about the proposed route for the road than Greeley. Leaving his assistant alone to run the field station the best he could, on the way to Washington, Abbot telegraphed to Walcott:

Ashfork, Arizona 11-22-20 Starting East arrive Washington Wednesday morning. Road requires six miles. All good road material. Grade one in ten no bridges cuts or switchbacks. Four miles easy made sample dig at rate two feet per hour. Estimate this part twelve thousand

dollars. Two miles harder rock work required but rocks
loose and broken plenty gravel fill. Estimate this part
thirteen thousand. Total twenty five. Am bringing photos
and information. Abbot

Chapter 4

Aiming at the Sun

On Harqua Hala, the observers aimed a variety of instruments toward the sun: they had a theodolite for measuring the sun's altitude above the horizon, and two silver-disk pyrheliometers and a pyranometer for measuring the energy of the sun. The pyrheliometers were mercury thermometers with shutters to open or close at set intervals; this action and the resulting thermometer readings provided a means to calculate heat both from the sun's direct rays and from rays reflected or scattered by the atmosphere. Conversely, the pyranometer, looking like a glass dish, was an electric instrument that measured heat from the atmosphere around the sun, excluding direct rays.

Readings from these instruments supported primary data from a recording spectrometer-bolometer, an electrical thermometer that Abbot claimed to be sensitive to a millionth of a degree.[29] Briefly explained, the bolometer used on Harqua Hala consisted of two very thin, narrow strips of blackened platinum, each built into half of an electrically balanced battery-charged circuit. The bolometer was housed in the basement of the observatory where one strip was hidden from the sun, the other exposed to a beam reflected from a coelostat – two opposing mirrors outside that tracked the sun's movement across the sky. Before it hit the bolometer, the incoming sunbeam passed through the spectrometer, which spread the beam into a spectrum, and through a rotating sector or beam chopper, which controlled the intensity of the beam.

The exposed platinum strip of the bolometer absorbed 97 percent of all parts of the sun's spectrum. Thus, the sun's energy heated the exposed strip and caused a change in the electrical balance of the bolometer's circuit. This produced a current flow on a galvanometer – a gauge that measured very small changes in electrical current.

To record data from the bolometer, the observer captured a secondary beam, split from the beam reflected into the dark basement. This beam fell on a very tiny mirror attached to the string "needle" of the galvanometer that reflected it, as a period-size

---

[29] Abbot, *The Sun*, p. 82.

spot, onto a photographic plate. As the galvanometer mirror moved in proportion to the rise and fall of temperature on the bolometer strip, a clock drive scanned the spectrometer through the spectrum and simultaneously moved the photographic plate. In seven minutes this apparatus scanned through the solar spectrum and produced a recorded plot of energy versus wavelength of the spectrum. During each seven minute run, the observer operated the rotating sector so he could compress the entire expanse of energy plots onto the eight-inch wide photographic plate.[30]

Harqua Hala
November 9, 1920

Dear Mother,

I will try to give a little description as to the object of our work and tell you what I have to do.

The object is to find the solar constant of the sun's radiation from day to day or in other words to find out how much heat the sun gives off every day outside the atmosphere of the earth. The sun's rays in passing thru the numerous layers of atmosphere, gases, water vapor, dust and other ingredients, are deflected and lose considerable heat, hence all these sensitive instruments we have to read to find out as near as possible how much heat was lost. Haven't got a very thorough understanding of the procedure yet as I have to stay outside most of the time reading the pyrheliometer while Chas is inside reading the rest of them - pyranometer, galvanometer, bolometer, etc.

Everything is timed and we have to get out readings at certain intervals, right on the second. The pyrheliometer consists of two mercury thermometers with shutters the latter are painted with lamp black to absorb heat. They can be opened or closed and it is my business to do this at set intervals of every few seconds recording the heat absorbed or the cooling that takes place while the shutters are closed. This instrument records the sun's heat not barring the atmosphere. The pyranometer measures the heat of the atmosphere around the sun and not the sun's rays direct. The bolometer with the aid of a glass prism splits the rays up into its spectrum which is measured.

---

[30] Intensities of various parts of the sun's spectrum differ enormously, being very slight in the ultraviolet and violet and very high in the red and infrared.

Another beam of light passing thru the bolometer is reflected to the galvanometer in which there is a little mirror about the size of a pin head. It is so arranged that it can swing from side to side. The little mirror reflects its light on a photographic plate which is run by clock work and arranged so it can slide up or down. The plate is set in motion and a beam of light let thru a shutter on to the mirror. The different variations of heat due to atmospheric conditions causes this mirror to swing one way or the other consequently it's little image of light on the plate swings too, photographing a little black line wherever it goes. Thus we get the wavelengths of light and Chas can tell by measuring these how much water vapor there is in the air. That's all the computing he does as it takes from three or four hours to read one plate. There is a good deal more to it than this vague description that I can't explain but then you'll probably be a little better informed than before.

Love,
Keg

Work on Harqua Hala began at sunrise. One observer would prepare breakfast in the upstairs living quarters, the other the instruments outside and in the basement.

Outside, the instrument preparer would first uncover the coelostat. He would breathe upon its stellite mirrors and polish them with clean hospital cotton. Then, he would set the coelostat in motion, aligning it to reflect a beam of sunlight into the basement observing chamber. Abbot described, "It is carefully adjusted until a single ray forms its pinhole image of the sun within a little circle, drawn with India ink on a bit of cardboard, ten feet back on the wall of the observing chamber. This is our guiding image. All through the observations, we must take care to keep it exactly central with the inked circle, so that the main sunbeam will enter the spectroscope squarely."[31]

Next, the observer carried out of doors a stand holding the two silver-disk pyrheliometers and the pyranometer; he aimed these instruments at the sun and briefly tested them. Likewise, he readied the theodolite for observing.

Checking the spectrometer-bolometer was more difficult. First, the observer set the spectrometer to the "oxygen band" at the extreme red end of the solar spectrum; he focused this band on the sensitive strip of the bolometer. Then, with the spectrometer's shutter closed, at the far end of the observing chamber, he looked for the secondary

---

[31] Abbot, *The Sun*, p. 121.

beam of light entering at the corner of the chamber, passing through a slot, reflected twice and falling upon the tiny galvanometer mirror and then onto the photographic-plate carrier. He made adjustments by moving tiny magnets on the galvanometer's needle. Gingerly, so he didn't send the needle of the galvanometer spinning, he closed the switch to start the bolometer and made small changes in the balancing resistance to swing the spot of light back to zero. Finally, putting everything together, the observer set the rotating sector spinning in front of the spectrometer, opened the spectrometer's shutter and checked the spot of light falling on the photographic-plate carrier, carefully aligning the carrier so he could record up to six bolographic curves on one plate during the day.

With all instruments ready, the instrument preparer went to breakfast. Usually, his colleague had found time to set the page in the field station's record book, placing another sheet and carbon paper over it for a copy to mail to Washington.

After breakfast, if the sky was clear, observing began with a measurement of the sun's altitude using the theodolite. Then, throughout the morning, this observer would make a series of readings with the theodolite and the two pyrheliometers.

Reading the pyrheliometers was not easy: it seemed as if seconds galloped by and things went wrong. When the observer should have opened the shutter, perhaps he left it closed. When he should have merely read the thermometer, he inadvertently closed the shutter. Invariably, these slips happened toward the end of an observation after four to five minutes of readings, requiring the observer to begin again, though the proper time to begin had passed away forever.[32]

Greeley took to the task easily, and by October 20th Abbot had enough confidence in his work to put his readings in the logbook. Usually, he made five sets of pyrheliometer observations a day. The first sets were only ten minutes apart because the path of the sun's rays changed rapidly early in the day. Later, a full hour elapsed between sets.

Each time Greeley made a pyrheliometer reading, Abbot was in the basement making a seven-minute run with the bolometer-galvanometer. There were sixteen exact instants within the seven-minute run, including times to check the pinhole solar image centered in the guide-circle, to open and close the shutter, to start and stop the rotating sectors, and to start and stop the runs. During bolometer runs, Abbot also periodically read the pyranometer five times successively, carefully avoiding conflicts with the bolometers.[33]

Inside and out, everything had to be timed so the observers read all instruments at certain intervals, right on the second.

---

[32] *Ibid*, p.124
[33] Although the pyranometer was outside, the observer measured its electrical output with the galvanometer when the bolometer was not operating.

In one letter to his mother, Keg Greeley explained, "Am sure I'll like this work as I learn more about it. Chas is a fine instructor. He has written a book on this kind of work describing the process and the instruments. It surely takes a book to describe it. Am reading it at piece meals. Every time I take it from the shelf I have to take down Webster too, and any words that aren't in there I have to refer to Abbot."

Abbot found satisfaction in piecing this observational puzzle together. "Every pyrheliometer reading affords its moment of expectancy and gratification if it falls in nicely with the series. The bolometric observer has rather less to carry along his interest during the observations, although for him the agreement among pyranometer readings is always to be looked for. At the end of the morning, when he develops the photographic plate and sees his five or six curves beautifully superposed, with never a mistake marring their similarity, he has a little moment of exultation."[34]

The observing routine was collectively "the long method" because, in addition to the tedium of daily observations, the observers spent several subsequent hours, often falling days behind, "computing" the observed data into a solar constant value. The long method used empirical "corrections" for water vapor absorption in the atmosphere, and for unobserved ultraviolet and infrared radiation. Langley had originated the long method when he first began his solar constant research.

For more practical daily measurements, Abbot began in 1919 to develop a quickly computed "short method" using a "function" that could be determined only from an accumulation of long method observations over an extended period at a given observatory. Thus, Abbot and his observers had to determine the function of the Harqua Hala site before they could make useful daily measurements of the solar constant.

---

[34] Abbot, *The Sun*, p. 126.

Chapter 5

Near Disaster

Although the U.S. Weather Bureau had dubbed Harqua Hala Mountain "one of the most cloudless regions in the world," right from the start Abbot and Greeley fought an almost overwhelming battle with wind. Combined with the wind, the relatively small amount of rain, ice and snow that fell on the mountain were enough to damage the adobe structure seriously. By early November, the new building's exterior adobe coating was falling, exposing the underlying adobe brick. And the south wall was beginning to sag, separating from the two story building where it connected with the roof. Abbot's trip to Washington, D.C., on November 21, 1920, came at a bad time – just when the work at Harqua Hala seemed more than two men could handle.

With Abbot off to Washington, Greeley was to be alone on the mountain for what he hoped would not be much more than ten days – the length of the round trip from Wenden to Washington. Before leaving, Abbot encouraged his young assistant to stay busy, keep up the observing as much as he could, and rely on himself, letters from home and Mr. Ellison for companionship. After ten days, there was no sign of problems in Keg's letter to his mother.

> Harqua Hala
> November 30, 1920
>
> Dear Mother,
>   Have held the fort now for ten days and am no worse off for the experience. My greatest foe has been Old Father Time and his blue army. Have had plenty of work to do so survived all his attacks and am now on the offensive. Dr. Chas expected to be back in ten days and in that case he will come sometime tomorrow, but I think his trip will take the greater part of two weeks as it takes about five days one way.

Have been reading the pyrheliometer every day. Only one cloudy day and that was today. Nine fair days out of ten is a pretty good record.

Received the cranberries OK, also your letter and they both hit the right spot. Cooked a little batch the first thing and they sure tasted Pelhamish alright.

I won't need my army overcoat as I have got plenty of other clothing to keep warm with. Mr. Ellison says we won't get more than six weeks of severe weather here and then it will be comfortable in the day time. The wind starts to blow like sixty after sun down every night, but calms down to a light breeze every morning. It has been delightful weather since Dr. Charles left. Have been around with shirt sleeves rolled up and collar unbuttoned but slip on my sweater at night.

Dr. C. left a lot of computing so have kept busy until ten every night. Didn't have anything extra for Thanksgiving dinner but Mr. Ellison came up in the afternoon and invited me down for supper. It was a rare night. Full moon, clear as a bell and so quiet I could almost hear him cooking supper from here. He shot a deer the day before so we had venison, also had all kinds of vegetables from his garden, fresh biscuits and a half of lemon pie apiece. He cooked everything, even the fluffy frosting on the pie made out of the whites of eggs. It was his treat and he took great pleasure in it. I am sure the pleasure was as much mine. He is one grand cook.

Did up a good sized washing this morning. Took a bath this afternoon and also scraped off a two weeks six days beard. Have killed so many flies on the windows that I had to wash them.

Love
Keg

Abbot's trip to Washington stretched to twenty-two days, even longer than Greeley had expected; the return trip probably seemed longer than normal because he still did not have Congressional funding for the Smithsonian's solar program. Arriving at the Wenden train station on December 13, 1920, Abbot was surprised to see Greeley waiting for him.

Wenden, Arizona
December 14, 1920

Dear Dr. Walcott,

Found Greeley at station. He had walked sixteen miles to meet me. Fine weather continually during my absence. Everything else gone to pot. Wet and dry thermometers smashed early. No fault of his, just wire broke. Theodolite smashed last Wednesday by a cyclonic gust of wind, luckily saved pyrheliometers. Mr. Ellison and burros gone for the winter.

Water tank leaks so must lug water a mile hereafter and perhaps supplies five miles. Building showing a fault in wall. Going up today to see what can be done to repair building and theodolite. Hope to get old Mexican[35] to pack up my supplies from foot of trail occasionally.

Devil appears to have claimed everything. Have to exorcise him.

Yours truly,
C. G. Abbot

With his ability to take charge, and his multitude of skills, Abbot immediately saw to stabilizing the wall, repairing, testing and resetting the water tank, repairing the instruments, and replacing the dry cells that powered the coelostat and spectrometer-bolometer, all while trying to maintain a reasonable schedule of observing. Within a week he could report a completely different situation to the secretary of the Smithsonian, in a letter that also clearly outlined the burden of this remote, poorly equipped field station.

---

[35] An old Mexican man lived near the trailhead at the foot of the mountain, probably raising a few cattle.

Harqua Hala
December 19, 1920

Dear Dr. Walcott,

All's well and the goose hangs high now. In order to fix the wall, which was really so dangerous looking Tuesday (December 14) that I moved my bed fearing a fall at anytime, Mr. Adams when he visited here November 13-15 took measurements and sent the necessary tie rods from Pasadena about two weeks ago. We had them carried to foot of trail when we came out last Tuesday. We lugged up on Tuesday my grip and about two meal sacks of provisions. On Wednesday after observing we went down again and lugged the 160 pounds of steel about one-third the way up. We were all in and could hardly make camp that night. But the wall looked so dangerous that down we went next morning as I had devised a new easier way to carry and also arranged for a hot dinner at the halfway water spring. We got the whole up here at 5 P.M. and then drilled two twelve inch holes through the south wall finishing by moonlight. Next morning we completed the job and pulled the south wall up true. It had sagged out about two inches so that a bird flew into my room through the crack. I suppose it was too high to build of adobe.

That afternoon I began to mend the theodolite. The main axle was broken off and bent, and several minor parts bent. I set two steel screws into the axle and then soldered it. After that I got it true enough so that the sensitive level does not swing over 0.5' of arc in a complete rotation. So far as I can see the instrument is now as accurate as ever.

Today, we went down to Mr. Ellison's camp, heated water out of doors, and took baths out of doors. Then we lugged up 20 gallons of water 1 mile, 1000 feet up, another 160 pounds of weight.

We had just gotten home when it began to rain. At noon today it was cloudless.

Altogether, we feel more cheerful than last Tuesday night.

We need here extremely an adding machine, perhaps the Monroe or Dalton. As there is no money at all I suppose we can't have it. But if some Regent would give us a Christmas present of one we could get on a little easier adding four figure columns of forty numbers.

With best wishes for a Merry Christmas and Happy New Year to you and Mrs. Walcott and everybody.

Yours truly,

C. G. Abbot

By the beginning of January 1921, Mr. Ellison had returned and resumed his water and supply runs for the observatory. With a few cloudy days, Abbot and Greeley caught up on computing and further improved the equipment set up.

Despite the early difficulties and near disaster with the wall, Abbot believed that the first months of observing on Harqua Hala were more favorable than expected. Clear skies permitted observing on more than seventy percent of the days. In addition, there was little difference in the clarity of the sky between morning and afternoon, a great improvement over the condition on Mt. Wilson.

Now, Abbot turned his attention to the temporary return of Lloyal Aldrich and eventual arrival of permanent field station manager, Alfred Moore. Abbot expected to return to Washington by February 1st. Aldrich had already left Washington before Christmas so he could move his expectant wife to be with family in the Midwest.

Harqua Hala
January 21, 1921

Dear Mr. Dorsey,

Am expecting Aldrich daily and when you get this it will be a sign that he has come, I think. I suppose you heard of his 6 1/2 pound boy at 6 am January 1.

I am leaving in a blaze of glory. This is the cloudiest month of the year by reports. We have observed thus far on 11 days in January. Day before yesterday it rained all day. First real rain I've seen here. We caught 150 gallons of water. We took fine bathes and washed our hair in the rain water! Great luxury after hard water with green growth in it for three months. The building stood the rain and furious wind finely, except a little more outside plaster fell.

If Aldrich comes I shall hope to leave the day following, and leave Pasadena about four days later so as to be in Washington about ten days after I leave here.

Yours truly,
C. G. Abbot

P.S. I've found an absolute cure for chilblains.[36] I was nearly frantic for several days, with both feet and hands. I shall bring a photograph of the patient under treatment. I wish I had known what to do when I was on Mt. Whitney in 1910.

---

[36] An inflammation followed by itchy irritation on the hands, feet or ears, resulting from exposure to moist cold. The photograph showed Abbot had wrapped his feet tightly in wool socks and canvas.

Chapter 6

Aldrich Returns

Late in January 1921, Loyal Aldrich returned to manage the Harqua Hala field station temporarily until Alfred Moore's arrival from Los Angeles; Charles Abbot left January 26th to return to Washington.

Arriving in Wenden, Aldrich was preoccupied with concerns for his wife in Milwaukee and their infant son who was having medical problems. Perhaps, much of the determination to run the field station, along with the necessary luck, left with Abbot. Immediately, Aldrich's letters and reports to Washington showed how difficult the scientific effort and even routine tasks could get on the mountain. The weather and day-to-day operations, especially communicating and dealing with Wenden merchants Bunker, Wilkinson, Harrington and Matteson, did not start well for Aldrich.

Harqua Hala
February 9, 1921

Dear Mr. Abbot,

Since you left we have obtained long method observations on January 29, February 1, 2 and 8, and short method observations on seven other days. Almost every day the sun has been out long enough for us to get all ready and then have to close up.

On Saturday following your departure, Mr. Ellison and his burros appeared, bringing up the adding machine (which has been a great blessing), wet and dry thermometers, pyranometer and potatoes, all of which he found at the foot. He had not been near Wenden and announced he had no intention of going there for some time to come.

We were entirely out of alcohol and pretty low in other supplies. Accordingly we asked Ellison if he could go down to the foot for them some time soon. He agreed to go the following

Monday and we made plans to signal Bunker asking that the
supplies you ordered be brought according to whatever
arrangement you made. Well Ellison suddenly decided to go down
on Sunday and camp until Monday when he would bring the
supplies. So we spent all Sunday evening frantically trying to get
Wenden without a flicker from them.

Monday morning we spent the entire morning trying to make
them understand our message without results. So I sent Fred
down the trail to ask Ellison to stay over a day. He found old
man Bunker and Wilkinson had been out in the morning (not even
bringing the mail) to see what was up. Saw our lights Sunday
night but their's wouldn't work and they thought we must be sick!
(Ellison is of the opinion they were all too drunk to signal.) Well,
Ellison waited over and Monday evening we again wasted almost
three hours in futile signaling. All they would reply was that they
would meet Ellison but refused to say whether or not they
understood our message.

That made a total of ten hours of nerve wracking efforts to
make them understand. And the replies they made were mostly
unintelligible.

Fred went to meet them on Monday with instructions from
me if they brought no supplies to return with them, find out what
was what and bring out the order to Ellison the same day. They
came out empty handed! Fred went back with them. They made
excuses that they couldn't read the signal. Harrington hadn't told
them he had an order, etc. Fred says the Bunkers acted rather
strangely - seemed jealous and put out that they had lost an
order. And we both think that either they are too careless and
slipshod for any use in signaling or they deliberately tried to
bungle it.

Well, Fred found Harrington waiting for Ellison to call
for the order. Fred bundled it into the auto and took it back to the
foot. But unfortunately Fred cashed a check in Bunker's store and
when they got back to the foot, Wilkinson demanded $18
immediately for his three trips. Said he was tired waiting so long
for his money! One of these trips you note was entirely

unauthorized. They thought we were sick, but I'd like to see either Wilkinson or old Bunker walk up to the top if we had been. Fred had no alternative but to pay and take a receipt.[37]

Believe me Bunker, Wilkinson, et al. will get no further opportunity from me to run that game. Doubtless they think the new man in charge has withdrawn patronage from them so they'll get even.

Well, to continue this harrowing tale. Harrington's order lacked the 10 lbs. butter, 5 gal. gasoline and the kerosene can leaked so Fred had to make an extra trip on Wednesday to the foot and rescue it. Also instead of 1 gal. alcohol which we so direly needed, he sent 1 gal. sheep dip!!

By good fortune on February 5 a storm was brewing and Ellison had to again go to lower regions. He has been our only comfort and he agreed to go to Wenden and straighten things out and get some other supplies we needed. (Fred had not been feeling well so I thought a change in diet would help him. We got some fresh vegetables, cheese, eggs, etc. He is all right now.) Ellison just returned yesterday with the additional news that having forgotten the butter, gas, etc., Harrington sent them out the following day by his own messenger! Ellison asked him if he thought he (Ellison) sat there at the foot all day every day like a dammed crow waits for food!!

I think my next order goes to Matteson and if possible I'll wait until another storm drives Ellison down to get it. I'm through with the present mode of signaling, at least with the Bunkers at the other end, unless I have to. I'm sorry affairs should be so bungled immediately after your departure, but I don't know how I could have done differently.

I have talked it over with Ellison and he agrees most heartily that we'll never get satisfaction with present methods. He himself suggested he get a second hand auto and keep it at the foot. Then he could go in to Wenden, get our order filled and back on top the same day. It would be an ideal arrangement and I think he only needs a little encouragement to do it.

---

[37] The normal procedure involved submitting bills to the field station manager; then, he sent them on to Washington for reimbursement.

If any improvements are to be made out here I would suggest that some change be made in the cook stove equipment. Fred and I have lost our tempers, cussed and wasted many weary hours trying to get our cooking done. We can get temporary service only by keeping the gasoline torch playing on them to keep them hot. And there is so much to do it seems a pity to use valuable time on them.

Well, for recreation and comfort we are making the most of the Victrola, sunsets and horseshoes.

The doctor is still in attendance on the baby. His digestive apparatus won't work right and naturally I feel considerable worries and would give a good deal for better mail service.

Yours sincerely,
LB Aldrich

PS. Don't think we have shown displeasure to any Wenden citizens. The enclosed are only our confidential opinions.

Without a reliable service link with Wenden, it was even difficult for the observers to get word of these problems to Abbot in Washington: Aldrich's letter of February 9th did not leave the mountain for a week and was not postmarked from Wenden until February 18th, by which time he had added another letter and another harrowing tale.

Harqua Hala
February 15. 1921

Dear Mr. Abbot,

The three days Feb 11, 12 and 13 were wonderful weather but yesterday it clouded and blew a gale. Last night the wind was terrible all night. Both Ellison and Fred say it was the worst wind since the house was built. I spent a miserable night for I surely expected either the roof to go or the side wall to cave in. I got up and dressed for I preferred being buried in my clothes. Today we find no damage except a drain pipe blown down. It cleared beautifully and wind abated and we got full observations.

Yours truly,
LB Aldrich

Back at the Smithsonian Institution in Washington, D.C., Abbot was now in a better position to manage the financial support from Roebling and address the needs on Harqua Hala Mountain. He recognized that continued moral support was crucial for success of the observatory and the well being of the observers. One of the first improvements he sent to the mountain was "Victor and Columbia records" for the observer's Victrola.

By return mail he told Aldrich, "We have the financial support to end some of the troubles which you so feelingly describe. The question is, how to carry through the improvements." Part of the situation was, which problems should be solved by Aldrich and which by Moore the permanent field station manger who was still in Los Angeles and not due on the mountain until April.

Through his letters from Washington, Abbot explained to Aldrich some of the improvements that Moore was already planning. He said, "Moore has found a place in Los Angeles where they make up special wireless telephone sets at very reasonable prices. I have instructed him that if he is convinced that the sets are satisfactory he should go ahead and get the necessary equipment for Harqua Hala. Naturally, it will be some time before that is installed." Abbot also asked Aldrich, "Do you think it is best to take up the matter of the regular supply service before Moore arrives on the ground? I leave it to your discretion. Of course the matter should be kept confidential from the people in Wenden and from Ellison too, unless you are quite ready to go on with it." Then, two days later he offered more specific advice.

SMITHSONIAN INSTITUTION
Washington, U.S.A.

February 25, 1921

Dear Aldrich:

The more I think of it, the more desirable it seems to me that you go and see Moore in Los Angeles and talk things over, in the light of your information and his, before you make any deal with Ellison in regard to the weekly mail and supply service which we now have the money to inaugurate at any time. Moore proposes to get a Ford. We have an appropriation of $250 to build a garage for it at the foot of the trail. We have also some unallotted funds with which, if you and Moore recommend, we could do something towards promoting the jitney end of Ellison's mail service if he should undertake it.

Very truly yours,

C. G. Abbot

Time, or perhaps the delay in return mail from Washington, always seemed to help the difficult situations for those who manned the Harqua Hala field station: Seemingly, writing a letter to Abbot was a way for Aldrich to vent frustrations at the end of a difficult week. Invariably, however, a letter full of frustrations was followed in a week or two, before receiving a reply from Abbot, by a letter that reflected greater tolerance to all the situations and surprises on the mountain.

Harqua Hala Mt.
February 27, 1921

Dear Mr. Abbot:

Fred puts it all over me with the horseshoes. He practices all his spare moments and is continually getting ringers.[38]

Every few days we take our empty water cans down to Ellison's in the evening. He tells us yarns about hunting, mining, etc. and is surely good to us. We always get something - some chocolate cake, a side of venison (he just got another deer), some oyster plant from his garden, sour dough starter for griddle cakes, etc. I don't know what we'd do without Ellison. He is the leaven that lightens our stay here He has been perfectly willing to go down to Wenden about once in two weeks for us. It was certainly a pleasure last time to get our supplies exactly as we asked for them and even better for he used his good judgement in bargaining with the Wenden grocers.

I think he is willing to go down this often because he is planning to build his house this spring and is ordering lumber, cement, etc.

To date we have caught 13 full grown mice in the galvanometer and bolometer room. They surely have no trouble getting in.

Last Friday we were surprised by a visit from two of the toughest looking Arizona cowpunchers I ever expect to see. They looked worse than the movie pictures, with leather breeches, broncos and armed to the teeth. I was a bit scared at first but they behaved very decently and only asked for tobacco. Said they were scouting around for new cattle pasturage. This is a terrible dry

---

[38] Having also been beaten by Greeley, Abbot wrote, "I believe Fred must be in league with some powers of the air . . . he was quite as likely to get a ringer by throwing four feet from the peg as by throwing anywhere near it."

season so far and the cattle and sheep men are hard put. There are 4000 sheep now in the canyons just below us. We hear them every day and they worry Ellison for fear they get up higher and ruin his water. The cow punchers said unless a rain came soon they would all die of thirst. Ellison says one of the cowboys is a fugitive who killed a man over at Bill Williams awhile ago. He looked it.

Our Victrola is in a bad way. The gears slipped when winding it and partially stripped them. We have filed and fussed with them but it rattles like a 10 year old Ford. The stoves are behaving a little better. We cleaned them inside and out and are using only Kerosene filtered through filter paper. We still use the torch to heat them. It's considerably cheaper than alcohol and much surer. We have made some grand oatmeal bread, cheese dishes and soups and yesterday Fred made a fine chocolate cake out of the "Excelo" package. Weather has been warmer this past week.

Yours truly,
LB Aldrich

Instead of Aldrich going to Los Angeles, as Abbot had suggested, Alfred Moore visited the mountain field station on March 2, 1921; Moore and his brother, Edgar, drove to Wenden from Los Angeles. Spending just one day on the mountain, Moore talked with the Wenden merchants and Ellison and spent some time with Aldrich and Greeley explaining the improvements he planned to start when he returned in April.

Aldrich was encouraged by the plans, but knew they would not change his tenure on Harqua Hala. While he was able to improve supply service to Wenden by relying on Ellison,[39] Aldrich's troubles now took a different form: increasingly he was plagued with difficulty running the sensitive instruments at the field station and making sense out of the scientific data. Results were erratic at best; problems emerged as an apparent error in the mathematical "correction factor" used to determine the solar constant; the observers applied this factor to the raw data taken from the daily bolographs.

As refined as the scientific procedure seemed, it was still very experimental; the scientific work at Harqua Hala could be explained theoretically, but day-to-day implementation was extremely difficult. Accuracy even depended on the eccentricities of

---

[39] Ellison arranged with Mr. Barnett of Wenden to deliver supplies weekly to the foot of the mountain, at $5.50 a trip.

the observers' pocket watches, which they used to time their measurements. Operational procedures were in the form of a handwritten "precept" that Abbot had left. In addition, Abbot continued to suggest procedural changes by mail.

Coming up with a solid correction factor and resulting solar constant meant that Aldrich had to ensure that all the delicate instruments were running correctly, but he constantly found functional problems particularly with the coelostat and the various beams of sunlight associated with the bolometer and galvanometer. In addition, with each tweak of an instrument he needed to verify proper operation with test runs to ensure measurements corresponded with previous data. Such test runs required days with continuously clear skies, a condition that was increasingly rare because during Aldrich's time on Harqua Hala the sky was often hazy.

Throughout March 1921, letters to Abbot discussed minuscule changes to the instrument setup and the effects on the calculated solar constant.

> Harqua Hala
> March 10, 1921
>
> Dear Mr. Abbot,
>
> Your three letters date February 19, 23 and 25 came in our mail on Saturday last. Also two books - Lipka's "Graphical and Math Computation" and Humphrey's "Physics of the Air" - besides three Atlantic Monthlys, National Geographic Magazine and the Monroe Calculating Machine.[40] This latter Fred is finding a great convenience.
>
> I immediately set to work to determine the scale uniformity of the galvanometer and much to my chagrin found it un-uniform. In changing to the position, I had gone too far on the old original side. So I fixed up a special mounting for the mirror on March 6. Then on March 8, my first chance, I redetermined the scale uniformity [and correction factors] as you suggested.
>
> The computing is rather in arrears due to a sort of chronic indigestion I have developed. I guess it is the results of poor cooking, irregular meals and worry about things at home. I am trying to vary the food and take better care of myself and think things will soon improve.

---

[40] Roebling paid for the calculating machine and had it delivered from Los Angeles. Abbot described it as "very quick for multiplying and dividing, which you can do with your eyes shut by simply listening to the ringing of the bell, so it is quite a restful thing to eyes."

After continued efforts our Victrola now runs far better and quieter than ever. 'The Rienzi' Overture, etc. show not the slightest wobble and we are enjoying all the records more than we ever supposed we could.

Fred and I clipped each other's hair close as we could with Ellison's clippers.[41]

This morning we had rain enough to put three inches of water in the tank. Hope it will clear the sky, for the past week has been very hazy and unsatisfactory.

Yours sincerely,
LB Aldrich

Increasingly, Aldrich's letters showed the physical and mental ups and downs, particularly mental, of life at the Arizona field station.

Harqua Hala
March 19, 1921

Dear Mr. Abbot,

I seem to be hoodooed in this matter of the correcting factors. Twice I have thought the matter settled and have written you so, yet I think now it is as bad as ever. I will try to test other things if we only get a clear sky.

Our physical barometer has risen since last writing due to improved digestion but my mental barometer has materially slumped as a result of this correcting factor mix-up. We are anxiously awaiting the new records to help maintain our spirits.

Yours truly,
LB Aldrich

---

[41] Greeley described them as "baldy hair cuts. If we had on striped clothes would easily pass for two 'birds' from Sing Sing tonight. We both had hair long enough to braid and the clippers were decidedly dull so the operation soon turned into a hair pulling contest."

By April, Aldrich obviously had Moore's pending arrival in mind to cheer him up as much as possible, as well as an occasional win at horseshoes. However, nothing seemed destined to change the plague of the weather or instrument problems.

Harqua Hala
April 4, 1921

Dear Mr. Abbot,

    With the possible exception of March 16 and 17 we didn't have a single respectable sky during the whole month of March. We managed to scrape out eleven day's complete observations, and ten other short method days. In addition to an abundance of wind and cloudiness there was a persistent haze and streakiness as bad as any we had on Mt. Wilson. Pyranometer values were twice as big as on former good days. Maximum transmission coefficients were much lower. There has not been a single opportunity to make further progress in the correcting factor trouble. We have the same brilliant red sunsets and fluting high up in the sky that we had so much at Mt. Wilson. I think the continued wind has carried much fine dust into the upper air. However, after four cloudy days, today a change came. This morning we had a tremendous gale and blizzard - 2 inches of snow! And tonight it is clearing with apparently a fine blue sky. So I have great hopes of the next few days.

    I plan to leave here April 19 or 20, depending upon our auto service. In the event Mr. Moore is delayed a day or two, I am confident Fred can get short method observations. I would like several days leave to arrange for the moving of my family, if you see no objection, and reach Washington on May 2 or 3.

Yours truly,
LB Aldrich

In a reply dated April 5, 1921, Abbot seemed to know he could not deter Aldrich from his planned departure. Abbot wrote, "Mr. Moore reports that it will be impossible for him to reach Mt. Harqua Hala until April 23, and he hopes very much that you will be there to instruct him in the details of the outfit. I have written that I feared that telegraphic communication would be out of the question and so was writing you and that it might be that you would receive this letter too late to alter your plans for that purpose."

Harqua Hala
April 11, 1921

Dear Mr. Abbot,

I think our worst wind yet is raging at present. I have to weight down papers on the table and dust and sand are falling all over me. The house actually rocks. The hoped for change in skies following our snow storm did not come, though we have observed a number of days in hazy skies. The wind is almost incessant.

For several days I have noticed a progressive decrease in sensitivities of the pyranometer. Finally today the deflections were only about 1/4 what they should be so after some meditation and much hesitation, I took it apart. In the process of finding the trouble, I made matters worse and broke several of the thermocouples. I spent the whole afternoon trying vainly to patch them up. I shall of course redetermine its constant (provided I get a clear sky).

I have written Mr. Moore that I leave April 20 and if he doesn't arrive before I go, I'll try to leave all information with Fred. He has run several practice bolographs successfully.

My walk down hill on April 20 will be the happiest one I've taken.

Yours truly,
LB Aldrich

Chapter 7

From the Comfort of L.A.

While Loyal Aldrich struggled to keep the Harqua Hala field station running, his replacement, Alfred Moore, was in Los Angeles. Staying at the home of his brother Edgar, Moore was using his vacation time before he completed his transfer from Chile to Harqua Hala: He was tending to problems with his eyesight, making arrangements for his move to Arizona, and looking forward to marrying Miss Chella Moore[42] in early March and a planned honeymoon at the Smithsonian's cottage on Mount Wilson.

> 753 Carondelet St.
> Los Angeles, Cal.
> February 3, 1921
>
> Dear Mr. Abbot:
>
> I was down at Chella's home last evening, and her mother seemed anxious to know just what the Institution had at Harqua Hala in the way of bed and table linen since she said she wanted to have Chella take all that would be necessary for our new home. Since Chella is a brave enough girl to be willing and even anxious to go up there with me, I certainly want to do all in my power to make the place as cozy as possible for her.
>
> If I thought that I would have any use of it in Arizona, I would buy me a Ford automobile. If a strong garage could be cheaply constructed at the foot of the trail, we might get a good deal of use out of the machine even though we had to walk the five miles up and down the trail. It would at least break the monotony of having to stay at the observatory continually.
>
> Yours sincerely,
> *Alfred F. Moore*

---

[42] Apparently, Alfred Moore and Chella Moore (Orange, Calif.) were not related before marriage.

Anticipating having his wife at Harqua Hala, Moore asked Abbot about his annual salary. "You mentioned $2500 and my subsistence. Of course, Chella will be with me most of the time. While she isn't a direct employee of the Smithsonian, and under ordinary conditions would not be supposed to share in the subsistence arrangement for her husband, still she will doubtless have a good deal to do in the subsistence department and will make the place more livable for both observers. As Fred will doubtless eat with us, I suppose this will have to be considered in arranging things also."

Moore and Abbot corresponded often between Los Angeles and Washington. They needed to arrange for further outfitting the Harqua Hala field station. Abbot was finalizing the financial support promised by John Roebling.

SMITHSONIAN INSTITUTION
Washington, U.S.A.

February 9, 1921

Dear Alfred,

In regard to the bed and table linen and table service on Mt. Harqua Hala, there are six sheets, six pillow cases, six blankets and two eiderdown blankets, either six or twelve small Turkish towels of very ordinary quality, almost nothing in the way of dishtowels or cloths, no tablecloths, a large lot of paper plates and paper sauce dishes, six plates, six cups, six saucers, six each of knives, forks, teaspoons and tablespoons, six oatmeal dishes, four vegetable dishes, and quite a collection of cooking utensils. All of the table service is of a very ordinary variety, although the knives, forks and spoons present rather a brave appearance. I believe there are a lot of paper napkins, but no linen ones.

Your suggestion to procure a Ford automobile is a very excellent one. I will include the proposed garage in my discussion of the financial question and will let you know about it in a few days.

Very truly yours,

C. G. Abbot

Assistant Secretary

The much needed financial support from John Roebling was a breath of life for Abbot's hopes for improving the APO field station on Mount Harqua Hala.

SMITHSONIAN INSTITUTION
Washington, U.S.A.

February 15, 1921

Dear Alfred:

I visited Mr. Roebling a few days ago, in response to his invitation "to discuss what might make life more livable on Harqua Hala." He has approved and given us money to carry out the items below.

```
Mail and supply service, 1 year . $750
Wireless telephone. . . . . . . . $1000
Cottage for director. . . . . . . $2500
Two cement tanks . . . . . . . . $1000
Garage at foot of trail . . . . . $250
Furniture and furnishings . . . . $500
Paint and brushes. . . . . . . . .$100
Books and musical records. . . . .$200
Foot power lathe . . . . . . . . . $200
Meteorological instruments . . . $200
Monroe calculating machine . . . $300
Grinder and small tools . . . . . .$100
Fly screens . . . . . . . . . . . . $100
Pressure cooker . . . . . . . . . .$100
Stoves . . . . . . . . . . . . . . .$100
            Total . . . . . . $7400
```

I would like to have you satisfy yourself that the wireless telephone outfit proposed will answer its intended use.

The matter of the mail and supply services, I have entered into consideration with Mr. J.E. Matteson, postmaster at Wenden.

In regard to the cottage, I think it should be located at several hundred yards distance from the observatory, preferably to the northeast to avoid contamination of the atmosphere by smoke issuing from the fires in the cottage. There should doubtless be a couple of small out buildings which you will attend to, one for the house and one for the observatory.[43] As you are to live in the house with your wife, I think you

---

[43] If this is a reference to toilet facilities, it is the only such reference in all the correspondence about the Harqua Hala field station.

should be the one to choose the plan, the material and arrange for the construction of it.

As for the garage at the foot of the trail, I had in view one of the ready-made structures which are now upon the market, but it might be necessary to add something to the security of it, and also you would doubtless wish to put irons on each of the four wheels of your Ford so that even if evil disposed persons should break into the garage they would still not be able to use the car.

As to the furniture and furnishings, they would evidently comprise two beds for the cottage, and such chairs, bookcases which are always necessary to make a house comfortable. In addition, there should be certain bookcases and tables and easy chairs for use at the observatory, but you can best select what will be needed after a visit there to see what is on the grounds at present. It is not necessary to spend all this money at the moment unless you see how you need to spend it, for it will be continued as the Roebling Fund until exhausted, whether this year or in some future time.

With regards to the paint and brushes, I shall order so much of these directly as are needed for coating the outside of the observatory, for the plaster has, much of it, fallen away, and the rest of it is loose.

We shall also spend a considerable part of the appropriation for books and musical records from here, and purchase the foot power lathe perhaps in Baltimore or New York. The recording meteorological instruments, Monroe calculating machine, grinder and tools are also being taken up from here.

You will attend to the proper screening of the observatory and cottage against flies, scorpions, centipedes, tarantulas, and other venomous creatures when you arrive.

Mr. Roebling and I thought Miss Chella might like one of the pressure cookers which are coming into such extensive use in your neighborhood, and as to the stove, we leave you free to select whatever you wish for in that line. Our experience with the Coleman blue-flame stoves is like that of Longfellow with the little girl — when they are good they are very, very good, and when they are bad they are horrid.

As for lamps, there are several ordinary small
kerosene lamps and lanterns on the mountain now, and you
will find that there is nothing equal to the Coleman man-
tle lamp which burns gasoline, one of which we have in the
observatory and another of which you will evidently want
for the cottage.

Mrs. Roebling also takes an interest in the station
and has suggested that she should subscribe for certain
magazines, including, I believe, Life, Literary Digest,
and others, as well as certain books, humorous and
otherwise.

Very truly yours,
C. G. Abbot

Alfred Moore had not yet been to Harqua Hala; his impression of the place had all
come from his correspondence with Abbot. While the list of improvements seemed
impressive, the comment about the building's outside plaster must have confused his
mental image of the new building. And perhaps he wondered about all those venomous creatures that he would have to screen out. To get a better feel for what was
needed at the observatory and to see if the place would be suitable for his wife, in
early March Alfred Moore visited Wenden and Harqua Hala Mountain (see previous
chapter).

753 Carondelet St.
Los Angeles, Calif.
March 9, 1921

Dear Mr. Abbot:

Edgar and I returned from Wenden this morning, arriving at seven o'clock after an all-night ride in his
auto. We left here last Friday evening, going as far as
Banning that night. The next day we had 90 miles of
abominable road to contend with, as well as engine trouble, so we only got to Blythe on the Colorado River that
night. The next morning we discovered that we had broken
a leaf of a spring the day before, and this held us back
the rest of the trip. We got to Wenden about five o'clock
that evening (Sunday), and after making the acquaintance
of Mr. Matteson, and having him tell us how to reach the
foot of the trail, we proceeded. I had never heard of the
old Mexican living there, and my meager knowledge of
Spanish came in good place, for he told us how to find the

trail in the pitch dark. I guess we were pretty lucky, for with the aid of our flashlights we went right up to the observatory without any trouble. We got up there about eleven o'clock, being three hours on the trail.

Aldrich and Fred were very much surprised to see us. We put in the next morning discussing matters with Aldrich and Ellison. We left about two o'clock. We made Parker that night, and left there yesterday morning for the trip home across the desert, via the Parker cutoff road. It was pretty bad too, so doubtless the longer route via Needles is the best way to go by auto.

Aldrich and I talked over many things in regard to the present and proposed arrangements. One of the most important things considered was the matter of the messenger service. Probably the best arrangement would be with Mr. Ellison, since he had expressed a willingness to do it.

I have bought me a Ford auto, for $750, but since it is brand new and has an electric starter and several other extras, I would of course prefer not to have other people run it. It seemed to Aldrich and me that it might be best to purchase a secondhand Ford truck for the use of the messenger. If approved by you, I will get the auto here in Los Angeles. I think I can get a suitable truck for about $300 or less. I would drive it out to Wenden when I go the first time. I would stay about a week or so, to get the present quarters in shape for Chella, and then return here and take her out. I think it would be best to defer the actual building of the cottage until after I go out to stay. Mr. Ellison expressed a willingness to help us build the garage, and I think he would probably like to help on the cottage too.

The old Mexican said we could put the garage at the foot of the trail, but from what Ellison said, I'm not sure that the Mexican has much title to the land. However, we want to keep on the good side of him, for his being there will be a good deal of protection to the garage.

Here in Los Angeles, I started the man to work on the wireless telephone this afternoon. He agrees to make all the wireless apparatus except the aerial, gas engine and dynamo, for $185 for both ends. He agrees to test it out to my satisfaction for a greater distance near here. He says he is giving us a price of actual cost plus 10% since he thinks it will be good advertisement for him.

Since we have to get a small gas engine anyway, it seems to me that we should get a 30 volt dynamo too, to charge the storage batteries[44] as in Chile.

I wonder if the Institution would object to paying Edgar the equivalent of the round trip rail and sleeper fare that I would have had to pay had I gone on the train. The single rail fare is $21.19 and the sleeper $4.86. The wear and tear is pretty heavy on a car on a 700 mile trip over such roads as those.

Sincerely yours,

Alfred F. Moore

A week after his first visit to Harqua Hala, Alfred and Chella Moore were married on March 16, 1921, in "a quiet little home wedding." While at first he did not voice his opinion about the conditions on Harqua Hala, a tone of disappointment began to grow with each letter to Washington. In addition, his honeymoon to the Smithsonian's cottage on more accessible Mount Wilson seemed to set his opinion that the APO's field station should have been moved to a better location within the mountains of Southern California, instead of Arizona.

Mt. Wilson
March 26, 1921

Dear Mr. Abbot,

We will try to get an apartment in Westlake Park when we leave here. I will try to reach Harqua Hala around the 20th of April, but will have to leave Chella in L.A. for a week or two until I can go out there and get things in shape for her to come. I want to calcimine the walls and paint the woodwork and floor - at least in our room in the present building - and give the place a thorough cleanup so it will be as homelike as possible for her.

Considering that I had to wait five months longer for my vacation and didn't leave Chile until December 27

---

[44] The storage batteries provided electric power for the observing instruments.

and spent about a week in my late trip to Harqua Hala on purely Smithsonian business, it doesn't seem to me that all my vacation will be spent by April 20, but I would prefer to have more time later on. I am sure we can arrange this satisfactorily afterwards. It seems to me that in view of the extreme isolation of Harqua Hala, so that we virtually give all our time to the Institution, instead of eight hours per day six days a week as in Washington, it will be necessary for us to have more time away from there than the thirty days per year as regularly allowed. I am sure that I could break Fred in so that the work can continue unbrokenly on all good days throughout the year and yet so that the observers will not suffer so much from the isolation. I am sure some such plan will have to be adopted if the men are to continue steadily with the work.

If possible, I think Aldrich should be at Harqua Hala when I get there as doubtless he should show me about several things in connection with the work.

Sincerely,
Alfred F. Moore

Of course, at the other end Aldrich was prodding Abbot to get Moore to Harqua Hala before he left on April 20th. His mind was set to return to his family and on to Washington; Aldrich had already told Abbot, "My walk down hill on April 20 will be the happiest one I've taken." He was simply not going to delay his exit from Harqua Hala, even if it meant a lapse in the solar constant work. Nor could Moore pull himself away from Los Angeles any sooner; he was busy with last minute plans and "many social events planned in our honor since our return from Mount Wilson." It seemed Moore dreaded leaving civilization as much as Aldrich wanted to return to it.

                              Jamieson Apts.
                              915 S. Carondelet St.
                              Los Angeles, Calif.
                              April 17, 1921

Dear Mr. Abbot:

     I have certainly been kept on the go, and I don't see
how I could have reached Wenden by the 20th. Considering
Aldrich's report of the weather conditions at Harqua
Hala for the same period, I think much better conditions
prevailed at Mt. Wilson. On only one day observations
would have been impossible although there was considerable haziness on many days.

     I have bought a secondhand Ford truck, furniture
for the present house and gas engines for the wireless
outfit. The wireless man has been held up in getting some
of the things for the outfit.

     I have written to several building material firms
of Phoenix getting their prices, but want to confer with
Mr. Ellison before taking definite steps with the new
cottage. We drew up some plans while on Mt. Wilson, but
have not decided definitely yet just what style of house
we will build.

                         Sincerely yours,

                         Alfred F. Moore

Chapter 8

Moore's Attitude Arrives

As both had planned, Alfred Moore left Los Angeles on April 20th headed for Wenden, Arizona, the same day that Loyal Aldrich left Mount Harqua Hala. From the mountain, Moore quickly established a routine of writing to his boss, Charles Abbot, in Washington; his unfavorable opinion of Harqua Hala was evident even in his first letter from the mountain.

> Mt. Harqua Hala
> April 26, 1921
>
> Dear Mr. Abbot,
>
> I left L.A. last Wednesday morning with the truck and arrived in Wenden Saturday and up here that evening. Fred had no trouble in observing alone during the interval between Mr. Aldrich's departure and my arrival. I have helped him observe every morning since I came.
>
> We have been putting in our time getting the present quarters in shape for Chella to be here. The furniture that I bought in L.A. for this place is now in Wenden and will be brought up this week. I expect to return to L.A. next Sunday night to get our things in shape and bring her out, for I'll have a lot of things to do including carrying that wireless telephone along. I'll probably have to be there about a week, but I will bring her out in the train.
>
> Fred and I sat down to talk over things with Mr. Ellison last night and I must confess that I am in quite a

quandary as to what to do about starting the cottage. In the first place Mr. Ellison says the water supply has dropped off very much the past few days and he fears he may not have water enough for the adobe bricks. He even said that if no big summer rains come he fears the domestic supply will be in danger of running out next fall. He suggests that a concrete house would require much less water, but would probably cost more. And then, since it is largely for Chella and myself that the house would be built, I'm wondering if it wouldn't be better sense to fix up this present building as comfortably as possible and see how she will like it up here. Chella is a mighty sweet girl, but this is an awfully isolated place for a woman to live in continually. And lastly, it seems to me that it is doubtful if the weather conditions here justify such an extremely isolated place. Edgar thinks this station is located too far east so as to be in the bounds of the eastern thunder cloud region, and I rather think this is the case. From what Aldrich said[45] and what I've seen of it on my two trips, it seems to cloud up very rapidly. (I have an idea that mountainous regions near Victorville, Calif. would be better in this regards.)

So altogether since Mr. Ellison says he will know more about the water condition in a month or six weeks, it seems it might be better to wait a little while before making definite arrangements to build the house.

I think the cistern for this house should be built soon and the garage built at the foot of the trail and the wireless telephone put in working order.

Sincerely yours,
Alfred F. Moore

[45] Here, Moore is referring to his brief meeting with Aldrich in March and to Aldrich's comments in the field station log books.

With each letter to Washington, Abbot was quick to reply with encouragement for his isolated observers. He thought that building a house would add a lot. Abbot told Moore, "If I were Mrs. Chella I could be a good deal more contented in a house of my own, perhaps, than I could in the station itself, especially if I had to be as quiet as a mouse every morning while the observations are being taken lest I interfere with the galvanometer or make a smoke which would interfere with the seeing."

Abbot held to his belief, and decision, that Harqua Hala was a promising location, reminding Moore that the site was selected "after an extensive survey of the matter by the Weather Bureau and a year of special observations of various localities in the Southwest compared with all available records of the cloudiness; we supposed we had picked the best in the United States."

Back in Washington, Aldrich seemed to have forgotten the unpleasantness of the place: Abbot relayed from Aldrich to Moore, "He said that you had gained a wrong impression from him that it was a poor place. On the contrary, he had never seen such fine conditions as in February, and the haziness of March and April were temporary and exceptional. Even when the haze was present, he found that sky very uniform all day, so that he believed good results were obtained even on the hazy days. He is of the impression that we would look very far to find so good a site, except for its isolated character."

Yet, from the mountain, obviously Moore was experiencing the same daily frustrations that had caused Aldrich sleepless nights, many of them caused by the experimental nature of this underfunded work to tie solar measurements to the earth's climate.

> Mt. Harqua Hala
> May 20, 1921
>
> Dear Mr. Abbot:
>
> I brought Chella out on the train, leaving Los Angeles a week ago last Tuesday, arriving in Wenden early the following morning.[46] Fred came down with the truck, and we went up to the foot of the trail in it, where Mr. Ellison had his burros. He had a saddle on one burro, and Chella rode most of the way up on it, and stood the trip very well.
>
> With the cleanup that we gave the place just before going to Los Angeles, and the work that Fred did during my absence, the place was looking pretty good when we got here, but there have been a thousand and one things to do

---

[46] According to Greeley, Chella Moore arrived on May 11, 1921, bringing with her "linoleum, curtains, oil cloth shelving and a real table cloth."

since our arrival. Putting things to rights, and adding a
little paint surely makes a marked improvement in a
place.

I was very much surprised at the great difference in
the methods of observing and computing here and in Chile.
I have almost had to learn the business all over again.
About the only similarity in the observing is in the
method of reading the pyrheliometers, and even in this
the computing is entirely different. I am wondering what
is the reason for this, for undoubtedly your instructions are being followed in both cases, and yet there is
very little similarity. The Chile method seems much
longer, although I am inclined to think it is much more
accurate. I surely had to dig out most of the computing
methods from your "precept," for aside from the pyrheliometer and air mass, Fred knew very little about this,
for he had never been shown, and Aldrich took away every
single reduction to date, so I had nothing to go by except
the precept.

I had much trouble in keeping the galvanometer spot
where I put it on the scale just preceding each bolograph. It seemed impossible to get a good looking bolograph. Fred said that Aldrich laid the trouble to air
currents stirred up when the observer walked past the
bolometer. For several days I did not have time to look
into the matter, but when I did I decided that such was
probably the cause of the trouble. It looked to me that
the easiest and most sensible thing to do would be to put
up some sort of housing around the bolometer and
spectroscopic instruments to shield the bolometer from
the air currents. So one morning Fred and I got busy, and
in about two hours we had constructed a housing of some of
that heavy roofing paper. It works admirably, so that now
the conditions as regards drift are very good indeed. I
am surprised that some such thing had not been gotten up
sooner, for undoubtedly with the bolometer so exposed to
air currents, much error has been introduced by fluctuations happening between zero readings.

We got a most unusual display of northern light last
Saturday night (May 14). Huge patches and streamers were
seen far to the south of the zenith, and at times the
whole northern sky was aglow.

The skies have been very poor most of the time since
I returned, in fact, I haven't seen a very good sky here
at any of the three times that I have been here. It seems
that this ought to be one of the best seasons of the year.

The wireless telephone fellow surely is taking his
time. With all my urging, he did not get it finished before I left Los Angeles. I told him I would not OK his bill
until I got it to working up here, since he did not get it
ready for a tryout over the required distance around Los
Angeles. I expect to test it out over a short distance in
Wenden before bringing it up here, so as to get the adjustments made there, where we can easily go back and
forth between the two ends.

It is a very dry year here. It seems to me that this
water has much more of a taste now than when Edgar and I
came up here in March, but none of us has gotten sick yet,
so it may be all right.

                                     Sincerely yours,

                                     Alfred F. Moore

With a brief, likely bewildering, reply about the tedious scientific method used on
Harqua Hala, Abbot confessed, "I had never done any computing of solar constant observations myself, with the exception of the very few days in Algeria, until I arrived at
Mt. Harqua Hala. I had nothing to go on there except what is included in the Annals[47]
and the data which we collected on Mt. Wilson this last summer, so that I manufac-
tured the whole method afresh."

                                     Mt. Harqua Hala
                                     Wenden, Arizona
                                     May 25, 1921

Dear Mr. Abbot:

We expect to go to the foot of the trail tomorrow to
start work on the garage. We will have a carpenter from
Wenden help us, and I think we will get it up in two days.
It will be of corrugated iron, as this will be more thief
and fire proof.[48]

I was certainly very much surprised to read what you
wrote about Aldrich's report about this station, and I
cannot help thinking that his ideas have changed very

---

[47] Smithsonian Institution Annals Vols. III and IV.
[48] After the carpenter quit because it was too hot, Greeley and Ellison completed the garage on May 29, 1921.

much since Edgar and I were up here, both as regards the
weather and the livability of the place. If you will read
over his weather notes on his February bolographs, I
think these will more nearly agree with what he told us,
than what he has told you since his arrival in Washington. As to the uniformity of the skies, I remember dis-
tinctly that he mentioned several times that he had
never seen a place where the sky conditions would change
so rapidly!

I did not mean to convey the idea to you that I consider this a poor place, as you mention in your letter,
but I do not think that the sky conditions justify the
extreme isolation, and general awkard conditions up
here. It is my opinion that when a place is selected for a
probable permanent station, one factor to be considered
is the livability of the place for the observers who must
stay there year in and year out. In this regard, a temporary station is vastly different from a permanent one. By
livability, among other things I mean its access to
civilization, for no normal human can be satisfied to be
continually tied up with his work alone. But aside from
Phoenix about one time, Los Angeles is about the only
place worth going to from here, and it cost over $100 for
railway fare alone each time Chella and I go to Los Angeles and back.

You have expressed much confidence in Edgar's
judgement, and he has said to me many times that he thinks
you have gotten too far east so as to be within the bounds
of the thunder cloud area. He thinks a much more favorable region is located a short distance north or east of
the Sierra Madre Mountains in California, and it certainly would be much more accessible to decent sized
cities. That "Rim of the World" auto road back of San
Bernardino, and reaching out on the Mojave Desert toward
Victorville, rises to elevations around 8000 feet, so
surely there is plenty of elevation.

I am glad to report that Chella finds this place
much more livable than she anticipated, but we both think
that it would be wiser to defer building the cottage until a more thorough tryout has been made of the place
generally. We have limited our purchases with Smithsonian money almost entirely to things that can be

carried out of here, and it seems to us that the permanent things should wait.

Sincerely yours,

Alfred F. Moore

With each letter to Washington, Moore's attitude about the unsuitability of Harqua Hala seemed to build. Finally, Abbot had to stop the complaining with a firm letter.

SMITHSONIAN INSTITUTION
Washington, U.S.A.

June 7, 1921

Dear Alfred:

Reports from many sections of the country incline me to the belief that abnormal weather is very widespread this spring, and I hope that further experience at Harqua Hala will tend to confirm the view we formed last year that the sky there is highly favorable to the work.

At the same time, I appreciate the isolation of which you complain, and which I presume you fear more for Chella than for yourself. Perhaps we can arrange to relieve this somewhat by financing an occasional trip to Los Angeles.[49] You will readily see, I am sure, that, having employed the Weather Bureau to survey the conditions of the Southwest and through their advice having settled upon this station, and having expended a considerable sum of Mr. Roebling's money on establishing it, it would require very strong reasons to justify my endeavoring to secure more money to bring about a removal to some other untried locality. I hope that the various items which Mr. Roebling has financed for making life more agreeable up there, and the cheerfulness of your companions, will altogether tend to make you as contented as the circumstances will allow.

Very truly yours,

C. G. Abbot

Assistant Secretary

---

[49] Already, Keg Greeley had received $100 for a vacation trip to Los Angeles, which he planned for June or July.

In a postscript added to a June 14th letter about the wireless system, Moore humbly told Abbot, "I have just received your good letter of the 7th. I can readily appreciate your position regarding the new station, and I'll do all in my power to make it a success. I think, like you, that probably the weather conditions are very unsettled now and from the wide variations which seem probable in old sol, don't you think it likely that, that is the cause in part at least. It is totally overcast again today. Wireless has not arrived so I'm sending Knight a letter to hurry him up."

Chapter 9

Troubles With Knight

Moore's hopes were that the wireless radio system ordered in Los Angeles would help with the isolation on Harqua Hala. First, with one radio station on the mountain and another at a merchant in Wenden, he could get telegram messages to Wenden, and on to Washington, without making a trip down the mountain; faster communications with Abbot were necessary to help solve the problems with the field station's instrumentation and the observing procedures. And, the wireless would help the observers order supplies and arrange for deliveries from Wenden. With the wireless overdue, Moore was getting frustrated.

                                        Wenden, Arizona
                                        June 12, 1921

Mr. G. M. Knight
6053 Hollywood Blvd.
Los Angeles, Calif.

Dear Sir:

    I received your letter of May 21, enclosing the statement and have been expecting the telephone sets ever since. Yesterday my assistant brought up a letter of June 5th, and I take it that you are holding our apparatus, awaiting my OK. I have received the gas engines and dynamos.[50]

    When the Smithsonian authorized me to place the order with you for the sets, it was with the understanding that they were to be tested out over a distance equal to that between Mt. Harqua Hala and Wenden and this test was to be carried out in my presence. You failed to get the sets ready for the test by the time I had to return here, and hence there is nothing else for me to do but to await

---

[50] Each wireless station required a gas engine ("prime mover") and a dynamo to generate power.

okaying your bill until the apparatus is found to work all right up here. I have no authority to change the Smithsonian's instructions.

Certainly you are not fearing that you will not receive your pay for the sets when they are shown to work all right. Should you have any fears in this regard, I can refer you to Fairbanks Morse where I got the engines, to the Advance Electric Co. and the International Electric Co., where the motors were gotten, to the J.M. Overell Furniture Co. and the Mathews Paint Co., where I have bought many things on Smithsonian orders. You may write to the Smithsonian Institution if you care to.

What I want to know is when are we to expect those telephone sets, for we are greatly in need of them, and if you cannot send them soon, it looks as though we must make other arrangements. It seems to me it is to your advantage to hurry them along, for if they prove successful, our prestige will probably help you in getting other business. And what is certain, if they work, the Institution will likely place an order with you for sets for Chile.

I have spent about ten years in electrical work, mostly in testing lines, so I don't think you need fear to trust the apparatus in my hands. If you have any doubts in this regard, please call up Mr. A.S. Price of the test department of Southern California Edison in Los Angeles.

Hoping to receive the sets by next Saturday, or if not a letter from you explaining things.

Very truly yours,

A.F.Moore

The heat of summer in 1921[51] made Moore change his plans for testing the wireless. He told Abbot, "I have decided that it would be wiser to test out the wireless telephones (if they ever arrive) up here instead of in Wenden, as I first planned. It is pretty warm here now, and it must be fierce down there. And besides, it would be conducive to much cussing to have trouble in getting it to work down there in all the heat, and with all those loafers and bums hanging around and making suggestions."

Constantly concerned with details and justifying all expenses at the field station, Moore added, "It will not be necessary to bring the Wenden gas engine and

---

[51] One letter explained that the observers were using correction factors in their calculations for 42°C (108°F) at the field station, which was one mile above sea level.

dynamo up here, for we can make one set do for the test, by putting wires between the two test stations. It will probably require about 300 or 400 feet of lamp cord to make the test up here, but this can be used in putting in some electric lights in the house here, for use during the hot weather. The Coleman lights are certainly dandy, except that they throw off a good deal of heat on warm nights."

In addition, with each letter Moore continued his subtle negative assessment of the Harqua Hala site. "We kill a lot of enormous big flat brown spiders in our rooms, but we haven't been bitten yet," he told Abbot. Moore added, "We are now boiling all our drinking water. Strangely enough, it does away with the bad taste about which I wrote you, and makes it pretty good to drink. But I think it contains a lot of inorganic salts, and I'm wondering if such will prove injurious to us after a time. We keep it very nice and cool by using wet canteens."

Mt. Harqua Hala
June 13, 1921

Dear Mr. Abbot:

    I told Mr. Knight it would be necessary for me to test the telephone sets out here. Personally, I am getting pretty tired of their un-business-like way of doing things. Mr. Ellison thinks that they are afraid their outfit will not work successfully, and are trying to get the money before we find it out. I am not so certain about this, for their sets look to be well made, and the Los Angeles Evening Express uses one of their sets, so I still have hopes that it will work, if we ever get it up here. However, I think we should hold them to their agreement to try it out first. I am pretty anxious to find out if he intends to send the things out here.

    Knight is a sort of erratic, pugnacious individual (the last time that I saw him he had a dandy black eye, and a badly banged up knuckle that he had just gotten in a fight), so he may fly off the handle and write to the Institution. I am enclosing a carbon copy of the letter I am sending to him, for your reference, should he write to you.

    As we get time we are getting the screen windows and doors put in, for we surely need them, with the choice collection of bees, wasps, yellow-jackets, bumble bees, etc. that we have here at this season of the year.

Sincerely yours,
Alfred F. Moore

Finally, while Keg Greeley was on vacation in Los Angeles, the wireless apparatus arrived. This seemed to brighten Moore's attitude and bring out his plans to improve Harqua Hala's living conditions.

Mt. Harqua Hala
July 12, 1921

Dear Mr. Abbot:

Mr. Ellison made the trip to Wenden and back in the flivver without mishap, it being his first trip alone with the car.[52]

He reported the wireless apparatus is in Wenden, but did not bring it up. I will telegraph you tomorrow to that effect, for it may be well for you to know as soon as possible, in view of the letter that I wrote to you about ten days ago. Fred and I will start in right away to test it out. It will be quite a little work to put up the aerials.

With the wireless apparatus, engine, dynamos, lathe, etc., I find it will be necessary to construct a small shop building just south of the present building. It will probably be well to get all that iron farther away from the galvanometer, anyway. Since I am in pretty much of a hurry to get this building up, I suppose it will be all right with you to go ahead and order the material for it, especially since it will not cost much, and will probably come within the balance left over from the $250 allowed for the garage. Fred and I will build it. I am planning it to use as little material as possible, and am going to make the roof of corrugated galvanized iron, so as to catch this much more rain water. My plan is to use the lower front room of the present building for the telephone apparatus, pyranometer, theodolite, and Edgar's large telescope which he has very kindly promised to loan us for a time. I think nine feet by twelve feet will be about right for the shop building.

We had a pretty good run of weather from the middle of June until a couple of days ago, but I guess we are now in for a lot of cloudiness of the thundercloud variety. We got 25 days without a break, but have lost yesterday and today. We have some "humdinger" electric storms in

---

[52] Moore and Greeley taught Ellison to drive so he could make trips to Wenden when they were too busy. Greeley said, "He finds the sensation of leading burros some different from being led by a Ford."

this vicinity, but this mountain itself, seems a little
less "favored" than the immediate region on all sides.
While I am writing this there is a grand bombardment going on toward Wenden. I never saw anything before to
equal the rapidity of the flashes, and their intensity in
a storm of several hours' duration to the south of us last
evening. I wonder if our telephone aerial will not prove
a grand thing to get hit by lightning, but if well
grounded I guess it will be safe. I will arrange to have
the apparatus entirely cut loose when not in use.

The tank holds water pretty well, but I think there
is still a very small leak, for about two inches goes out
of it every 24 hours, and I don't think the evaporation
would be nearly that much. Mr. Ellison was fearful a week
or so ago that his spring was failing, but with the rains
that we are now getting, I guess there will be no danger
of our having to leave the mountain for lack of water this
summer.

I have put up a lot of much-needed shelves, etc.,
and painted them, as well as put up some railings alongside the steep steps of the house to keep Chella from
taking a bad fall. Chella has also been busy getting curtains fixed for the windows, and arranging coverings for
clothes shelves for Fred's and our room. I wish you could
see the house now, for I think it would present a pretty
homelike appearance. If you come west you must be sure to
make us a visit.

Sincerely yours,

Alfred F. Moore

P.S. Wenden, 7/13 - Fred returned this morning.

One can imagine the trek up the trail on July 13th. Perhaps all Alfred Moore could think about was his anticipations for the wireless. Keg Greeley, on the other hand, had mixed emotions after spending two weeks visiting relatives and friends in Los Angeles. Greeley wrote to an aunt in New Hampshire, "I started back on the 12th with lasting memories of California, its good generous people and the fine time I had. Alfred met me in Wenden the next morning and then came the worst part of the trip, walking up the mountain after I had been riding around in autos, trains and electric cars for two weeks. The old canyon was boiling hot with no wind stirring. It took us over three hours to come up and the canteen was dry when we got here." Like Keg, Moore's happy thoughts were soon brought back to reality.

> Mt. Harqua Hala
> July 16, 1921

Dear Mr. Abbot:

When I was in Wenden last Wednesday I sent you a telegram relative to the wireless telephone. We brought it up here, and when we opened it I found to my dismay and disgust that Knight had proven himself to be crooked, along with his other failings. There are eight vacuum tubes in the outfit, two for receiving and two for sending at each end, and when I looked them over I found that he had "honored" us with seven out of the eight burned out and utterly worthless! I thought they looked rather smoked up for new ones when I took them from the box. The apparatus was well packed and came through in good shape, so there is no ground for thinking that they were injured in transit, for they look old and used.

Knight had written me to have the pay sent to the International Electric Co. in L.A. as he owned them money. I am writing them by this mail, explaining about the burned out tubes, and telling them that they will have to make Knight replace them with new ones, unless we deduct the value of them from the bill. The cost of the burned-out tubes will amount to nearly $50. I am so thoroughly disgusted with Knight, and he is so utterly irresponsible, that I see no use in writing to him. Aside from the tubes, his apparatus is pretty well made. Were it not for this I would recommend sending the whole thing back to him, and inform him that the deal is off as far as we are concerned. If there were a shadow of a doubt that he did not knowingly send the burned-out tubes, I would give him the benefit of the doubt. Possibly he has it in for the Electric Co. I am certainly sorry that I ever got in with this fellow, for he has been nothing but a source of worry and trouble from the start.

> Sincerely yours,
>
> Alfred F. Moore

P.S. We really should have two 0-500 volt D.C. voltmeters, to use in keeping the voltage right at both

telephone stations, for this is pretty important in
wireless telephone communications.[53]

Adding to his problems with the wireless apparatus, the Post Office returned Moore's June 12th letter to Knight; Moore concluded that Knight had "flown the coop" and that the only recourse was to discuss the matter with officials at the International Electric Co. in Los Angeles. Fortunately, he and Chella were planning a trip there beginning July 29th.

With the dream of a useful wireless link to Wenden not yet realized, Moore came up with three more ideas to make the isolation of the Harqua Hala field station more tolerable.

Mt. Harqua Hala
July 24, 1921

Dear Mr. Abbot:

Fred has often wished we had a shower bath to cool
off under. Since we have a little gas engine, and I am going to build a little shop just south of the observatory,
the idea struck me that if I could procure a little sec-
ondhand pump I could easily and cheaply rig up a little
shower bath near the shop, fixing it so that the pump will
keep the water running round and round, so that two or
three gallons of water will suffice for a fine shower
bath, and one would easily imagine he had a whole ocean to
draw upon.

In order to better keep the bugs, centipedes, etc.
out of the cistern, I think it would be well if I would get
a cheap hand pump, and then board it over carefully, just
leaving a little trap-door to examine the interior of the
cistern occasionally. It does not leak at all now, and
keeps us supplied with nice rain water for everything
except drinking.

Since we get tired of playing horseshoe all the time
for out-of-door exercise, I wonder if it will be all
right for me to get a cheap set of croquet, for we can find
room for that near the observatory. I don't think it will
cost over $5, and likely less.

Chella is counting the days until we are to start
for L.A., and I guess I am too. With these occasional

---

[53] Author's speculation: this postscript certainly leads one to wonder if Moore did not burn out the vacuum tubes himself because he did not properly control the voltage of the dynamos?

little trips I think we will be very contented here for
sometime.

                              Sincerely yours,
                              Alfred F. Moore

P.S. Sunday evening, July 24th - When it was hopelessly
cloudy Fred and I took a hike down a ridge to the north of
the observatory, to see if a road would be possible down
that way. It looked quite promising for quite a long way,
but at last the hogback dropped off suddenly into a big
canyon running east and west. It looks to me like it will
cost a pretty large sum of money to construct a road to
the top of this mountain, and that the upkeep of such a
road would cost a good deal every year. To me the chances
really look better to the south and east, for there do not
seem to be such precipitous ledges in that direction, and
the descent into the valley is much more gradual, but a
big trouble there would be that the road would land so far
away from any town on the railroad. A.F.M.[54]

Back in Washington Abbot and Roebling had already decided against constructing a
road. Abbot replied to Moore, "Mr. Roebling and I discussed it sometime ago, but he
is of the opinion that if we should build a road, although it would relieve the isolation
of the mountain to a considerable extent, it would do so at the expense of bringing up
a horde of prospectors and fake mining concerns whose operations might make observatory work there quite impossible. On that account we decided to defer indefinitely
the consideration of building a road."

With the Moores off to Los Angeles, again Keg Greeley was alone to operate the Harqua Hala field station. Curiously, Greeley's attitude about the remote mountain site always seemed better than Moore's.

                              Harqua Hala
                              August 12, 1921

Dear Dad,
*   Every evening a delightful breeze breezes thru my*
room and before morning I have to employ the warmth

---

[54] Today, the road to the summit of Harqua Hala ascends from the south; this road was built circa 1979 to provide assess to a modern solar-
powered communications facility for the Bureau of Reclamation and the Central Arizona Project canal system from the Colorado River to
Phoenix and Tucson. An earlier road up the south side of the mountain gave ranchers access to high pastures and the mountain's springs.

of a comforter. One reason for the cool atmosphere is because of the incessant thunder showers. They start in about 3 o'clock every afternoon and die out in the night. Not much of them pass over this mountain, although we get a ragged edge once in a while.

Have been pretty busy the last two weeks, all alone. Painting, digging post holes for our new shop and leveling off a place for the same. Then I've had to try my luck at cooking again. I got indigestion one night and between that and a couple of blistered shoulders that old sol donated I didn't get much sleep for a couple of nights. I observed seven days and did my part of the computing on them. Shot a rabbit with the 22 rifle and invited Mr. Ellison in one noon to help eat it as he happened along with a load of lumber about time.

The dog[55] and I added quite a lot to our menagerie the past two weeks. We were down to Mr. Ellison's one day and he discovered a Gila Monster. I poked him into a can and put the lid on. A day or so later he discovered a Tarantula around the tank so I got another can and canned it. Alfred has a collection of scorpions, centipedes and vinegaroons in a glass jar filled with alcohol so when he gets back I imaging G-M and I will have a chance to violate the Volstead Act.[56]

Alfred and Chella are coming back tomorrow so I've got to pile out tomorrow morning about 4 o'clock and make Wenden by breakfast time. Mr. Ellison and I went down last Sunday and the roads were so bad we had to shovel ourselves out of sand three times. It was worth it though for when we got there we had three dishes of ice cream apiece. I also got four nice letters and a shower bath. One of the fellows down there has rigged up a shower and told me to make use of it anytime, which I'll do all right.

Love to you and mother,
Keg

---

[55] There is no mention in the letters written from Harqua Hala where the dog came from, but it was probably a stray from Wenden or from the Mexican's camp at the foot of the trail.

[56] Prohibition, or the period (1920-1933) during which the 18th Amendment banned the manufacture and sale of alcoholic beverages, was in force in the United States.

Chapter 10

After One Year

Following two weeks away from Harqua Hala, Alfred and Chella Moore returned from Southern California by train on the morning of August 13, 1921. As always, an arrival at the Wenden depot was an event for the little town. And with the Moores returning, this arrival was an excuse for Keg Greeley to get off the mountain; he and Ellison met the Moores at the train station and drove them out to the base of the mountain where Ellison had left his burros. Then, "Chella rode up in state on 'Jack Sprat' or 'General Jackson' as Mr. Ellison sometimes calls him," Moore wrote to Abbot.

Refreshed, Alfred Moore seemed to return from California with a renewed attitude, ready to make living conditions better at the field station. He had settled the bill for the wireless apparatus with the International Electric Co., and brought with him the parts needed to make the wireless work properly and other supplies to build a shower bath. In addition, Alfred's brother Edgar had given Chella a croquet set for her birthday.

Keg's letters to his family on the east coast always seemed to capture the positive side of living on Harqua Hala and the progress being made, along with the continued adventure of the place.

> Harqua Hala
> October 19, 1921
>
> Dear Aunt Grace,
> The fine box of candy you sent came as a very pleasant surprise a few days ago. I shared it with the rest of the family here and we all pronounced it as excellent. We hadn't had any chocolates all summer except on our trips to L.A. for the merchants in Wenden don't keep them during the summer because they melt.

News is about as scarce as the hair on a cow's horn, nevertheless I'll start about August 1st and give you some idea of the slow moving matters on the mountain.

Mr. and Mrs. Moore went to L.A. the first two weeks of August, which added fourteen more days of blessed singleness to my already unenviable record. It was showery most of the time so only had a chance to observe six days. There was considerable painting to do inside during their absence which with cooking and several odd jobs kept me busy. I also leveled off a place for our little nine-by-twelve shop and dug four post holes for the corners which in this rocky, camelback mountain was no cinch.

We built the shop soon after Mr. Moore got back as a real necessity. It houses about 57 varieties of tools, a two horsepower engine, three small dynamos for the telephone, a lathe and work bench, paint, lumber, old newspapers and bailing wire, in fact about everything including the dog, fleas and all.

There is also a little centrifugal pump which supplies water for the shower bath built on the back of the shop. The shower is quite economical as we have it so arranged as to use the same water over and over. It is a fine addition and we all like it.[57]

Received your nice letter from Greensboro[58] around the last of August and well I remember the day. I went to town with Mr. Ellison as there had been heavy showers in the valley the day previous and the road was a fright. The car was working bad, choked up with carbon, and we had to shovel ourselves out of the sand in three different washes. It was after three o'clock when we arrived in Wenden and never got started back till about five. Of course we ran into a shower. Although there is a top on the car, the rain and wind came with such fierceness that it blew right thru the sides and drenched us both. It rained all evening so we couldn't build a fire outside to get some supper, but built a small one in the garage and made some tea which with bread and butter constituted the bill of fare

---

[57] Moore had already told Abbot, "The bath uses only two gallons of water, but one would think he was drawing on the whole ocean."
[58] It's uncertain where this Greensboro was.

that night. Hot tea never tasted better to me in my life. There are a couple of cots in the garage so we stayed there all night. There aren't many climates you can sleep in your wet clothes all night and not catch cold.

Mr. Ellison shot a deer lately and has been treating us to venison and liver. It sure tastes good as we haven't had fresh meat for over a month. He has moved into his new home so I go down once in awhile of an evening and have a smoke talk with him and he always has some interesting yarn (and some pie or cake) as he has traveled quite a bit in his day.

I recently sent to L.A. for a Kodak and have been trying my luck at picture making. We have the apparatus and material to develop films and print pictures. It was my first attempt and you will notice some of the pictures have dark spots because I didn't wash the negative thoroughly.

With very much love,
Keg

Despite the hope for progress, it didn't take long before Alfred Moore was again berating the Arizona site. He continued to compare observing conditions on Harqua Hala with his brief views of the sky while traveling through California's deserts and valleys. Just before leaving for California, Moore had experienced a run of "five days in a stretch with practically total cloudiness all of every day." Referring to his train ride to California in late July, Moore wrote to Abbot, "I was quite surprised when I awoke on the train the morning of the 30th, out near Barstow, and saw an almost perfect sky! It remained so until we got across the Cajon Pass, when we ran into low fog, which turned into a high fog as we got lower down."

Of course, Moore's judgment didn't always consider that Arizona was in the midst of its summer thunderstorm season. By autumn, writing in October to his Aunt, Greeley said, "We have had fairly good weather for observing since the last of August. Got twenty-three consecutive days in September and twenty-seven in all for the month. This month we have sixteen chalked up and the sky has been perfectly clear all day today."

Abbot had directed the observers to run a long method on all days possible for six months. But even when sky conditions allowed the observers to make their solar-constant measurements, the measurement method and instruments continued to be a problem. Writing about the pyranometer, Moore reported, "I am now changing the value for K',[59] and really should have done so a couple of months ago, I suppose, but yours and Aldrich's constants agreed so well that I was a little afraid to change it. This will have the effect of decreasing the function value, increasing the transmission, and decreasing the solar constant. I looked into the matter today and was surprised to find that it makes as much difference as it does. Most certainly, very little dependence should be placed on anything that was gotten in July after the 7th. Personally, I have very little faith in ever getting a very satisfactory set of curves on Harqua Hala, for the sky conditions are too changeable."

Moore added, "We have so many things to do that must be done soon, that I wonder if you want us to take long measurements every day with low functions. We have been putting in very long hours, I think averaging about eleven hours per day ever since I took charge, and I think we will have to have considerable help with the computing if we are to get so many long methods. I know from various things that Fred has said of late that he is getting pretty tired of this continual grind of long hours, and I guess I must fess up that I am too."

Along with the observing conditions, increasingly, Moore worried about the deteriorating field station building. "The heavy rain of last Saturday night surely about ruined the paint on the adobe outside the house. It peels off bodily. Since some of the same paint is peeling off of woodwork, possibly it is poor paint. I do not see much use in putting more of it on, but do not know just what to do. When I look at this house and see the cracks widening in the adobe, I wonder if it is worth spending much money upon. I think it will probably be necessary to get some more tie rods before long to go in the other direction at the south end of the house."

And there was a new problem: the "awful state that the trail to the landing is in." Moore told Abbot, "Mr. Ellison asked me the other day if I thought that you would be willing to furnish some funds with which to have it put in repair. I tried to get out of him what he thought it would take, and the best that I could do was to find out that he thought it would take two men about a month. I don't think he wants to work on it himself. Since the Mexicans use part of the trail, it seems nothing but right that they should help repair the part that they use, but from what Mr. Ellison says, I doubt if they will do much to help."

Back in Washington, forever optimistic Charles Abbot, the recipient of all of Moore's written complaints, knew that a valuable solar constant measurement depended on correlating measurements made at his field stations in Chile and Arizona. Abbot also knew the Arizona field station would not be a success unless Moore's attitude about the work and living conditions changed.

---

[59] "K prime" was a constant used with calculations that reduced observations to a solar constant value.

SMITHSONIAN INSTITUTION
Washington, U.S.A.

September 12, 1921

Dear Alfred:

Your first letter, besides enumerating the centipedes, scorpions, rattlesnakes, tarantulas and Gila monsters, goes on to say that the paint is all off the building, the walls are sagging east and west as well as north and south, and the tank leaking, and you question whether it is worth while to do anything with the house other than let it go to ruin. That house cost $4000, and a stone and cement construction would have cost between $6000 and $7000. At that time we had not the money to build the stone one. It seems to me best to tie the walls together east and west and try some other variety of paint if the Sears Roebuck paint is worthless.

As for the tank, we have money to build cement tanks, but I know that you are inclined not to put any expense on the mountain, with a view to moving away. All your experience is so diametrically opposite to mine.

This summer has been the most extraordinary one everywhere that I can recall, so far as weather goes. Possibly we may never see another like it. If we now move to another place, all the long method observations which have been taken will be worthless for establishing the short method and we must wait another year after the removal before the work can get settled into a groove.

As to the pyranometer, I am sorry that the calibration of the one you have had so long has so certainly changed, but the change only confirms the view which I expressed to you that the pyranometer is not reliable as a standardizing instrument, however, satisfactory it may be for single day observations.

Mr. Roebling has made it possible for me to go to South America and Arizona. The work is so promising, in view of the results some of which I am sending you, that I am in the highest degree anxious to get the two stations cooperating in a thoroughly satisfactory manner.

Very truly yours,

C. G. Abbot

Assistant Secretary

In a subsequent letter Abbot added, "As for the trail, suppose we appropriate $200 to the repairing of it, and when that is exhausted and more is needed let me know. I do not think it is wise to inform anybody just what amount is appropriated for that object, but only to go about repairing the worst places first and to stop when the result appears tolerably satisfactory."

About the instrumentation, Abbot added, "I have long believed the principal causes of the poorer definition at Harqua Hala are two. First, that the bolometer slit width is quite a little greater than you employed at South America, and second, that probably the neck of the glass flask which encloses the bolometer happens not to be as good and optically perfect as the neck of the flask which is used in Chile. Perhaps, there may be some striae, or it may be that the bolometer strip is not strictly parallel with the elements of the cylindrical neck."

Whenever things got tough on Harqua Hala, Moore seemed to find refuge in working on the challenge of establishing easier communications with Wenden and Ellison.

                                                        Mt. Harqua Hala
                                                        September 16, 1921
Dear Mr. Abbot:
        Fred and I had a general straightening up yester-
day, getting things in order to try to get the wireless
telephone going. We will have it in the little room in
front downstairs. We have the engine and dynamo all
mounted up here, and as the engine drives the dynamo at
considerable over rated speed, we get 350 volts, which is
just what our transmitting vacuum tubes are rated at. We
are now working on the aerials, and I wish we had them up,
for it is no fun getting them thirty-five feet above the
ground.
        Mr. Ellison was up the other day and was wondering
if we could get a little telephone between his place and
the observatory, of the wire variety of course. He suggested having a friend of his save some baling wire in
Wenden, but I hardly think this would serve very well, as
well as taking a mighty long time, for it would take a lot
of baled hay to get 5500 feet of it. I looked in Sears &
Roebuck's catalogue, and they have small magneto telephones, including transmitter, receiver, magneto and
bell, for $28.80 for two phone. The wire would cost about
$12.20 and the freight about $6.00. No poles would be required, but the wire should be fastened to bushes with

some sort of insulators, so the whole thing would cost
about $50. While this is not an absolute necessity, since
Mr. Ellison goes to Wenden for us and packs our water up
here from his spring, it would be pretty convenient both
to him and to us. It would not take a day to install it. It
would save Fred quite a lot of running down to his place.

I don't know whether I wrote you about the croquet
set or not. We have leveled off a place between the house
and the peak, where we get a lot of enjoyment out of it
every evening after supper.

Chella and I are celebrating our sixth (month) anniversary of our wedding today.

Sincerely yours,

Alfred F. Moore

Keeping busy, with a few breaks for croquet, was still not enough; two weeks later the
tone of Moore's letters changed dramatically.

Mt. Harqua Hala
October 1, 1921

Dear Mr. Abbot:

As I am writing this it is still pouring. It began
about two o'clock yesterday morning, and rained quite a
bit during the day yesterday. Late in the afternoon I
rigged up a rain gauge, and up to dark this evening it
registered three inches. Early this morning the rain got
into the cracks at both south corners of the house and
softened the adobe so that chunks of it fell from both
corners. Fred and I covered it as best we could with canvas, but about an hour later a great big piece fell from
the southeast corner. Only the outer row of adobe bricks
have fallen thus far, but if the rain keeps up much
longer, it would not surprise me if the whole south end of
the house should go down. Chella and I have moved out of
our room into the computing room. The inner layer of
bricks are so poorly put together that it will not take
much to put them out of business. If it gets no worse, we
may be able to fix it by building up the place with concrete, placing the concrete on the stone foundation, and
reinforcing it in some way. I am in a quandary to know
just how to protect the whole house, for in a recent

letter, in which you seemed to think I was greatly exag-
gerating conditions, you instructed me to go ahead and
fix the house up. I am absolutely certain that, that
paint arrangement is no good at all, for in the part that
went down today, the paint was little injured by the
August storms.

     Chella suggested a plan today, that seems to me
about the only way to save the house, and that is to build
practically another house around it of corrugated iron.
This would probably cost between $300 and $400 with galvanized iron, and about 20 per cent cheaper with painted
iron. In this way the adobe would be protected from the
weather, and the iron could be nailed to timbers that
could be easily fastened to the rafters and floor. Please
let me know soon what you think of this plan, and if you
approve of it, let me know whether to order galvanized or
painted iron.

                              Sincerely yours,

                              Alfred E. Moore

Moore's disconcerting letter did not arrive in Washington for over a week; Abbot replied immediately, but not by telegram.

                    SMITHSONIAN INSTITUTION
                    Washington, U.S.A.

                              October 10, 1921
Dear Alfred:

     I do not think it would be proper to cover the whole
house with galvanized iron, as Chella suggested, because
it would altogether change the magnetic conditions
around the galvanometer.

     It is quite impossible for me to come out there be-
fore I go to South America; transportation is engaged for
October 26th. Would it not be practical to replace the
south wall with stone and cement or reinforced concrete,
and drive the balance of the walls with projecting ten-
penny nails and then plaster the whole house? If you approve of it you are authorized to have it done. I am
obliged to leave the matter in your hands to do the best
you can, and if the worst should come to the worst, so

that you see no way out of it at all, I shall have to
authorize you to close the station until my return.
                    Very truly yours,
                    C. G. Abbot
                    Assistant Secretary

A day later, Abbot changed his mind, added a small variation to the concept, and
wired Moore, "Approve plain thin galvanized iron use zinc ten feet each side west
door. Cannot south wall be patched. Tie rods sent. This corrects letter." Moore proceeded by ordering the necessary materials (and ordering a telephone set to install to
Ellison's place).

Then, in an exchange of letters, Moore and Abbot were on the verge of parting
ways. First, Moore bared his soul.

                    Harqua Hala
                    October 11, 1921
Dear Mr. Abbot:
        As to myself and isolation, I guess this is not a new
subject to be discussed between us, but since it figures
in this plan, it looks as though it must be up for discussion again. As you know, I have now been four and one half
years at this isolated work with the Institution, and I
feel that I must ask you what is in store for me in the future in this work as regards isolation, especially since
at the present time I have up for consideration another
proposition, which I cannot decide about until I know
better what to expect as regards isolation. I am not
writing this in a complaining mood, and I am certainly
grateful to you and Mr. Roebling for the many things that
have been allowed to help ward off the ill effects of
isolation. But, at the same time, I think you must agree
with me that four and one half years is a long time to be
virtually deprived of the benefits of social life.
        And last, but certainly not least, is the fact that
there is now another one to be considered in this connection, and that one is Chella. She is not of the complaining sort, and says that she will be perfectly happy in
whatever I am happy. Yet, certainly, you must agree with
me that an isolated place like this must be harder for a
woman than for a man, and surely you can't blame me for
wishing to better her conditions as soon as I can arrange

it, but I wish to make it clear to you that she is not urging me in any way to make any change for her benefit.

Sincerely yours,

Alfred F. Moore

Only five days before he was scheduled to depart for his field station on Mt. Montezuma in Chile, Abbot replied firmly, baring a little of his soul also.

SMITHSONIAN INSTITUTION
Washington, U.S.A.

October 22, 1921

Dear Alfred:

I do not know that you fully appreciate the impor-
tance which I attach to getting the present series of
measurements at Mt. Harqua Hala and at Mt. Montezuma on
every possible day for the coming two years, until July
1, 1923. We have requests from government meteorological
establishments in India and in England for the solar
constant results, in order that they may be compared with
the meteorological elements with a view to their value in
forecasting. The United States Weather Bureau is also
deeply engaged in the study of our results, and I feel
that it is up to us to give a really satisfactory basis
from comparative observations at two first-rate stations so that it may be definitely decided by these government agencies whether or not it is worth while to
carry on the solar constant work forever, or whether it
may be discontinued as of no practical benefit in
forecasting.

I do not expect to live forever and intend, if it is
humanly possible, to get this piece of work accomplished
right now. This is a piece of work that we set our minds to
accomplish and which, to use an expression you may have
heard, we intend to carry through if hell freezes over.

We place the most implicit confidence in your work
on this solar constant job. Your results in Calama are
far and away the best that we have. You, no doubt, take as
much pride as I do in the work, and, if you can stand it, I
feel perfectly sure you will be enthusiastic to see the
end of this two-year job that I have in mind. If you

cannot stand it or if you feel it is too much of a sacrifice, of course you will have to get out, but I do not see
my way clear, financially or otherwise, to transfer you
to Mt. Wilson.

                              Very truly yours,
                              C. G. Abbot
                              Assistant Secretary

Chapter 11

A Voice From Stockton

Charles Abbot returned to Washington from Chile on January 7, 1922. He seemed mellowed from his three weeks at the Montezuma field station where the equipment needed "careful readjustment and repair." His experiences there included a "dreadful time with the Ford," problems with the gas engine, and keeping the piano tuned. Sounding more like Moore than himself, about the weather in Chile Abbot wrote, "It was certainly very discouraging to lose so many days in the month in which we hoped to get observations. There seems to be a fatality operating against us, for when we had only the Mt. Wilson station in the early days, 1905-1910, it seems to me that the sky was much better there than it ever was during the times that we had cooperating stations, and now it seems the same with respect to North and South America. Last year in the spring in Calama you had a run of nearly every day for almost four months, whereas this year in the corresponding period the weather was abominable, and in fact it has been very discouraging at both stations during the whole of 1921. Let us hope that 1922 will reform itself."

Abbot asked Moore, "I should like to know more particularly how things are going at Harqua Hala, whether you found out the cause of the depression of the last bolograph of which you were writing when I went away, whether you succeeded in repairing the house, whether the wireless works now, how the weather has treated you, and in short what the general outlook is and the number of observations hitherto."

> Mt. Harqua Hala
> January 17, 1922
>
> Dear Mr. Abbot:
>
> I was glad indeed to receive your letter of the 7th a few days ago. If it does not storm Fred is planning to go to Wenden today, so I'll write a few lines for him to mail.
>
> We at last got the house fixed up, so it give us no more concern during bad weather. We got the corners fixed

in good shape with concrete and then covered the whole
house to keep the rain off the adobe. We used corrugated
galvanized iron, except for a 20 foot strip near the galvanometer, where we used zinc, as you requested. It makes
the place look a lot better too. We have the space under
the eaves made airtight with adobe bricks and adobe mor-
tar, so the house is a lot more comfortable during windy,
cold weather than when you were here.

    The wireless has proven the worst hoodoo up here,
but we now have it in a fair way to be working before long.
When I was home Christmas,[60] I went around to the Brode
Electric Co. and showed him one of Knight's sets, which I
took back with me for the purpose. I got nearly a complete
receiving set from him and tried it out in Los Angeles to
make sure it would work. Since bringing it up here it
works even better than it did in L.A. for I have a much
better aerial. We hear concerts ever day from Los Angeles, San Francisco and Stockton, California, and quite
often from Denver, Colorado. I also get the time signals
every day at one o'clock, and they come very strong. Besides the concerts we get daily news, weather forecasts,
stock and market reports, etc., so it aids quite a bit
with the isolation. I am wondering if the Institution
would sanction our getting some sort of a "loud speaker,"
which is an arrangement like a phonograph horn, to make
the concerts and speaking audible throughout the room. I
think the prices range from $30 to about $90.

    I have to do a lot of changing around on Knight's
transmitters to make them practical for 12 miles, and as
soon as I do this I will test them out, and then have the
aerial put up in Wenden, and get the thing to working one
way to make sure it is all right before getting the
necessary things for the other way.

    The weather has been quite a bit worse for observing
this year than last. We lost six days in October, nine in
November, twenty in December, and seven thus far in
January. We got thirteen long methods in September,
eleven in October, five in November, four in December and
four thus far this month.

---

[60] Moore's "first Christmas at home in five years." Also, while Abbot was in Chile, Keg Greeley went to Los Angeles in November 1921 riding back with Moore's brother. Greeley told Abbot, "We started from here early in the morning (moonlight) and reached LA the next morning.
Nearly twenty three hours on the road. It was a rough and rather tedious trip towards the end."

                    I hope you will find it possible to visit us soon,
            for there are many things that we should discuss.
                                          Sincerely yours,
                                          Alfred F. Moore

Although Abbot had previously said his trip to Arizona would follow his trip to Chile, he replied, "I am arranging to be on Mt. Wilson, probably with Mr. Aldrich, for one or two months this summer,[61] and I wonder if that might not answer. It is quite an expensive and time-consuming trip from here to Arizona and return, and naturally there is a great deal here which I ought to attend to. However, if you think it is indispensable, I will try to take it up."

Abbot approved purchasing a loud speaker and again encouraged Moore to build "a cottage for the director and his family" if Moore felt it was necessary. He also told Moore that he had agreed to keep a rain record on Mt. Harqua Hala for the Weather Bureau.

On the mountain, Moore seemed almost obsessed with the receiving end of his wireless apparatus and its ability to connect him with society. While Moore couldn't find time to work on Knight's transmitters, and perhaps stealing time from his observing duties, seemingly he could always find time to work on the receivers.

                                          Wenden
                                          January 24, 1922

          Dear Mr. Abbot:
                I'm planning to make our aerials higher on the
          mountain so as to get distant stations more clearly. This
          is one of the best isolation aids that I've struck. I'm having
          trouble getting Knights transmitting sets to working, but
          haven't had much time since my return from California
          to work on them.
                                          Sincerely,
                                          A.F.M.

---

[61] Abbot's plans on Mt. Wilson included "observing the energy spectra of the brighter stars with the 100-inch telescope. My computations show that we may reasonably hope to get curves of stars of the zero to first magnitude, like Sirius, Vega, or Arcturus, which will approach very sensibly in their appearance and detail the energy curves which we are now obtaining from the sun, and it will be possible to obtain information of real value in regard to spectrum distribution from stars even as faint as second or third magnitude."

Increasingly, in every letter, Moore talked about radio reception and potential problems with his aerial, at the expense of other work on the mountain.

Mt. Harqua Hala
January 27, 1922

Dear Mr. Abbot:

I have decided that in view of the terrific electrical storms up here in summer, it would be unwise to have the aerial pole joined onto the south of the house as it now is, so when we put up the higher one, we will put it away from the house. I think the buildings up here should be protected with lightning rods, for we had some very scary electrical storms last summer, and with the station being so high up, and with so few other projecting objects for the lightning to hit, it seems we should protect it as well as possible. Of course, I think the corrugated iron covering together with the adobe walls, is quite a bit of protection, as doubtless the whole house is pretty well grounded.

It seems that the art of wireless telephony is fast progressing. Last evening I was listening in on a concert at the Fitzsimmons General Hospital in Denver, and the fellow called out to stations in Winnipeg, Canada, Washington, D.C., Houston, Texas, and San Diego, California, who had written him that they had heard him during former concerts. Chella and I had quite a surprise about ten days ago. We listen quite frequently to the concerts from Stockton, California, and one night the fellow requested persons hearing him to write and he would send them a copy of his list of concert and news broadcasting stations on the coast. He also asked for names of Victrola records that should be desired. So I wrote to him and named two records for him to play. A week ago last Tuesday night, Chella and I were listening to the Stockton concert, and were surprised when the fellow called out very clearly, "Good evening, Mr. and Mrs. Alfred F. Moore, Mt. Harqua Hala, Wenden, Arizona. I hope you are hearing this well. We will now play one of your selections." Later on, he played the other selection. They both came in fine and clear.

We are having it cloudy today, the tenth day we have lost thus far in January. But we have managed to get eight

long methods, all but one with some sort of excellent
grade.
                              Sincerely yours,

                              Alfred

Even with all the work on the receiving end of his wireless apparatus, Moore did recognize that he needed to spend time this winter to improve water storage capacity at the field station.

                              Mt. Harqua Hala
                              February 7, 1922
Dear Mr. Abbot:
        If it is not storming tomorrow I'll probably go to
Wenden as there are several things that I should attend
to there.
        We are now putting in spare time getting the "Mt.
Harqua Hala Water Works" in better operating condition.
Just after I returned from Los Angeles, Fred and I put in
a small concrete cistern back of the shop, which will
hold about 300 gallons, and which will likely take care
of the water from the shop roof. Today we took out the
galvanized iron tank north of the house, and set it on top
of the ground within reach of the eaves pipes from the
house so that it can save any water that we may get while
we are constructing the concrete cistern.[62] When the latter is finished, we will keep the old tank for a reserve,
either for the house or shop. If we do not encounter too
hard rock north of the house, I expect to make the cistern
large enough to hold from 1000 to 1200 gallons. It will be
of concrete and all underground. Thus we expect to have a
total water storage capacity of about 1800 gallons which
will nearly keep us going with usual rainfall. From all
accounts this region is liable to have rain almost any
time of year except about three months in the later
spring and early summer and a month or two in the fall.
        I am glad that you approve of our getting a loud
speaker for the wireless receiving set, for I think it
will add a great deal to our pleasure. I have written to
the company which makes the Magnavox which is the best

---

[62] The digging task was Greeley's; he told his mother, "I spent a couple of days last week excavating a place for the cement water cistern. It was mostly rock and the process was slow. I got a hole dug five feet square and five and one-half feet deep."

loud speaker. They have gotten out a new model for a small
room which sells for $45, which I think is about what we
need. Since writing to you, I have joined up a two stage
amplifier, in place of the one stage one I had at first.
Of course this calls for using some of the set intended
for Wenden. We can hear lots better with the two stage
amplifier. Last Friday evening the Stockton company gave
a concert at which several Victor artists sang in person.
We could hear them just fine, with the headsets, of
course. I now have the material[63] here to put the aerial
up sixty feet or so in the air, and this will doubtless
help a good deal. Since the signals are rather weak this
far away, except from the powerful sending stations. I
suppose we really should have three or four stages of amplification when working with very distant stations.
Each stage of amplification, costs, including the
amplifier vacuum tube, about $20. I picked up a concert
from Roswell, New Mexico, last Sunday evening, but the
signals came in pretty weak, even with the two
amplifiers.

I confess that I hardly know just what to do in regard to the transmitting arrangements between here and
Wenden. I think that Knight's layout along this line is
almost a fizzle, and it will cost quite a lot to put the
two sets into working condition. In the meantime I'll try
to find time to thoroughly try out Knight's arrangement,
to see if there is any possibility of using it, or many of
its parts.

As to the additional house, I think it would be best
to not build that now. It may be necessary to add a room to
the present building, but I am not sure that this is
needed. It seems to me that since the money will not
likely be spent for the cottage, and since the cisterns,
etc. are costing much less than the appropriation, if you
and Mr. Roebling approve, it might be best to put in a
good receiving set for the wireless here, and probably
the transmitting arrangement between here and Wenden. I
think Mr. Matteson plans on putting in several amplifiers at his own expense so he can pick up concerts, etc.,
so I guess it is only up to us to put in the aerial and

---

[63] To his aunt, Keg explained that the aerials "are made out of four-inch by four-inch Oregon pine twelve-feet long and spliced together with two-by-fours. We got them up with a pair of pulley blocks."

detector and one amplifier, as would be necessary for use
between Wenden and the mountain.

Sincerely yours,

Alfred F. Moore

Wenden: Feb 8th. I don't consider it necessary to make a special trip out here, but hope you will stop in route to Mt. Wilson. I think I'll likely be in L.A. the first part of April so we can be home at the time of Mother's birthday. We may go through in the Ford, as with two this is much less expensive. In summer it is too hot for an auto trip. A.F.M.

Chapter 12

Taking Care of Lightning

As 1922 proceeded, the situation on Mt. Harqua Hala progressed ever so slightly. However, for every problem solved new ones emerged, or at least Alfred Moore seemed to be able to find them. As always, his solutions anticipated eventually moving from the Arizona site.

> Mt. Harqua Hala
> February 14, 1922[64]

Dear Mr. Abbot:

> I sent the box of bolograph plates by express a couple of days ago. Some of the plates seem to begin to show the lack of water up here, but I guess they are all legible.

> We have been having a run of cloudy weather this month, having lost seven of the fourteen days thus far, and only got today with one poor short method this afternoon.

> As to the lightning rod protection, I am not sure just how is the best way to go about it. From what I have read up about high frequency currents, iron is a very poor conductor for such, and should not be used.[65] Would you think it advisable to have Mr. Kramer cut some copper or brass tubing, perhaps about three-eighths inch in diameter, thread the ends and send fittings for same. In this way, the material could be saved whenever we should leave here. It could all, except the rods themselves, which should be solid, be of eight foot lengths, since the slope distance on each side of the gable to eaves is eight feet and the length of the house is a trifle over

---

[64] Greeley told his mother, "Chella got up a Valentines' supper tonight. Decorated the table with crepe paper that had hearts and cupids printed all over it. Roast pork and lemon pie constituted the main dishes."

[65] Oddly, Moore ended up buying three-eights inch galvanized iron cable because he could not find copper cable in Los Angeles.

forty feet, a multiple of eight feet. The distance from
eaves to the ground is twelve feet, which could take two
lengths, and be buried four feet in the ground, which is
about as deep as is possible without blasting rock, which
we could not do up here. If, on the other hand you think I
should install heavy copper wire, I suppose we could get
this ready. But since this mountain is subject to such
terrific electrical storms, and this house is so very
much exposed, it seems that it should be petty well protected. Of course it will be several months before they
begin, but everything should be fixed by June.

Fred and I have gotten one of the high aerial poles
up, it being 72 feet long. It was quite a trick to get such
a long pole up, but we managed it all right.[66] I put a
fairly heavy copper lightning rod on it, and soldered it
to the four heavy iron guy wires. These are usually insulated, but we will install means of grounding them well
before electrical storms commence. I also put a weather
vane on top of the 72 foot pole, so we can better tell the
wind direction. It is marvelous how very changeable the
wind direction is here.

By this mail I am ordering a Magnavox loud speaker
from the manufacturer at Oakland, California. It is considered the best make. The size for our need cost $45.
Fred and I listened to about the best concerts last night
that we have heard, due to our higher aerial I suppose.
First we caught a new station to us, at Los Altos, about
twenty miles from San Francisco. When they finished, we
swung over to Hamburgers at Los Angeles, and then jumped
up to the Fairmont Hotel at San Francisco. The fellow at
Stockton had a message for Chella and me last Friday
night, and played a selection that Chella had asked for.
Sunday I caught part of a sermon from Denver.

Sincerely yours,

Alfred F. Moore

---

[66] Greeley told his mother, "It took us two whole days to get it up straight and guyed into position."

Moore seemed almost obsessed with his wireless radio set-up; his letters to Abbot in Washington showed that the wireless installation occupied much of his time.

Mt. Harqua Hala

February 19, 1922

Dear Mr. Abbot:

Since I last wrote you we have lost one more day en-tirely, making eight for February, but have had to sand-wich in observing between clouds a good deal the past week.

It has been fairly free from wind of late so Fred and I have taken advantage of it to get the higher aerials up in the air. Yesterday we succeeded in getting the other to the same height. They surely loom up above the house. I have taken some pictures and will send some as soon as I can get them finished.

It is possible that I may be able to use the aerial for another purpose beside the wireless telephone, in connection with experimenting on some solar phenomena that I have been thinking over of late. I wonder if you could send out some sort of measuring electroscope as I would need some sort of fairly delicate electrostatic potential measurer for the test I have in mind.

Our shoe repairing outfit went smash proper the other day when I was putting some nails in my shoes. Since such is very much needed up here and there is not reliable cobbler in Wenden, I am taking the liberty of ordering another last and stand from Los Angeles. This is the worst place on shoes that I ever saw, being even worse than Chile. It is impossible to get any sole leather that is of any account in Wenden. We find that soles made out of old auto tires last much better, but just now we are out of old tires.

We now have some new "neighbors," in the way of sheep herders with their sheep, in the canyons to the west of us.[67] There is now a small stream of water running down that canyon, but I guess it will not last long.

Mr. Ellison told me the other day that he is expect-ing a couple of men up to look over his claim. I have never been informed as to what arrangement the Institution has with Mr. Ellison, regarding this property, and Fred does

---

[67] The observers would see the campfires of the sheep herders at night.

not seem to know. If there is any possibility of his
selling out his claims, probably I should know what is
what. However, he has not sold them yet, and since I think
he is asking $25,000, I doubt very much if he sells in the
near future.
      With best regards, in which Chella joins me.
                      Sincerely yours,

Alfred

Abbot patiently replied to all of Moore's requests and ideas: When Moore asked if he should consider buying a new De Forest wireless apparatus,[68] particularly because he doubted that it would be safe for Chella to operate the gas engines and dynamos that the Knight set-up required, Abbot replied, "I should think that if you were able to get the contrivance so that you can communicate to Wenden whenever either you or Fred is on Mt. Harqua Hala, it might answer for all usual purposes and perhaps would be about as costly as we ought to install at present. I wish you would go ahead as far as you can with what you have and then make a definite recommendation as to what further apparatus is required, with costs, and we will see what can be done." In other letters, Abbot replied, "I will take up the matter of the electrometer and see what can be obtained.[69] I will send you an old tire or two so that you and Fred can keep your feet off the ground. I send you a copy verbatim of the writing he (Ellison) gave us. I tried to get a better one from him, but that was the best he was willing to sign." Then, Abbot provided a solution for the lightning protection.

SMITHSONIAN INSTITUTION
Washington, U.S.A.

March 3, 1922

Dear Alfred:
      We have received replies on the lightning protec-
tion proposition. I enclose that from the Weather Bureau
which includes Farmer's Bulletin 842. In view of their
recommendations, it would seem desirable for you to bury
two or three feet deep in the ground a copper ribbon one
by one-eighth inch in section extending all the way round
your building, and to erect a drain pipe leading down to
it at some convenient point where you could pour the

---

[68] Constantly trying to educate himself about wireless radio phones, Moore wrote to various suppliers, including Lee De Forest, Inc., San Francisco, and Wm. B. Duck Co., Toledo, Ohio.

[69] In a subsequent letter Abbot said, "They have recommended the Compton Quadrant Electrometer, although not fully understanding your purpose, and I am inquiring the cost and will hope to purchase one and forward it to you in a little while."

tolerably clean water, such as used for plate washing and
for washing the hands, so as to moisten the trench.

From this copper ribbon might go a number of one-
half inch copper cables which could be frayed at the top
and soldered to the galvanized iron sides of the house,
and the galvanized iron sides should be connected simi-
larly by such copper cable to the roof, on which should be
erected three aerials, two or three feet high, which
might also very well be of one-half inch copper cable
frayed out and pointed at the ends. These aerials could
be supported by means of angle-irons bent and bolted to
the roof.

Very truly yours,

C. G. Abbot

Abbot advised that Moore should "order the cable from Los Angeles. It would be
cheaper than for us to order it in the east and have it sent out there."

Throughout the month of March 1922, Moore's work and thoughts at Harqua Hala,
and the cooperation of the weather, and Abbot's needs for a valid field station again
began to drift apart.

Mt. Harqua Hala
March 5, 1922

Dear Mr. Abbot:

Long method days have been few of late due to the
extremely poor observing weather of February. Thirteen
days were lost altogether in February and no long methods
were possible after the 16th. March is showing some improvement, but the quality of the skies has not been good
the past two or three days.

Fred and I are busily engaged now getting the main
cistern in shape. We started cementing it yesterday, and
as it proved a much bigger job than we had thought, we had
to put in a half day at it today (Sunday), and will try to
get it done tomorrow. It will hold 1227 gallons.

As soon as I get the cistern done,[70] I will try to get
at that wireless transmitter. I have thought of one or
two other schemes to try, and then I will let you know

---

[70] The completed cement tanks included a cover to "try to make it bug proof, if it is possible." It held about 1265 gallons making a total water storage capacity with three tanks of 1875 gallons.

what seems to be the best thing to do, and about what the
cost will be for extra material needed. I got Knight's
set to sending out high frequency current the other day,
but had to force the tubes to do it, and wound up by burning out one of the tubes!

     There are about as many kinds of hook-ups on wire-
less telephone transmitters as there are fleas on a dog,
so it is pretty hard to take a jumbled-up set like
Knight's, with several of the necessary things missing,
and get it to working.

                                   Sincerely yours,

                                   Alfred

Curiously, in a March 22nd letter to John Roebling, Abbot reported about the Harqua Hala field station, "They have been getting results very regularly and very excellent ones. We have not published any of them as yet, for I felt it was highly undesirable to have to make systematic corrections after publication such as we had to make for Calama."

In the same letter Abbot continued, "We have gone over the whole list of long method results obtained up to the first of February and from them have constructed the curves necessary for the short method work. These are now in use at Mt. Harqua Hala. We are working up the short method results from the beginning up to February 1, 1922, which will be a long process of computation. We find that the long method and presumably the short method work, too, will require a secondary correction for water vapor just about the same as we had to apply at Mt. Wilson. It is a little curious that this is not required in South America, but possibly it may be because the definition of the spectroscope is very decidedly better than that which we have had a Mt. Harqua Hala, and also the quantity of water prevailing in the atmosphere from the station at Montezuma is naturally very small. I hope to go out to Mt. Wilson by the first of June. On the way, I shall stop at Mt. Harqua Hala and talk things over with Mr. Moore. Mr. Fred Greeley, his assistant, wishes to go home this summer for a month, in August, and I have approved of this and will arrange that either Mr. Aldrich or myself shall take his place while he is gone."[71]

Seemingly contradicting his report to Roebling, Abbot wrote to Moore, "I find it very hard to decide just how to draw the plots, and possibly improvements might be made, but we are trying to get them as consistent for the different air masses as possible."

---

[71] When Greeley requested a vacation, Abbot told him, ". . . everyone in the Government service has a right to thirty days leave, not including Sundays and holidays, so that if you should plan your trip to include, for instance, Labor Day, which is Monday, September 4, you could leave the mountain on Saturday, July 29, and be back Tuesday, September 5."

While Alfred Moore was used to difficulties with the observing conditions on Harqua Hala, one can imagine his utter disappointment when disaster struck his wireless radio aerial, a situation that Keg Greeley described vividly to his mother.

Harqua Hala
March 15, '22

Dear Mother,

We had another snow storm last Friday and Saturday which is leaving a vivid impression in our memories. It started nice and gentle late Friday P.M. but Saturday morning it was going good and continued to gain speed as the time flew by. By Saturday night it was a free for all blizzard. I had just retired in hopes to be purred to sleep by the wind when Bang! something lit on the roof and caused me to come to a sitting posture. Alfred was still up and he went to the door and saw that the aerial rope had broken and let the aerial down. The wind was so strong it blew it off of the house and it lit about 100 feet the other side. The next morning (Sunday) the storm was over and so was one of the aerial poles. It was flat on the ground and broken in two about the middle.

It was rather a discouraging sight and as it was Sunday and a lot of snow on the ground we contented ourselves with looking at it and lamenting.

Anyway we got busy with the shovels and filled all the tanks with snow. Most of it has melted now so there is an abundance of dish water on hand. It snowed down at the garage this time, something quite unusual.[72]

Monday, we spliced the pole together again and got it ready to go up. Tuesday we pulled it up slow but sure and surely slow.[73] It took us all day and we were lucky to strike a remarkably quiet day for March too. Today we put strain insulators on the guy wires and tightened the wires on the other pole which had become stretched from ice and wind.

Tomorrow, Alfred and Chella are going to celebrate their first wedding anniversary. Chella is planning on a

---

[72] The garage, at the base of the mountain, was 2600 feet above sea level.

[73] Moore said to Abbot, "We put it up again making it 60 feet in height, instead of 72 feet, as the latter seemed almost too high for best results with the wireless anyway."

big feed including a chicken which Alfred got in Wenden and has been trying to fatten the past week.[74] Guess I'll be ready to do justice to it. The generators on both our gasoline lights have gone bad so we have been using the little kerosene lights for a few nights. I am in hopes to get some generators tomorrow as the little old kerosene light seem quite tame after using a brilliant gas light.

Very much love to you,
Keg

In March, Moore received the Magnavox loud speaker and found "it works quite well, but will work very much better when I get another amplifier or two hooked up with it. It certainly seems strange to hear a 'phonograph' being played from 600 to 800 miles away, and no wires intervening. One night everything was very freaky and I could hear talking going on at Avalon, California, just by using my body as an aerial. I had the aerial entirely disconnected, and stood on an insulated platform, and held the regular aerial post in my hand."

Finally, the task of digging the trench for the lightning protection apparatus fell on Keg.

Harqua Hala
April 4, 1922

Dear Mother,

Tomorrow is the big day as Alfred and Chella leave for L.A. for a two week's or more stay. Sad to say it looks very much like rain tonight, but Chella says she's going rain or shine. They have been preparing for the last week or so and we plan to get an early start tomorrow morning, at least they do for if it looks like observing I'll stick around awhile and get a short method then come along and probably catch them before they reach the garage as Chella is rather a slow walker on trails with high heels. Mrs. Matteson one of the store-keeper's wives (one wife) in Wenden has asked us to come to her house and have supper. The last time I was in Wenden, she insisted I stay for supper also so that means I'll get back to the observatory about midnight. We are hoping it don't rain tomorrow.

---

[74] Moore said that the meal also included "frozen custard, cake and candy."

Alfred and I have been working on some short method days that have accumulated since the first of last September. The new curves came about two weeks ago and we have computed 50 days along with the regular work during that time. There are 20 left so I guess I can compute to my hearts content for the next two weeks.

We are going to put lightning rods on the house so I have another job cut out and dried for me. Namely digging a trench around this house three feet deep.

I have been digging holes at the foot of all the guy wires on the aerial poles. The aerial poles have lightning rods on top soldered to the guy wires. The wires have strain insulators on them now which doesn't give them a proper grounding for lightning so we are going to bury copper plates in the holes and run a wire to above the strain insulators and have a switch we can throw in when a storm comes along.

Alfred is going to let me run the phone while he is gone so I guess I won't get lonesome during the evenings.

I'll bet we had something to eat last Sunday you didn't have. Ice cream! It was vanilly. We froze it with snow and salt and without a freezer. We got the snow out of the cement cistern. Chella put it in a large coffee can and we packed this can in a pail full of snow and salt then took turns whirling the coffee can around. The cream would freeze to the sides of the can and then we would scrape it off with a knife and let the liquid get to the sides of the can. We got it fairly hard this way then packed it with more snow and by noon it was just like the confectioners make.

Last Sunday, was April fools day and Alfred took the prize here for the best joke. He went down stairs that night as usual to get the weather reports over the radio phones. Chella and I were sitting here reading when the phone from here to Mr. Ellison's rang. I answered it and Mr. E said hello on the other end, silence for a few seconds then I said what do you want and he said nothing, what do you want? Then I said didn't you ring? And he said no you did the ringing. It then dawned on me that

Alfred had tapped the wire. He used the magneto to ring both phones at the same time. Then he put on one of the radio head sets and heard the whole conversation.

Tonight Alfred connected the radio phone onto the wire phone so Mr. Ellison has been hearing selections on the Victrola from Denver.

Very much love,
Keg

Chapter 13

Plans for Continued Work

Increasingly, Abbot devoted more attention to validating the solar constant measurement method. He was plagued with problems finding the right "corrections" and "function" to use at his Harqua Hala field station; while he was able to provide some temporary correction curves for the Harqua Hala observers, he could not accurately correlate the values between Arizona and Chile. As yet, Moore had not been able to obtain enough long-method measurements to statistically determine the right way to apply the newer short method.

Abbot told Moore, "It is already plain that the high values of the function give high solar constants, and vice versa. But I think there is probability that the correction will be so small that we ought to get it with sufficient accuracy. I feel very anxious about the situation. It would be such a blow to us if the comparison of North and South America, which we shall be able to make in the course of another month or so, should go badly."

With less than a scientific approach to the matter, Moore doubted they were on the right track at all. He told Abbot, "Personally, it seems to me that most likely there is a variation in the sun, probably of short periods, and that this variation has a very direct affect on the weather on the earth, but I am pretty much on the fence as to whether this is a variation of radiation, at least entirely. But I guess we will have a chance to discuss this more at length when you come out to Harqua Hala."

SMITHSONIAN INSTITUTION
Washington, U.S.A.

April 29, 1922

Dear Mr. Roebling:

There are so many matters connected with the solar work about which I should like to consult you before I leave for the summer campaign at Mt. Wilson.

The most important is the consideration of what we
shall do after July, 1923, when it will probably be necessary to make a change in the directors of the Mt. Harqua
Hala and Montezuma observatories. The young men have
been in the desert so long that they feel indisposed to
sacrifice the society of friends further, and one cannot
blame them for that. The two assistants are first rate in
their way, but neither has sufficiently broad education
to be suitable to put in charge of such delicate and responsible work. Accordingly we shall have to make in-
quiries very soon for the purpose of finding the right
men, if the stations are to be continued after July 1923.
But that question has to be decided first of all, and I
wish to lay before you the considerations, pro and con,
in regard to it.

Mr. Clayton is now in the United States, near Boston, on furlough, and has a great deal of very interesting data, part of which he has brought to my attention in
the last few days, which tends strongly to confirm the
value of solar radiation work for forecasting purposes.
I can give you some idea of some of his results and also of
the present tendency of the United States Weather
Bureau.

Very truly yours,

C. G. Abbot

More specifically, Abbot wrote to Moore, "Mr. Clayton called upon me for confer-
ences twice last week.[75] He has brought along some of his eight-day forecasts based on
solar variability, and these seem to correspond surprisingly closely with the actual
weather.[76] He feels very sanguine of the values of our work, and indeed believes that
he would be able, if he had the resources of the United States Weather Bureau, to predict better for the United States than for Argentina because the changes here are so
much larger and more definite. I wish that it may prove so. On the other hand, Mr.
Clough of the Weather Bureau was down here with data which seemed to him to
prove that there is no variability of the sun whatever. So we find people looking, some
on the red shield, some on the blue."

---

[75] Abbot and Clayton met the week of April 24, 1922.

[76] Abbot plotted six weeks of Clayton's eight day predictions of the temperature for Buenos Aires versus actual temperature. He reported,
"There is a well marked correlation between the two which, in view of the piecemeal character of the solar data which he uses and some other
considerations, seems to me to be quite a confirmation of the view that he is working on the right track."

Moore returned to Harqua Hala from his trip to Los Angeles, picking up with the work where he had left off seventeen days earlier, and immediately planning his next chance to get away from the mountain.

> Mt. Harqua Hala
> April 27, 1922

Dear Mr. Abbot:

I intended to write to you while in Los Angeles, but with going to the dentist about every day including the very day we left, and in keeping up with Edgar in his many attentions he showed to us, I had to postpone letter writing. Chella and I both managed to catch a little gripe or something just before coming back, and were laid up a day or two the early part of the week, but are about all right now.

We have quite a number of short methods computed by the new curves, and I am sending them under separate cover. But we are now putting in our time when not observing at getting the lightning protection arranged.

As to Fred's vacation, I do not think he should be expected to remain up here until August. He thinks he will have a short enough stay at home as it is, since the going and coming take so much time. He has been here continuously since December 3rd. Personally, I think we should be allowed to get out of here every three months. The Government employees in Washington are supposed to have sixteen hours of every twenty-four and one day of every week for their own desires, and have a very delightful city in which to spend their leisure time. In our case we virtually give twenty-four hours of every day, and seven days each week to the Government, hence it does not seem to me to be just to expect us to come strictly under the thirty day a year vacation limit. It is my opinion that if a place as isolated as this is to be run continuously, the vacation trips should be taken before the person has been here long enough to begin to hate the place, for then it is too late.

I think Fred should be allowed to take any trip he sees fit out of here as soon as we get the lightning protection arranged.[77] He says he really prefers going east a little later than August, since the trip will be such a

---

[77] Greeley wanted to take a trip to the Grand Canyon in addition to his one month vacation to visit his family back east.

hot one at that time. I hope that Chella and I can get out
of here around August 1st for a breathing spell from the
hot summer.

As for you or Mr. Aldrich taking Fred's place while
he is east, I don't think that will be necessary if it
will not be convenient for either of you to be here. I can
do the observing alone, and probably most of the
computing.

Thanks for sending the Government book on wireless.
It is about the best thing on the subject that I have
seen. We are having an awful time with static interfering
with our hearing, and I guess it will get steadily worse
as summer approaches. I am sorry that you will be here
during the season for such poor hearing on the radio, for
when static does not bother we hear very plainly indeed.

Owning to the large amount of snow and rain this
spring the desert and the mountain look very different
from the way they did a year ago. Tonight I noticed some
very beautiful white lilly-like flowers, which grow on a
very common looking plant resembling dandelions. The
blossoms come out just at sundown. The are exceedingly
fragrant.[78]

We hope to see you out here before many weeks.

Sincerely yours,

Alfred

On May 10, 1922, Keg Greeley left on a ten day trip to Phoenix and the Grand Canyon, catching the train in Wenden at 2:15 A.M. The Moores took advantage of his absence to invite a house guest to the mountain. And, increasingly they looked forward to Abbot's planned visit.

Mt. Harqua Hala
May 16, 1922

Dear Mr. Abbot:

I am going to Wenden after I finish observing
tomorrow to bring up Mrs. Matteson, the wife of the store
keeper, to spend a few days with us. Chella has everything looking spic and span in honor of her first lady
guest to the mountain.

---

[78] In a later letter, Moore sent a pressed flower to the Smithsonian to help identify it. He further described the plant, saying, "The buds pop open just about sundown, and do so very rapidly. They bloom all night and in the afternoon of the following day they wilt and other buds open." Subsequently Abbot wrote that Dr. Rose of the Institution identified the flower as a primrose and wanted more specimens.

We are hoping that you can bring Mrs. Abbot up to Harqua Hala with you. With an extra single bed and cot I am sure we can easily accommodate all. It might be rather hot in the valley, but she could come up on one of Mr. Ellison's burros, and it would not be uncomfortably warm up here in June.

I had a rather exciting time during observations yesterday morning. I was running a long method, and just at the close of the third bolograph, I heard the greatest crash in the galvanometer room. I went in and found that the sixty-five pounds of lead weight had fallen. At first I thought that merely the wire had broken and went right on with the succeeding pyrheliometry. But when I looked into it, I found that the trouble was much more serious, and at first thought it might put us out of business for several weeks. One of the shaft bearings of the plate carrier clock had broken off flush, letting the shaft and gear fall free. This evidently allowed the lead weight to drop, and was the cause of the trouble. I took the clock out into the shop, and saw that I could probably fix it by screwing a brass collar bearing on both ends of the shaft, for the bearing had broken off on the other end too. I did this and it works better than it did before. It is a wonder to me that the thing had not broken long before now, for the bearing was not much larger than a pin and must have been subject to quite a severe strain. This caused me to lose the long method yesterday, but got two short methods, and got a long method today. This makes two long methods I have run since Fred left. I haven't lost any days since he left.

I must close now. With best regards to all.

Sincerely,

Alfred

The many trips on the trail to Wenden obviously gave Moore time to think about the needs of the observatory; he did seem to genuinely want to improve conditions at the Harqua Hala field station.

                                        Mt. Harqua Hala
                                        May 19, 1922

Dear Mr. Abbot:

As Mr. Ellison and I were coming up the trail yesterday morning, he said that having to walk up the trail each week was getting to be almost too much for him, especially since the hot weather is again coming on. Since our loads usually require the three burros, he thought it would be necessary to get a horse or riding burro. I was rather surprised that he suggested getting a horse since he once said that horses tear up the trail much worse than burros. Since it is quite necessary for Fred, Chella and I to have means of riding, I thought it might be well to ask you if it would be possible for the Institution to get a horse and saddle, and then Mr. Ellison can use it on his trips, and we can have means of transportation without being dependent upon Mr. Ellison wholly when we want to make the trip to Wenden, or to bring up anybody. I think $100 would cover the cost of horse or large riding burro and saddle.

Mr. Ellison talked as though he was thinking strongly of selling his claims up here to some cattlemen who were up to look them over a few weeks ago. He said that he thought that he could very likely make the Smithsonian a much better proposition than formerly for a small tract of land where the station is, and a first right on his spring. I told him that you expected to be up here next month, and had better talk it over with you when you come.

Mrs. Matteson returns to Wenden tomorrow. The burro got out of the corral when I went to bring her up on Wednesday so she had to walk up the trail.

I think Fred will be back tomorrow. I haven't lost any days since he left. We had a terrific wind last night, but no damage was done except the breaking of three panes of glass in one of the windows.

                                        Sincerely yours,
                                        Alfred

Abbot also thought the horse was a good idea and authorized purchasing one. In the meantime, Alfred Moore laid the plans for Abbot's visit to the mountain.

                                        Mt. Harqua Hala
                                        June 6, 1922
Dear Mr. Abbot:

I am glad that you will be out here soon. I am not quite certain which would be the best time to arrange to come up. Your train arrives in Wenden about 9 P.M. As you know the hotels are a very poor excuse in Wenden, and unless you have arranged to stay over night with Mr. Harrington, I'd think the best plan would be for me to meet you when the train arrives and bring you both up here that night. There would not be much moon, but we have a good lantern at the garage, and I know the trail. It would be much cooler coming up at night than the following morning, for it would be nearly noon before we could get here in that case. If we should come up at night, we would arrive at the observatory about one o'clock A.M. I'll be glad to meet you at any time you think best, but it seems to me that it would probably be best to come up at night.

I expect to go to Wenden on Wednesday of next week (June 14th) if you should wish to reach me by wire to advise me of your plans. Mr. Ellison goes regularly to Wenden each Saturday. I have arranged with him for Mrs. Abbot to ride his burro "Jack" if she comes.

Under separate cover I am sending some more completed bolographs. I am holding out the one for May 24th for it was evidently a very unusual day, and I think we should look it over together after you come. Business seems to be picking up on Harqua Hala, for we have lost but one day in the last twenty-eight. But many of the May days were afflicted with a lot of haze and rather poor skies generally. They seem to be getting clearer now, and will probably continue this way until the July and August summer rains begin.

Having a lot of scrap material from the cistern lumber, corrugated iron and zinc. It struck me that it would be a good plan to have a porch on the east side of the house for use in the summer months, so Fred and I have been getting it ready the past couple of days. We have the

lightning rods nearly installed. I think you will note
many changes in Harqua Hala when you arrive.

I have told Mr. Ellison about getting a riding horse
or burro and saddle. He will look into the matter when he
goes to Wenden. I think it would be best for him to buy the
outfit and we purchase it from him, as he can doubtless
get a much better buy than we could.

We hope to see you up here soon and we do hope you can
bring Mrs. Abbot with you. Chella seems so anxious for
her to come, and for her sake too, I hope she will come
with you. Chella is writing her by this mail.

Sincerely yours,

Alfred

Abbot planned to arrive in Wenden by train the night of June 17, 1922, almost two
years since his first trip. Prior to leaving Washington, he wired his plans to Wenden.

Washington, DC 6-12-22 Accept proposal ascent Saturday
night, Lillian also. CG Abbot

Chapter 14

Settling Down Until 1925

When Keg Greeley returned from his vacation at the Grand Canyon, he and Alfred Moore turned their attention to preparing for Charles Abbot's visit to Harqua Hala.

Harqua Hala
June 16, 1922

Dear Mother,

The days are getting so pesky hot now. I reckon it's going to be hotter than last summer the way it's starting out.

Alfred observed every day I was away so these observations with some other back work caused us about ten days or more of solid computing. I sure was glad when that grind was over.

Since then we have been primping the place up in general. Finished soldering the lightening rods on the house. Soldered the old tank and it was quite a job as all the old tar had to be scraped off. We set it in a cement base and if it doesn't hold water now will roll it down over the mountain. We built a porch on the east side of the house and have given it two coats of paint. It adds quite a bit of dignity to the ark and when coming in the door now it seems more like entering a real house.

This afternoon we gave the shop and cellar a thorough cleaning out. If a second hand junk man had been around to see the pile of stuff it would have done his eyes good. We would have sold him most anything from a rat trap to a bed. I am going to sleep in the shop while the

Abbots are here, on the little cot I use when staying over at the garage.

Went to Wenden on the seventh and sure had some time. Found one of the hind tires flat when I got to the garage. Got down under it to jack it up when a scorpion stung me on the knee. I thought at first I had put my knee on a tack but when I looked down and saw this little devil running away I knew different. Made the wound bleed good with my knife and then applied some strong ammonia which we always keep in a bottle at the garage for just such emergencies. Felt no ill effects from the sting other than it made me walk stiff legged for a day or two.

Will write again when the Abbots leave. Very much love to you and dad.

Keg

As planned, Charles and Lillian Abbot arrived in Wenden on June 17th "on the night train" and ascended Harqua Hala during the cool of the night, arriving at the field station at 3 A.M. Greeley told his mother, "They slept pretty late that morning and got up with sticks in their eyes."

During his brief stay at Harqua Hala,[79] before going on to Mt. Wilson, Abbot raised the morale of Moore and Greeley, at least temporarily.

Harqua Hala
June skidoo, 1922

Dear Mother,

Charles seemed to be delighted with the improvements made in the past year, and he suggested some more himself. He is going to send Chella a sink from L.A. and is also going to try and find a small ice making plant. It will be a fine and much needed addition here. Our wireless is practically out of commission on account of the static electricity in the air so he suggested putting in a wire phone from here to Wenden. It will go along the trail and road so we can watch for broken wires. We will also have a phone at the garage. Mr. Roebling is anxious to

---

[79] It is not clear how long Abbot and his wife stayed at Harqua Hala, but it was likely not much more than a few days and certainly no longer than a week; Abbot wrote his first letter to Moore from Los Angeles on June 24, 1922.

carry on the work until July 1925 and has appropriated money for any necessary improvements.

Alfred bought twelve hens while in Wenden last week so "there'll be aigs for our breakfast in the mor-on-in" now. I built a yard for them today, that is, dug post holes and set the poles.

I would love to get home this fall but don't you think it's more sensible to wait until next May?

Very much love to you and dad.

Keg

Keg changed his travel plans to visit his parents in the Fall of 1922 because Abbot planned to shuffle the duties of his field station observers. Plans called for Aldrich to go to Chile in October. Then, in May 1923, Keg would swap places with his brother Paul, Keg going to Chile and Paul coming to Arizona. Keg told his mother, "Dr. Chas. is going to arrange it so that Paul and I will be home at the same time. I have been thinking it over and think I had better wait until next May before coming home as the Smithsonian will pay my fare then, and I would like to make another trip or two to California in the meantime."

As he had discussed with the observers on Harqua Hala, when Abbot arrived in California he quickly arranged for a sink and a Kelvinator refrigeration unit[80] to be shipped to Arizona. Abbot also arranged for the phone wire from Harqua Hala to Wenden to be strung on the Santa Fe poles where the line would parallel the train tracks for seven miles into Wenden.

The refrigerator immediately became a concern for Moore; he seemed to have an ability to analyze concern into any situation. About the Kelvinator, he told Abbot, "The only thing that I am afraid of is whether it is supposed to run a good share of every day. The gas engine requires considerable attention, although I can arrange the oiling and cooling device so that we will only have to look at it every couple of hours, fixing it so that the engine will be automatically stopped should the cooling water get low." Moore expressed even more concern about working with Santa Fe. In addition, his letter to Abbot in California showed that Abbot's visit to Harqua Hala had not resolved the difficulties with the observing method.

---

[80] To his dad, Keg described it: "The Kelvinator is not an ice making plant, but is a cooling system. It is claimed that it will make a refrigerator 10 degrees colder than ice."

Mt. Harqua Hala
June 30, 1922

Dear Mr. Abbot:

I am wondering if it could be arranged for their men
to string the wires, for from what I've heard, railways
are always very fussy about all work, and since I really
know very little about the orthodox way of stringing
telephone wires, and I doubt if anyone could be gotten in
Wenden who would know much more about it. I rather hate to
tackle the job on their poles. I'll have to stay in Wenden
while working down in the valley, for it is a pretty hard
day's work just going down there and back, and not much
time would be left for working on the phone line. I think
Fred and I can string it to the garage. Then I'll get
someone from Wenden to set the necessary poles from the
railroad to the garage and help me with that stringing.

The thunderstorms have ceased for a time at least,
and we succeeded in getting two long methods this week,
although the days were extremely wet, and the skies
rather hazy. But these two days have managed to stir up
quite a lot of trouble up here. The days showed pretty
good agreement with the former points on the curve,
especially the first day. I congratulated myself on
this, but I guess I did not tap on wood, for when I went to
plot the areas, instead of falling on the almost perfect
curve that I had gotten formerly, they all lay on a good
curve, but about 10% removed from the other curve. As I
told you when you were here, I now have somewhat poorer
definition than formerly.[81]

The definition here has gradually been getting
poorer for sometime, but a sudden change for the worse
came the day after you got here.[82] I worked some with the
galvanometer, and then tried to get the bolometer in
better focus. I am quite certain that the trouble lies in
the galvanometer, especially since the bolometer had not
been touched for many months, and since I had to adjust
the control magnets to get a larger deflection the day
the poorer definition started. I do not think that the
galvanometer here is nearly sensitive enough, but just
why it should be getting worse in this regard isn't at all

---

[81] Here, Moore is referring to the plot ("definition") of the resulting bolograph falling as expected on the photographic plates.

[82] The observing data was not analyzed until after Abbot left Harqua Hala.

clear to me. I hate to think of having to start all over
again, but it does seem to me that this definition business should be brought equal with that in Chile, and
probably both stations improved in this regard, before
Aldrich starts some real work going down there. I think
this past neglect of this definition business is one of
the weakest links in the chain of our work.

I am wondering if the pile of large rocks that you
have under the galvanometer here, together with the rock
wall just back of it may not be responsible for some of
the troubles, for the rocks up here are quite magnetic.

Yesterday evening after dinner I went out hunting
and managed to bag two dandy rabbits. Wish you folks
could have been here to enjoy the grand dinner that
Chella got up this evening.

I am sending in Mr. Ellison's bill for April, May
and June. It totals $143.50 for the three months.

Sincerely yours,

Alfred

Despite the apparent disaster that still lurked with the observing method, Moore's subsequent letters to Abbot seemed to focus on the every day problems that he could solve
more easily. He wrote, "We are getting a good deal of comfort out of the hens. The
store-bought eggs are very poor this time of year, and it is fine to have some fresh ones
to eat. The first week that they were here they laid nine eggs and the next week seventeen. They seem very contented up here, and really, I'd think they would, after having
come from that furnace of Wenden. It got up to 120 degrees down there a few days
ago. We had it pretty hot up here, but nothing like that."

Keg elaborated on the heat to his mother. "The thermometer registered 120 degrees in the shade in Wenden, and it was about 100 degrees here. Every degree counts
when it gets up that high, and we considered ourselves lucky to be up here on the
mountain where there is a breeze. There have been only two evenings that I had to
sleep on top of the bed clothes. The rest of the time I've needed a sheet and blanket."
Keg added, "Last night I couldn't sleep at all until after three o'clock. It wasn't hot, and
I didn't feel sick. Alfred thinks its the altitude. Both he and Chella get those spells once
in awhile. Says he used to have them when in Chile after being up on the mountain for
any length of time."

The observers looked forward to relief from the heat with the planned refrigeration unit. Moore attacked its installation like he had the wireless receiver.

Mt. Harqua Hala
July 14, 1922

Dear Mr. Abbot:

The Kelvinator is up here. We have looked the place over and about the only available place for the refrigerator is on the north side of the kitchen, under the shelves. Fred and I laid out a rope the way the copper tubing will have to run, and strange as it may seem it will require about 86 feet from the place the compressor will have to sit in the shop.

We have been racking our brains this afternoon deciding on a place for the refrigerator and its construction. It is highly important that we make it as well insulated as possible, since we do not want to run the engine any more than necessary. Also it is necessary to have it arranged so as not to open the doors any more than we have to. Since the drinking water would be the main reason for our opening the doors except at meal time, at Fred's suggestion we planned to have a sort of drawer containing a zinc tank with a faucet on the outside for drawing the drinking water. This drawer can be taken out and the tank scalded, to keep it sanitary, without heating up the refrigerator. The food compartment is just under the drawer, and to the right of these there is the brine tank and a small extra compartment under it. I'll build it of tongue and groove boards, and line the interior with that heavy roll paper we have here. The partitions will be of zinc. I have considerable cotton batting here, and may have to order some more in Los Angeles, if I find I do not have enough.

We had considerable excitement on Harqua Hala Wednesday and Thursday. A party of three county surveyors were up here putting a signal on the peak. They came up unprovided with food or bedding, so we supplied them. Mr. Ellison brought up some provisions for them from their truck at the landing, and when they left they presented us with a lot of canned goods, and nearly a whole side of Swift's Premium bacon.

We have a circus every time we give the pup a bone watching him trying to keep the hens from taking it away.

Sincerely yours,

Alfred

Indeed, in latter June 1922 installation of the Kelvinator seemed to occupy most of Moore's spare time. He told Abbot, "We have just finished putting in the sink in the kitchen. It had to be put in before we could start on the building of the refrigerator. It will not take long to get the ice plant going after the refrigerator is built.

                                            Mt. Harqua Hala
                                            July 17, 1922
Dear Mr. Abbot:
     Mr. Ellison brought up some more parts for the
Kelvinator and the instruction manual. In reading it
over I noticed that they do not at all favor long runs of
copper tubing between the compressor and condenser and
the brine tank. I rather expect that my proposed distance
would be considered a pretty long distance, especially
since a good deal of it would be in soil that is continually very warm at this season of the year. The idea struck
me yesterday that it would be very much better if we could
have the compressor-condenser in the basement, or at
least very much nearer the refrigerator.
     I made a temperature comparison yesterday after-
noon. I used a Fahrenheit thermometer, and the results
were as follows. In the shop with both windows and the
door wide open, and a good breeze blowing through, the
temperature was 94 degrees. Under the house, where I
would put the machine, the temperature was 79 degrees.
And on the front porch with a good breeze blowing, it was
87 degrees. This seems to me a pretty strong argument in
favor of the basement.
     We had a pretty fierce wind and electrical storm
late last night, but only got 0.11 inches of rain out of
it. The wind managed to blow down the surveyor's sighting
signal. I was not surprised at all. I told the head man
that I thought he was not putting it up securely enough
for the Harqua Hala winds, but he thought he knew better.
     We have a couple of riding horses lined up, so maybe
you won't have to walk up the trail next time. One is for
$50 and the other $35. I think the former is a pretty good
animal for our purpose.
                              Sincerely yours,
                              Alfred

It seems that another trip to Los Angeles was about the only thing that could interrupt installation of the refrigerator and Kelvinator.

Harqua Hala
August 12, 1922

Dear Dad,

Alfred left for L.A. July 28 and Chella a week before that.[83] I have calcimined[84] all the walls and ceilings inside the house and have given most of the woodwork and floors a fresh coat of paint. I tackle one room at a time. Have to move everything out of it into the other rooms and it makes traffic rather congested. The weather has been pretty rotten for observing. Have gotten only five days since Alfred left. One of them was a long method which was somewhat of a surprise as we didn't get a long method at all during last July and August. There are thundershowers booming around every day and occasionally one passes over here. We have caught between eight and nine hundred gallons of water in our tanks.

Alfred and I built a refrigerator for the Kelvinator and when he gets back are going to try and get the thing working. There were some things he didn't understand about setting it up so he's going to find out about it in L.A.

The hens are laying about three eggs a day and that helps out a lot in figuring out the breakfast menu. Every time I go down to Mr. E's he loads me up with green corn and cucumbers. They sure hit the right spot.

Mr. E. and I went to town last Saturday afternoon. Got there in time for supper, then did our shopping and came back to the landing where we stayed over night. Bought a big watermelon in town and wrapped it in a wet meal bag. When we got to the landing it was almost as cool as ice. It was a dandy and about the sweetest one I ever ate. Got up at 4 o'clock next morning and arrived on top between 8 and 9 o'clock. It

---

[83] An expense account memo detailed Chella Moore's trip: "Ticket to Los Angeles & return for Mrs. Moore, $26.50 one way; Pullman ticket to Los Angeles, $4.50; tip porter, $0.25."

[84] Like a paint, calcimine is a solution of zinc oxide, water, glue, and coloring, used as a wash for walls and ceilings.

beats coming up in that heat. Alfred and Chella will be back on the 19th.

My love to you and mother.

Keg

Chapter 15

Finally, Good Results

The Moore's had planned to be gone from Harqua Hala for three weeks, but their summer trip home to Los Angeles stretched to a month because of unforeseen circumstances. When they did return, Alfred Moore immediately resumed his work and written communications with Charles Abbot who was still at Mt. Wilson in California.

Mt. Harqua Hala
August 25, 1922

Dear Mr. Abbot:

After a few days delay and considerable worry due to the Santa Fe strike, we finally managed to get back to our mountain home. We had all our plans made to return in our Ford on the following day when I found out that the strike had been called off. The Phoenix line was without any trains for ten days.

When we got back we found that everything had been going fine except the weather, and it has been pretty bad since our return. Thus far we have lost fifteen days entirely in August, and only one long method has been possible this month.

We now nearly have our cisterns and tanks full, which is a fine thing. We have gotten over three inches in July. Another inch of rain will fill everything up. I am planning to extend the concrete on the shop cistern up to the top of the corrugated iron, thus increase its capacity about 150 gallons. A rain while we were away cut up the lower part of the trail very badly. After the summer rains are over I think we will have to get those two men to work on the trail again.[85]

---

[85] Ellison took on this task for pay, starting in early October 1922.

In L.A. I called around to see Mr. Bassett of the
Santa Fe. He says that he expects their gang will be
stringing wires near Wenden in October, and that he will
be glad to have them string our wire at that time. I am
writing about insulators, poles, etc., by this mail. I
wrote a letter to Mr. Roebling before going on my vacation, thanking him for the phone and other favors since I
last wrote to him, and describing the many improvements
up here which his generosity has made possible. I also
invited him and Mrs. Roebling to make us a visit whenever
convenient to them. When I got back I found a letter from
Mrs. Roebling. She said that Mr. Roebling wasn't very
well, and asked her to write to me.

I have been working on the refrigerator ever since
my return as it is a very tedious task. I have it nearly
done now, and hope to get it ready to try out in a few
days. I went around to the agency in Los Angeles several
times for instructions.

Chella initiated our horse "George" by riding him
up the trail on our return from Los Angeles. She pro-
nounces him first class. His sores have healed, and he
has put on a good deal of flesh, so he is a pretty good
looking animal now. He is a regular pet, too. I think he
and Mr. Ellison are getting real chummy. Mr. Ellison
gives him a little barley every day, and he stays around
very close to his house. He doesn't have to hobble him any
more, and we can go right up to him when we want him.

Mr. Moore, the man from whom we bought George, has
piped the water from the spring[86] down to a trough near the
corral at the landing, and expects to put some cattle
down there soon. Mr. Ellison is still dickering with Mr.
Stokes, the cow man of Aguila.[87] While we were away,
eleven people from Aguila came up and camped for about
two weeks down near Mr. Ellison's.

Fred thinks that our lightning protection is great
thing. During a big storm lightning was hitting all
around, and Fred says he could plainly hear the guy wires
sizzling. No harm was done.

---

[86] Moore is referring to the spring half way up the trail from the foot of the mountain. Today, there is still a mile or two section of old three-quarter inch galvanized pipe; while this could be the pipe originally installed, it could also have been replaced by later ranchers.
[87] Greeley told his mother, "He is a cattleman and wants to buy a right to Mr. Ellison's spring. He has offered him $2500 for the right to water his cattle. That's what a good spring is worth."

> We now have the house about as bug-proof as it is
> possible to make it. Fred re-calcimined the walls, care-
> fully filling up even the smallest cracks. If any bug en-
> ters our abode now, he will have to come in at the door
> like a gentleman.
>
> Sincerely yours,
>
> *Alfred*

The addition of the refrigerator was certainly a morale builder on Harqua Hala. In the first week of September Moore wrote to Abbot, "We have the Kelvinator working since last Saturday, and it seems to be doing fine. We have had an ice cream and a sherbet in the time it has been running. It took a good many hours running the first couple of days to get the refrigerator cooled off, but since then we have not had any trouble to speak of. We have ice tea twice each day. The compressor still heats up more than it should, but with more use I think this will be all right. It now takes between four and five hours of running out of twenty-four, but when the thing gets limbered up I think this will be cut down somewhat, although in very hot weather it will take more running. I am enclosing a couple of pictures of it. The drawer at the upper left corner contains a four and a half gallon zinc water tank, for drinking water. When we use this part of it, we merely have to press the faucet knob, thus not having to open the refrigerator each time we want a drink."

Keg described the refrigerator to his mother: "Down cellar we have a coil of copper pipe filled with sulfur dioxide gas. One end of this pipe is connected to a compressor, and the other end leads from another pipe to the brine tank which is located in the refrigerator in the kitchen upstairs. The compressor compresses the gas into a liquid state and pumps it to the brine tank where it passes thru an expansion valve and expands into a gas again. When expanding into a gas it cools off very rapidly and of course send out this cold into the brine. This process is kept up till the brine is ice cold. Power to run the compressor is furnished in relays. First, a dynamo in the shop is belted to the engine and then a wire runs from that dynamo to another dynamo in the cellar which is belted to the fly wheel of the compressor. It has been quite a job to get the thing set up and have the Kelvinator part of it air tight for we can't afford to lose any of the gas up here.[88] A little of it escaped today, and it sure is pungent smelling stuff. Makes you think of the lower regions."

---

[88] They tested for sulfur dioxide leaks with "strong ammonia," the reaction producing a small cloud.

Harqua Hala
September 15, 1922

Dear Mother,

Friday night and we had fish. California tuna by name.[89] I never heard of it till Alfred and Chella introduced it into the menu here. They are caught off the California coast and some of the big uns weigh one hundred pounds. It tastes something like salmon, but not nearly as fishy. The meat is white and looks something like chicken.

Remember my telling you about some surveyors that were up here last July? They came up again day before yesterday to finish up their job and a sad day it was too. The chief of the party was struck by lightning and killed outright. A small shower gathered over this range of mountains about noon. There was very little thunder and lightning most of the lightning flashing up in the clouds. Only one bolt came to earth in the whole shower and this one killed Mr. Thompson. The fatality happened about two o'clock a mile northeast of the observatory. A couple other fellows were severely shocked, but were not harmed beyond the further upsetting of their equilibrium. They wrapped the body up in a canvas we loaned them and packed it down the trail on one of the mules they had with them. I took them to Wenden where we arrived about eight o'clock. We built a box on the depot platform, packed the body in ice and shipped it to Phoenix on the morning train. Quite a bit of difficulty was experienced in obtaining lumber and straightening out all the laws governing the shipment of a dead body.

Got a letter from the motorcycle fellow yesterday, and he said my machine ought to be there next week.

Must say good night now and perhaps I'll be dropping post cards along the line next week.

Very much love to you and dad.

Keg

---

[89] Most likely this was canned fish.

Greeley had ordered a motorcycle from the Harley Davidson dealer in Phoenix. As soon as it arrived, he set out on another vacation to Los Angeles. Leaving Harqua Hala on September 19th, he told his mother, "I went to Phoenix to get the machine. Rode it around town for two or three days to get it broken in and running right. The first day I left Phoenix, I rode as far as Wenden, about 115 miles. It was a tough old grind thru sand and ruts, and I had to ride every minute to keep right side up. I was terribly hot too which I think took more out of me than the riding. Left Phoenix at 8:15 in the morning and arrived at Wenden at sundown." After spending the night in Wenden, Keg rode on to Parker, Arizona. There, because he was advised that the road from Parker to Victorville, California, "was in fierce shape," he crated the motorcycle and had it shipped by train while he rode in coach, both for "about $20." Then, from Victorville, he cycled into Los Angeles.

Certainly the tragedy experienced by the county surveyors was a reminder of how difficult life on Harqua Hala could be, but it seemed as if conditions on the mountain were genuinely improving. While Greeley was on vacation, Alfred Moore continued the grind of getting everything working properly. Once the summer rainy season waned, the radio reception improved again with less static. Moore told Abbot, "We heard pretty good over the radio last night, the best since last spring. There was some static so we only used one amplifier most of the time. We were surprised to hear Kansas City as we had never heard that far before. We also heard some good music from Salt Lake City, Denver and San Francisco. Strangely enough we could not hear much from Los Angeles last night, except Avalon."

Even the observing results started to look reasonable. At Mt. Wilson for the summer, Abbot and his assistant Aldrich had found time to plan an experimental course of action to solve the equipment problems at the Arizona field station. On his way back to Washington, Abbot return to Harqua Hala for three days in late September. Keg told his mother, "Dr. Chas was here for a couple of days while I was away, and he left Alfred so much experimental work to do that he hasn't had time to do any computing." All of Abbot's experimental procedures with the observing apparatus started to pay off: the scientific results from Harqua Hala seemed to be falling in line with the results from the field station in Chile. A postscript on an October letter showed that even Moore's attitude was improving.

Mt. Harqua Hala
October 13, 1922

Dear Mr. Abbot:

By Wednesday's mail I sent you prints of bolographs as now taken here so you can probably see what the definition looks like, and compare it with Chile bolographs. I have prints of some Chile bolographs here, and by comparing ours with them it seems to me that with the exception of a somewhat smaller deflection, our bolographs now look about as nearly like those of Chile as it will be possible to make them.

With so many things on tap at present we are somewhat behind in computing, but from the ones that I have finished there does not seem to be as much increase in the solar constant as I had looked for, with so much change in definition. But the values had been very low just before we changed so that possibly there is more change than at first seems to be.

I found the cause of the "jumps" on the bolograph curves, at last. It seems that the cord holding the plate carrier got placed in the wrong hole at the top, and was causing friction. This was part of the trouble, and the rest was in the plate carrier worm gear. I spent a whole evening working on it, and finally got it all right.

Chella joins in best regards.

Sincerely yours,

Alfred

P.S. It seems that some scientist claims that he can revive life in a dead body provided the vital organs are in good condition. The L.A. Times commented upon it editorially. But it seems that the fellow cannot make the brain work, so that there is no mentality. The Times did not seem too enthuse very much upon it, and wound up by saying that about all the fellow could do would be to make some more Democrats!

Abbot was elated with the observing results; he wrote, "I am pleased down to the ground by the new appearance of the bolographs of Mt. Harqua Hala. They are so nearly identical with those from South America now that it is hard to say how there can be any prejudicial difference after we have introduced the new form of the energy curve alike in both stations. Mr. Fowle has had a great deal of trouble in getting the results straightened out, but now he has nearly finished it, and I hope to send you the new data very soon."

While the sky conditions were beyond the control of the observers, Moore now began to interpret the data gathered at Harqua Hala as meaningful.

                                        Mt. Harqua Hala
                                        October 21, 1922

Dear Mr. Abbot:

        I am sending the completed bolographs from September 21 to October 20 inclusive. The only missing day in this interval was September 22, when I had trouble with the galvanometer, and it clouded over before I could get it fixed. But the last few days have been rather poor skies, so we are probably in for rain soon. We thought we would lose today, but got a couple of short methods later this afternoon.

        On plotting the solar constants for this month, a very interesting curve is gotten, with two very marked sudden rises, followed during the last thirteen days, with possibly one exception on the 17th, by a gradual decrease, so that the value is very low now. I have plotted the accompanying values and there seems to be no similarity, which indicates that this unusual curve is likely not due to water vapor changes. If Chile is awake it will be interesting to see if they get a similar curve.

                                        Sincerely,

                                        Alfred

Chapter 16

A Wire to Wenden

Keg Greely's nineteen days away from Harqua Hala, most of them in Los Angeles being "dated up for shows or auto rides" by Edgar Moore, soon came to an end. Recalling the difficulty traveling by motorcycle across Arizona's desert, Keg returned to Wenden by train on October 7, 1922. Writing home and to Abbot in Washington about his trip, he said, "Left my machine at the Harley place. They will store it and keep the battery charged for two dollars a month. It behaves better out there than in Arizona. Think next time I go out I will try to ride it back when the weather is cooler."

With both observers back on the mountain, fresh from a vacation to cooler California, they took on the task of installing the proposed telephone line to Wenden, in addition to observing and other tasks.

> Harqua Hala
> October 25, 1922
>
> Dear Auntie Grace,
>
> Alfred has been to Wenden nine times since I got back, trying to get things started on the new telephone line so I've had a good deal of the observing to do and most of the computing. We have observed forty-two days in a stretch now without a miss. The days have been about sixteen hours long so not much chance for letter writing.
>
> Alfred and I are going to run the phone line from here to the garage, and he has contracted the rest of the job from the garage to Wenden to some other fellows. Going down over the mountain we are going to use big boulders. Drill holes in them and cement iron rods in the holes. Farther down where there are no suitable boulders we will use giant cactuses as poles. We spent one whole day picking

133

out the best route and found out that we will have to set only about six poles in all. From the garage to the Santa Fe tracks, poles will have to be set all the way. The Santa Fe has given us permission to string wires on their poles from there to Wenden. We are in hopes to be in direct communication with the metropolis sometime between now and 1923.

Alfred and I started to build an addition onto the garage last Monday. Got the frame built and the doors made so all that's left to do is nail the galvanized iron on the sides and roof. He expects to drive his own car out from L.A. next time he comes back.

Sometime between now and the first snow storms we have got to erect a shelter for George, our noble steed.

Next week Mr. Ellison and I are going to drill the holes for the telephone line. We will camp down in the canyon by the spring and work from there. It will probably take all week so I'll have a real camping out trip. It will be a real change from computing and am looking forward to some of his dutch oven biscuits.

Very much love,
Keg

As funding for the field station was always a concern, Moore's plan to string the telephone wire across boulders and cacti was cheaper, and he thought easier, than packing poles up the mountain, digging holes and setting the poles. However, near the field station, because their were no suitable rocks, Keg did have to set six poles from the observatory across the summit to the edge of the mountain.

Mt. Harqua Hala
November 3, 1922

Dear Mr. Abbot:

We have been so busy with the observing and working on the telephone line that I have been too tired at night to write many letters of late.

I have placed the contract for the construction of the four miles of telephone from the railway to the garage to Messrs. Lawson and Fitts of Wenden. I put up a notice for bids in the post office. These fellows' bid was

the only one forthcoming for a long time. Finally Mr.
Boggs, who loafs around Bunkers' most of the time, put in
a bid. It was lower than the other one, but I don't think
he would do any kind of job, and especially since he was
in with the Bunker crowd, I preferred letting the other
fellows do the work, as they are both hustlers. I thought
that their price was a little too high, but since they
will have to dynamite most of the holes on the upper mile
or two, perhaps it isn't. Their price ($250) includes all
labor of setting poles and stringing wires, all hauling
of their material, they to furnish all dynamite needed,
and all tools and keeping them in repair. After all material is laid down in Wenden, they have thirty days in
which to complete the work. They also put in a bid of $50
to string the seven miles of wire along the railway. I
have not placed this yet, for I want to see what the railway will do in regard to their gang. Another fellow, Mr.
Reid, who is a professional lineman, loomed up just as it
was too late for the other deal, and I think that if the
railway will not do it, I will get his bid, as he will
probably do the work more to the railway's liking. Fred,
Mr. Ellison and I have been plugging away at the part from
the garage to the first spring, the wire laid on the
ground a little farther than that, and the holes dug for
the poles needed on top. Fred and I have also finished the
addition to the garage.

We have been kept pretty busy with the observing,
too. We have everything computed including two long
methods in this interval, but only partial since clouds
interfered. In fact the skies have been poor the past
week. It has been very cold. On October 28th we had some
snow and sleet. I am enclosing a plot of the march of the
solar constant for the month of October as far as we have
it completed. It seems to me the most remarkable thing of
its kind that I have seen. As most of the days were fine
and the values fall smoothly, it looks as though something must have been doing on Old Sol. I am wondering if
any other phenomena connected with the sun corroborate
the steady drop from the 8th to the 21st of October.

Our hens seem to be slowing down on egg laying, but
one of them, "Henrietta," the one that "talks" to us,
laid two egg in one day, a few days ago. She lays a

peculiarly marked egg, and has a nest all to herself. We
did not have very much luck with the hatching of eggs that
we sent away for, only five hatching.[90] But we have lost
none of the ones that did hatch. One hatched out lame,
having no use of one leg, but even he is getting along
fine. He hops around on one foot, but I haven't seen him
do any scratching yet, like the other four do. Chella is
making quite a pet out of him.

Sincerely yours,

Alfred

Abbot indeed found Moore's "remarkable" solar plot from late October interesting. He wrote, "The plot of the solar work is quite as remarkable as the one you obtained in Chile in March 1920, and is even more continuous. It happens to have occurred at the identical time of the month. One could almost lay one curve on top of the other with a slight difference for absolute magnitudes. I called Mr. Peters of the Naval Observatory who photographs the sun daily, and he tells me that beginning between the 15th and the 20th there was a sunspot group developed out of nothing somewhat beyond the center of the sun's disk and advancing towards the limb. It grew bigger and bigger until it disappeared. This is extremely interesting in connection with your curve, and will be more so if after we correct your results, if necessary, for water vapor, the form of it still remains approximately as at present."

With the more promising, yet not conclusive, scientific results, Moore let his speculation run a little wild suggesting that the measurements being made on Harqua Hala might be connected to local weather conditions. He wrote to Abbot, "We are having it very much colder this November than we did a year ago at this time. We had quite a snowstorm last Monday. Strangely enough it was accompanied by thunder and lightning to the north of us. A night or two previous the static was as bad on the radio as it is in summer. I see that a big sunspot was on about this time. Don't you think it likely that all these things are closely related?"

Mt. Harqua Hala
December 13, 1922

Dear Mr. Abbot:
         Yesterday we went down to the landing and completed
the phone line. This made eight out of nine days that I
went down the trail. The Santa Fe has not as yet notified
us as to whether our wire is to go under the bridge or
overhead on high poles. I have been after them since

---

[90] Moore had ordered fertilized chicken eggs from Phoenix.

October 20th. Meanwhile we have the wire laid temporarily under the bridge, and tied onto the Matteson-Salome line at Wenden. We have been using the phone to Wenden since last Saturday. It seems to work very well, and probably will work better when we get loose from the Salome line.[91]

Chella and I are going to Los Angeles next week for the holidays. We had a very pleasant visit from Edgar at Thanksgiving. He had a great trip out here. He came via San Diego, Imperial Valley, Yuma and Phoenix. He struck a big rain storm between Yuma and Phoenix and had to be towed several times. When he got to Phoenix he found that the roads were impassable to Wenden, so left his auto there and came here on the train. He got here about noon Thanksgiving day, and stayed until early the following Monday.[92] It rained nearly all the time that he was here. We had no chance to look through the telescope at the stars, but tried to look at Wenden one day.[93] I have rigged up a pretty rigid altazimuth mounting up near the croquet ground. Could you send out a blue glass to use in looking at the sun?

We have built a small horse shed down below the garden. We will also have to build a similar structure down at Mr. Ellison's for George spends a good deal of his time down there.[94] A horse can't stand the cold weather such as we have up here without protection. I have also gotten a blanket for him.

Today, we enclosed the space under the porch with iron, so we can keep our wood dry. Chella would very much like to have a small screen porch at the kitchen door, so she can keep the vegetables out there. I have a good deal of the material that would be needed. May I order the other that would be needed and build it in the spring? We have two doors to take the place of the screen doors in winter and keep out the cold wind, but have not had time yet to hang them.

---

[91] Salome is five miles west of Wenden.

[92] On the return trip, the roads were so rough, Edgar Moore's car "broke both front and rear springs and had to have a brand new set put in."

[93] Abbot had sent a telescope to the field station, principally for the enjoyment of the observers.

[94] Greeley and Moore built the second shed on December 15, 1922, Moore described them as "both nine feet by five and a half feet, large enough to protect him from the snow and cold."

I wonder if you can have four Smithsonian calendars sent out. We need two here, and Mrs. Matteson[95] and Mr. Ellison would very much like to have one each.

All this will reach you not far from Christmas time. Chella joins me in wishing you and Mrs. Abbot a very Merry Christmas and Happy New Year.

Sincerely yours,

Alfred

P.S. Wenden: Have tested out the phone here when disconnected from the Salome line and it works in great shape. Am OKing the bill for $50 for stringing wire along RR. AFM

Moore was confident about the newly installed telephone and the positive observing results; his attitude about Harqua Hala certainly improved throughout the Fall of 1922. But just before leaving on December 18th for Los Angeles, he wrote to tell Abbot about the latest news from Wenden, still showing his disdain for much of its citizenry: "A bunch of prohibition agents swooped down on Wenden Saturday night and grabbed a couple of moon shiners. But they missed the worst offenders along this line. I think those Mexicans down at the landing are at this business, but they evidently got a tip and got out of the way before the officers arrived."

With the addition to the garage at the landing completed, Alfred and Chella Moore planned to return from their Christmas trip to California in their Ford, or "flivver" as Keg called it. Greeley was left alone for Christmas on Harqua Hala, but the newly installed telephone kept him in touch with the social life in Wenden.

Harqua Hala
January 10, 1923

Dear Mother,

Your good letter of late and the fine box of candy with the necktie in it and the box of partridge berries all gratefully received. So you had roast pork for Christmas, so did I too with cranberries, celery and mashed spuds. The only drawback was I had to eat it alone, Spot was an attentive looker on and every time I would look at him

---

[95] Mrs. Matteson, the Wenden merchant's wife, had visited Chella again on November 15th.

he would sit up on his hind legs and bark till I threw him a morsel.

I was unable to revive the partridge berries, but just the same I showed them to a lot of people in Wenden so they could see one of the things that grow in New Hampshire and not out thiser-way.

Had quite a bit of company for this place. Mr. Lawson, he is the fellow who put in our phone line from the garage to Wenden, called up one day and wanted to know if it would be convenient for him to come up and bring his sister-in-law along who was visiting them. They came to the garage in his car and I met them there with George. They stayed that night, and I entertained them with the radio. They said it was a treat as neither one had listened in before. Another visitor was a cowboy from Wenden. He rode up on his horse and stayed two days and nights. He is a pretty good sort of fellow, and I enjoyed having him around.

Went to a couple of dances in Wenden, one on Christmas night and the other the Saturday before New Years. The first one was at Mrs. Matteson's and the other at Mrs. Harrington's. Practically the same bunch was at both parties, senoritas, cowboys, "lungers" and married ladies with their children. Dancing doesn't start till after the train comes and goes at nine o'clock. We danced till twelve and then after being revived with ice cream, cake and coffee started in again and danced till 2 AM. I had a dandy time at both parties and didn't know there were so many pretty girls in the surrounding towns of Aquila and Salome.

The weather has been marvelously warm for this time of year. We haven't had a freeze since the first week or so in November. It's too good to last tho, I guess.

Aunt Grace sent a fine box of "assorteds" as I called it, silk hose, after dinner mints, tube of tooth paste, bar of Hershey chocolate. Alfred and Chella sent a box of chocolates. Mrs. Roebling also sent a big box of candy so I've been having a sweet time of it. Received many cards

from both coasts, but at that it didn't seem like a real New England Christmas. The seasons are so undefined here.
                    Very much love,
                    Keg

With Fred Greeley pending transfer to Chile, this was his last letter home from Harqua Hala. He looked forward to seeing his family again in the Spring of 1923.

Chapter 17

Ready for a Real Test

The new year had all the markings of a turning point for scientific results from Harqua Hala. It began with Charles Abbot and John Roebling meeting on December 30, 1922, in Bernardsville, New Jersey, to review the status of the solar constant program. In addition to solid results from the Smithsonian stations in Chile and Arizona, Abbot was preparing to equip two new independent solar constant stations: one in Australia for its government's Committee on the Solar Radiation Station and Rev. E. F. Pigot at Riverview College[96] and another at La Quiaca, Argentina, for the Argentine government.

With Alfred Moore back on Harqua Hala January 7th, Abbot filled him in on the latest developments.

SMITHSONIAN INSTITUTION
Washington, U.S.A.

January 5, 1923

Dear Alfred:

Your letters of December were duly received as I was leaving to attend the meeting of the American Association for the Advancement of Sciences in Boston. While in Boston I attended a meeting of the Meteorological Society at which Clayton was present and described his studies of the variation of the sun for forecasting of weather a week in advance, as it is now being carried on in Buenos Aires. The excellence of the showing of Clayton was, I think, favorable to impressing those present with the probable future value of our work for meteorology.[97]

---

[96] Part of the Australian apparatus was built by William Gaertner & Co. Chicago, Ill.
[97] At the meeting, Clayton's results were favorably received, according to Abbot, by "Marvin, director of our Weather Bureau and Sir Frederick Stupart, director of the Canadian Weather Bureau."

The next day after the meeting I visited Mr. Roebling in New Jersey, and he showed even more interest
than common in our work. He has arranged to provide me
with a new assistant, to be secured as soon as possible so
as to help me in the preparation of the delicate parts of
the outfits for Australia and Argentina. It has been my
intention to go myself to Australia to set up the apparatus there, but in the course of our conversation Mr. Roebling and I discussed quite extensively the desirability
of starting Mr. Clayton on intensive study of the weather
of the United States as depending on our solar radiation
results.[98]

Mr. Roebling authorized me to get an estimate from
Clayton as to the cost of starting a private forecasting
bureau to make eight-day forecasts, similar to those he
has made in South America, for selected stations in the
United States. This is confidential, for the present, as
we do not wish to have any inkling of it get out to make
possible friction with the Weather Bureau. This would
involve daily telegrams from Chile and from Arizona, and
Mr. Roebling contemplates standing back of the whole
proposition financially.

He asked why someone else could not be sent to Australia. He asked me to consider the proposed new assistant, who would at all events be in training for the
directorship of the Argentine station, and whether he
with Paul Greeley could not run the Harqua Hala station,
sending you to Australia to set up the outfit there in my
place. I pointed out to him that it was doubtful if you
would care to go without Chella, and he at once offered to
pay Chella's way to Australia and back, including her
subsistence while there, and made an appropriation on
the spot of $1000 for that purpose. I understand, of
course, that the Australians interested in the project
will pay the transportation and subsistence of the observer sent out there to set up their outfit.

The matter would have to be delayed until the exchange of the Greeleys has taken place, and until I can go
out to Mt. Wilson to be somewhere near the ground so as to
look after Harqua Hala in case anything should go wrong

[98] Interestingly, Abbot was also aware of "Fabry's work on variable ozone in the upper atmosphere." He and Roebling wanted to study "the high probability that variations in ozone are influential in affecting the weather of the earth."

there, so that the journey might perhaps start before the first of July and extend for some three months. It would be quite a change for you both, would enable Chella to get a glimpse of Hawaii, the South Sea Islands, New Zealand and Australia, and would save me from having to go so far away from the Smithsonian Institution, which is, after all, a thing very undesirable. This also, if you please, you may keep confidential for the present.

Tell Fred I saw his father and rode down with him from Nashau to Lowell last week. Remembering how good Fred's cranberries were the year I was there, I sent out for you all a box of them, a while ago, and hope that they came in nicely.

Very truly yours,

C. G. Abbot

Moore was elated; he wrote to Abbot, "I received your very interesting letter of the 5th a few days ago. When I read it to Chella, she was just as much excited about the contents as I was when I first read it! I know she would have the time of her life on a trip like that."

Moore also reported on good weather and stated, "We have run three long methods since the 9th, all of excellent grade, and showing fine agreement between long and short method values, so I guess we are on solid ground after our change of definition."

As Abbot had explained to Roebling during their meeting, measurement results through 1922 from Arizona[99] and Chile verified "the introduction of the new form of solar energy curve. The new abbreviation of the short method will permit additional observations and higher accuracy each day." Abbot proclaimed "the two stations are at the highest level of efficiency and exactly on the same basis."

Arrangements for private forecasting were in place by the first of February. Abbot wrote to Moore, "To whet your interest, I may inform you confidentially that Mr. Clayton, Mr. Roebling and myself had a conference yesterday[100] and all the preliminaries were arranged to start Mr. Clayton on his private forecasting bureau. He will make quantitative forecasts of temperature and pressure at several stations long enough so that we can see how they go, and if the result is satisfactory we shall then be in

---

[99] Abbot told Moore, at the Smithsonian, human "computers," Mr. Fowle and Mrs. Bond "had completed the discussion of nearly 500 days of solar constant measurements at Harqua Hala. Apparently they are coming out beautifully, although it is necessary to use a systematic correction just as we did at Calama for the short methods, depending on the humidity."

[100] February 8, 1923.

position to show the Weather Bureau that we have accomplished something." In another letter Abbot explained, "Mr. Clayton thinks it will be something like May and June before he will be ready for the daily reports."

At Harqua Hala, attention turned once again to daily operations, what were now more routine problems with the equipment not working on occasion, and to the Greeley brothers exchanging posts. Moore wrote to Abbot, "As soon as we hear when Paul is to sail, we will arrange the date of Fred's leaving here." Keg Greeley was planning on one more trip to California. Moore added, "One of the cloudy days Fred and I put the new steps on the front porch. They are a lot easier than the old 'ladder' we had there formerly. Did I write you that I picked up a concert from the broadcasting station of the General Electric Co. at Schenectady, New York, a couple of weeks ago? It came in clearly with but one amplifier."

New construction also included a corral for George at the landing because, as explained by Greeley, "There are so many horses, cows, dogs, goats, sheep and hens around down there now that every time we feed him it is necessary to stand around with a club to see he gets his share." Moore also asked permission "to build a small screen porch off the kitchen door. We are getting pretty crowded for room, for the space under the house is rapidly filling up."

SMITHSONIAN INSTITUTION
Washington, U.S.A.

February 20, 1923

Dear Alfred and Fred:

I have a cable from Paul saying that he sails north on March 9th by the Santa Elisa. That will bring him to New Hampshire about March 29th, and it seems to me that it would be desirable for Fred to have arrived earlier so as to have had part of his vacation before that and after staying a couple of weeks at home while Paul is there he might be ready to go on to Chile about the middle of April.

In regard to the passport, I think it would be difficult or impossible for Fred to get that in the West, but think he will be able to obtain it at Nashua or thereabouts while at home. We are looking up the matter and will send him a letter to Pelham.

We shall probably wish to send some boxes of supplies to Aldrich along with him. It may be necessary for

him to come by way of Washington to sail, but we will let
him know about that later on.

> Very truly yours,
>
> *C. G. Abbot*
>
> Assistant Secretary

Immediately, Keg Greeley made plans to leave Harqua Hala on March 17th. In addition, Alfred and Chella Moore planned a brief trip to Phoenix early in March because it would be their "last chance to get out of here before June" and the trip to Australia.

A telegram from Abbot changed Greeley's plans: "Paul delayed to twenty-third. Hold Fred two weeks."

Wenden
March 16, 1923

Dear Mr. Abbot,

Chella has been visiting Mrs. Matteson for several days and last evening they had a dandy goose dinner in honor of our second anniversary.

As I wired you yesterday on receipt of your telegram, Fred will leave for the East on Sunday April 1st unless we hear otherwise from you.

We had a very pleasant trip to Phoenix. Were surprised at the big improvements in that vicinity.

We had a terrific windstorm day before yesterday. It picked up the horse shed and set it bodily 25 feet down the mountain - right side up and no damage done. The huge clouds of dust and sand from the valley kept us from getting more than one bolograph, and it looks poor.

We have the computing nearly done for the new short method. It has been some task! But it is well worth while I am sure.

Sincerely yours,
Alfred

PS. I have just received and signed the telephone tri-party agreement and am returning same to Mr. Bassett. They have made an elaborate map, etc. It is 6.39 mile along the railroad poles. When the bill comes I'll send to. Mr. Adams for payment. AFM

Moore welcomed the delay of Greeley's departure from Harqua Hala because he needed help to repair the phone line to Wenden. As he explained to Abbot, "The Western Union wire stringing gang that worked through Wenden region the past few days played havoc with our phone line on the railway poles. When I went down today to locate the trouble, I found the wire broken and on the ground in one place, and so loose as to nearly touch the ground in three other places. In making their transpositions, they had found it necessary to cut our wire frequently, and instead of phoning me about it, and having me take them some steel wire they very poorly spliced it back, and left it in a very poor condition indeed, so that I fear we will have to go down and tie in all their splices in those seven miles to keep it from blowing down with every windstorm."

Moore caught up with the Western Union crew working near Golden, twelve miles east of Wenden. He just missed the foreman, Mr. Fancher, but "some of his flunkies were there and said they knew the crew left the line in bad shape, but thought the 'old man' did not know about it." Moore told Abbot, "I wrote a note asking him if he would kindly have the trouble remedied. I told him that the line was the property of the Smithsonian, a branch of the Government, and that we had put it in as per arrangements with Mr. Bassett of the Santa Fe and Mr. Ord of the Western Union."

A few days latter, seemingly the line was repaired. The foreman "sent one of his men back to put the line in shape, and afterwards addressed a letter to me, in which he stated that our line had been put in good order." But still there was trouble, at least enough temporary trouble to cause Alfred Moore to vent his feelings.

```
                                        Mt. Harqua Hala
                                        March 19, 1923
Dear Mr. Abbot:
        It looks as though Fred and I will have to put in a
day's work tomorrow, further repairing the damage done
our phone line by the Western Union outfit. The whole
thing is such an unusual piece of business procedure.
Today I was quite surprised when Mr. Stauffer, the chief
electrician of the Santa Fe in this vicinity, telephoned
```

me that I would have to lower our line in places, so that the new copper lines just installed for the railway would not touch our wire. Now that the Western Union gang did a poor job stringing their wire, so that it sags too much, the Santa Fe figures that it is up to the Smithsonian to be the goat instead of making the Western Union put their line in proper shape.

If fixing the wire in a few places tomorrow were the only thing, it would not be so bad, but I have an idea that we will be troubled in this way whenever they take a notion.

Since they put the other two wires on the poles, we have been troubled a good deal with considerable noise in the phone, sometimes so noisy that it is hard to understand what is said. It does not seem to be the telegraph so much as a very noisy hum.

I think I wrote you that I had signed the tri-party agreement which was sent to me by Mr. Bassett. A couple of weeks ago I also signed the crossing permit papers, and paid the Santa Fe agent at Wenden five dollars each for the two permits. This afternoon Mr. Mann, the agent at Wenden called me up on the phone, and said he had a communication from Los Angeles in which they asked Mr., Mann to inquire as to my "official title" and if I had authority to sign the papers in behalf of the Smithsonian. Talking over the phone with his usual loud voice, I suppose every loafer in Matteson's store knows more about my business than I do myself before now!

As soon as I get through working for the Santa Fe and the Western Union, I hope to get you a lot of back bolographs which we have stacked up here.

Sincerely yours,

Alfred

P.S. Fred and I fixed the line today - having to lower our line in 29 places. It was cloudy this A.M. but about one P.M. it suddenly cleared off so we lost a chance to observe by the Western Union carelessness. However, I think it would probably be best not to complain to them as we don't want them to refuse the use of their poles to us. AFM

Fred Greeley left the Harqua Hala field station for the last time on Sunday, April 1, 1923, after serving there thirty months. Finally, he headed home to visit his parents.

Chapter 18

Changing the Staff

Early in March 1923 Abbot hired William Hoover to fill the position that Roebling had agreed to. With so many new projects pending for the burgeoning solar constant program, especially Moore's trip to Australia, Abbot wanted to train his new assistant as soon as possible.

SMITHSONIAN INSTITUTION
Washington, U.S.A.

April 5, 1923

Dear Alfred:

   Mr. Hoover seems to be just of the right sort. It occurs to me that the best way to get him thoroughly acquainted with the work, and at the same time to give you a little aid in it, will be to send him out to Mt. Harqua Hala about April 15th and let him stay with you for about three weeks and then return to Washington to help me in packing up the outfit for Australia. I spoke to Mr. Hoover about this, and he is quite agreeable to going, so that if you see no objection I will have him do so. You will find him a very quiet but very pleasant fellow, and one who is quite skilled with his hands, and he seems to understand perfectly and be able to carry out with large independence whatever one tells him to do. The idea, of course, would be for you to teach him every detail of your practice both in observing and computing, so that he could carry on the work during your absence with a good deal of confidence.

   These are very happy days here. We have been trudging along on this solar variation for years, spending thousands of dollars and enormous thought and care and

trouble in the faith and hope that the two stations will
support one another and indicate a substantial variation
of the sun. Now, at last, we have the Harqua Hala work all
treated for its systematic errors and have made a comparison between the two stations. The average deviation
of individual daily observations on acceptable days is
0.6 per cent. The average deviation of monthly means is
about 0.3 per cent. Naturally the agreement would be much
better if the days in the individual months were identical. However, both stations show substantially the same
march of the solar variation, confirming one another
with highly gratifying continuity.

    In short, we can walk by sight rather than by faith
from now on.

    With kindest regards.

                      Yours truly,

                      G. C. Abbot

                      Assistant Secretary

In a follow-up telegram, Abbot told Moore, "I plan to start Hoover from here Sunday
evening, April 15th, via the Pennsylvania and Santa Fe,[101] so that he will probably
reach Wenden on April 19th." While Hoover would train at Harqua Hala for only
three weeks, longer plans called for him, with his wife, to report back to Harqua Hala
"so that the Hoovers and Paul Greeley could hold the fort on Mt. Harqua Hala during
Moore's absence, from approximately July 1st to September 1st." Alfred and Chella
Moore expected to leave Wenden by June 12th, going first to Los Angeles and then on
to San Francisco, preparing to sail June 26th on the Oceanic Line's Sonoma.[102] Also,
during the summer months of 1923, Abbot planned to be on Mt. Wilson doing more
research measuring solar variation of stars; he would be readily available for the observers on Harqua Hala.

                      Mt. Harqua Hala
                      April 27, 1923

Dear Mr. Abbot:

    The poor observing weather continues, which is
somewhat bad for breaking in Mr. Hoover, but he is

---

[101] This route would take Hoover through Phoenix, rather than transfer at Ashfork, Arizona.

[102] Moore had expressed the desire to travel to Australia by Union Line; he told Abbot, "I think the Union Line offers better steamers and a better schedule, with more interesting ports. The Oceanic Line has on the Sonoma and Ventura, which were old tubs when you and I went to Tahiti.." But, Abbot, wanting Moore to sail at an earlier time than the Union Line offered, convinced Moore, saying, "Not withstanding your
disparaging remarks on the Oceanic Line, I would prefer to have the sailing made on June 26th. It would also have the advantage of being an
American line where there is not so much fuss and feathers for dinner as there is on the British line which you speak of."

getting along very well indeed. I have shown him practically all the computing methods, and he catches on very
quickly, and gets a thorough understanding of it all very
readily. It took him a little while to read the pyrehe-
liometers accurately, but I guess this is a stumbling
block for many. He is doing much better now. I'll break
him in at the other end of the observing the first of the
week, and then I think we will alternate on succeeding
mornings, and probably at the last I'll let him practice
at running the whole thing himself. Besides being good at
his work, he seems to be a very agreeable fellow, and from
my observation thus far, I think you made a good choice.

Fred has not honored us with any letters thus far
since he left here. I guess he is pretty busy at home. Do
you know about what time Paul will come out to Harqua
Hala? Chella is anxious for her father to visit us[103] before Paul comes, and after Mr. Hoover goes back to
Washington.

Sincerely yours,

Alfred

In transit from Chile to Arizona, Paul Greeley arrived home in Pelham, New Hampshire, on April 10, 1923, anticipating a four month vacation. Abbot told him, however, "I wish very much that you could go out to Harqua Hala soon after the first of June in order to get the hang of it before Mr. Moore goes away." Paul Greeley willingly agreed and immediately made plans to arrive at Harqua Hala about June 6th.

Hoover completed his training and left Arizona May 12th. Advising Abbot that Hoover "should be there for work the morning of the 17th," Moore reported, "I have shown him about the observing and computing, and I think he will easily be able to keep things going satisfactorily during my absence. We have run quite a few long methods, and he has done all parts of the computing, including the extrapolation." Moore added, "I hope that we may be able to start for Los Angeles in our car on June 10th or 11th, but if Mr. Hoover is not here by then, Paul will not have much time in which to get onto running the station here along. It has been quite warm of late and we get much comfort out of the ice plant, and also the screen porch,[104] where we frequently eat, as I have built a folding table out there, large enough for five persons."

---

[103]There is no indication in the letters in the Smithsonian Archives that Chella's father made this visit to Harqua Hala.
[104]Moore had completed the new screen porch the first week in April.

Mt. Harqua Hala
June 7, 1923

Dear Mr. Abbot:

I expect to go to Wenden tomorrow afternoon to meet
Paul and bring him up here tomorrow night. I would let him
wait in Wenden overnight and come up with Mr. Ellison
Saturday, but as it is imperative that we get away from
here Monday, I want to have as much time as possible to
show Paul about the observing at this station. I am sorry
that he did not get here several days earlier, but I do
not see how we can possibly put off starting for Los
Angeles later than Monday, as there are many things to do
there, and we must start for San Francisco the latter
part of the following week at the latest.

I was sorry to learn that you may not be able to get
to California before I start for Australia. There are
many things that we would do well to talk over, but if you
cannot get there by that time I suppose we must make the
best of it.

Sincerely yours,

Alfred

Obviously, arrangements were not falling into place the way Moore had anticipated
they would: Hoover had not yet returned, and Moore only had two days to acquaint
Paul Greeley with the procedures on Harqua Hala. It must have been a tense weekend,
but the Moore's did leave the mountain on time June 10th, only to have more serious
problems in Los Angeles. From his brother's home, on Thursday, June 14th, Alfred
Moore wired to Abbot, "Chella threatened appendicitis, possibly necessary postpone
trip, will wire later." Abbot replied, "Shocked your wire. Hope speedy recovery. Wire
frequently. Will cancel trip if necessary."

753 S. Carondelet St.
Los Angeles, Calif.
June 15, 1923

Dear Mr. Abbot:

I have telegraphed a couple of times in regard to
Chella's illness, and received your answer to my first
telegram, but thought you might want to know more of the
particulars.

We had it pretty hot crossing the desert, and the
road was none too smooth, and we found it necessary to

drive a good deal of the night, so that Chella was pretty tired when we got to Los Angeles Tuesday morning. We got caught in a heavy windstorm about 115 miles from Los Angeles about midnight, and fearing the top would be blown off, we had to pull up under a sheltering hill and sleep in the car until daybreak. We stopped in Banning for breakfast, and Chella thought she ate something there that did not agree with her, for she felt a heaviness in her stomach shortly after reaching L.A. This rather grew worse as the day wore on, but she slept fairly well that night and felt a little better Wednesday, but still not very well. About one o'clock Thursday morning she was taken with very severe pains in her abdomen, but we still thought they were caused by her stomach. A couple of times I started to call the doctor, and then she got better, and finally went to sleep. But yesterday morning I thought I ought to call the doctor, and when he examined her, he said it looked very much like appendicitis, and he thought she should be taken to the hospital right away for a blood test. So I called the ambulance, and went with her over to the hospital. They took a blood test, which showed some pus, and the doctor called in another doctor to examine her, to decide about operating. They decided that it might be best to wait a day or two, and ordered her put on a starvation diet and ice packs kept on her abdomen. This morning I saw the doctor at the hospital and he said she was getting along very well, and he did not think an operation would be necessary. I asked him about the chances of her sailing on the 26th of this month, and he said he thought she should have from two to four weeks to rest and recuperate before starting on such a long trip.

This evening I went over to see her and found her very much improved, in fact she looked better than I have seen her since her return from Arizona. So I am very hopeful that she is well on the road to recovery, although I think she will have to be very careful for several weeks, so she won't over-exert herself.

Of course if I had had any inkling of what was before her, I would have insisted on her coming back on the train. But I had to drive the auto back, and as she is always such a good sport, she wanted to come back with me. I

do not intend to take my car back to Arizona, for I think
those desert roads are too much for her.

I thought that Father Pigot could probably look after the apparatus after it reaches Sydney. It might be
well to get it started on its way by the boat we intended
going on, so that it would be there ready when I'd get
there. In this case it would be necessary for me to get it
started on its way at San Francisco, and I said in my
telegram today that I thought I could leave Chella for a
few days next week to attend to this if it seemed desirable to you.

As the Union Line has a steamer sailing on July 20th
which is eleven days in advance of the next Oceanic boat,
I thought that possibly you might want to try to arrange
with the steamship company to go via the Union and return
via the Oceanic.

As Chella is getting along so well, I think I'll be
free to do anything you may wish in the line of the work
within a few days, but I do not think it would be advis-
able for her to go out to Harqua Hala during the hot summer weather.

Sincerely yours,

Alfred

Pleased to hear of Chella recovery and knowing that the Australian trip would not be
canceled, Abbot once again concentrated on details for his observing stations. He
asked Moore, "It seems to me that it would be very desirable, if you can arrange to do
so, to go back to Harqua Hala for a few days and see to it that everything is being done
just as you would wish it to be in your absence. They have now been there long
enough to have run up against some difficulties which you could straighten out. If,
however, anything should make this journey irksome, I do not feel that it is indispensable, but wish you to have everything in readiness for the Australian trip."

While Moore did go to San Francisco to arrange shipping the observing apparatus on to Australia, he found a reason for not returning to Harqua Hala, as Abbot had
asked.

753 S. Carondelet St.
Los Angeles, Calif.
June 30, 1923

Dear Mr. Abbot:

A while after I went over to the hospital this morning to see Chella, the doctor came in. He noted much improvement in Chella, but since she is contemplating the
trip, he said he thought she should use the greatest
care, and thought she should remain in the hospital about
a week longer. I asked him what he now thought about our
sailing July 20th, and he said he thought she would be
able to start then. I then broached the question about my
making a trip to Harqua Hala, but he frowned on this.
Chella wants me to see her two or three times each day,
and I think he thought if I were away three days or so, it
might not be the best thing for her. She got pretty lonesome while I was away in Frisco.

So I wrote a short letter for Mrs. Matteson to phone
up to Mr. Hoover. I told him that if they had struck any
snags, to let me know and I would try to take a run out
there soon. I also suggested that he send me a long method
and a short method that they have finished reducing, for
I can tell a good deal from them, both as regards computing and to some extent the observing.

From what the doctor said this morning, I think he
now rather doubts whether she had appendicitis, but more
likely inflammation of the bowels. This of course might
be more serious than appendicitis, but with proper care
now, not so likely to re-occur as appendicitis would be.
Now that she is recovering from the attack I rather hope
this is the proper diagnosis, for she would be in constant fear of another attack were it appendicitis, and an
attack in the middle of the Pacific Ocean or on Mt. Harqua
Hala after our return might easily prove very serious
indeed. I did not realize it before we left the mountain,
but she was pretty thoroughly tired out, and I guess this
had made it harder for her to get over the attack quickly.

Los Angeles is getting worse and worse as regards
the traffic congestion, so it is really hard to get
across streets on foot many times. I often wonder what
they will do when they get 200,000 or 300,000 more autos

here. It is certainly no pleasure to drive a car around
and not much more to walk across the street.

Sincerely yours,

Alfred

Once Chella recovered fully, she and Alfred left Los Angeles by train the night of July
18th, then sailed from San Francisco July 20, 1923, on the steamer Tahiti. They arrived in Sydney, Australia, August 26th to begin advising Father Pigot on setting up
his solar constant observing station at Riverview College. He advised Abbot, "We expect to sail from Sydney on the Union boat Tahiti, leaving October 25th and arriving
San Francisco November 19th."

Chapter 19

Paul and Bill

With the Moores on their way to Australia, the Harqua Hala field station was now manned by Paul Greeley. While he adapted to the mountain easily, right away he had trouble because of his short training with Alfred Moore and his lack of experience with all the accouterments Moore had installed.

Mt. Harqua Hala
June 26, 1923

Dear Cousin Charles,

It was a hot trip out here, but I enjoyed it all the same. It was the hottest in Chicago, so instead of going to the ball game went to the Chicago State Theater. The trains were hot too, but stood out on the observation platform whenever there was standing room. I caught the afternoon freight from Wickenburg to Wenden, and Alfred met me there. It is fine up here, and I like it much better than Montezuma. I think the trail is grand, that is the scenery.

The same day that Alfred left I got back here and started the engine.[105] It ran fine for about an hour then stopped with a crash and bang. Went out and found half of the governor gone and the governor spring broken. I took the remains off and also the little rod that works automatically with the air valve and made a small piece of wood the right length that holds the air valve in a certain place. With a steady load it runs OK.

Yesterday I took a shower and set it too fast. Gosh, it was more like being out in the Garden of Eden in a hale and sleet storm. Finally the belt came off and I was thankful.

---

[105] This was the engine used to charge the instrument batteries and run the Kelvinator.

Mr. Ellison and I are good friends already. He is quite interesting to listen to and has one habit of beginning every other sentence with a "Thinks I," as you probably know.

Sincerely yours,
Paul

Paul's new assistant William Hoover returned to Harqua Hala, this time with his wife Sally, later the same week that the Moores left.

Wenden, Arizona

Dear Mr. Abbot:

Mrs. Hoover and I had a very fine visit at my home in Indiana and a very pleasant trip out here. We arrived in Wenden last Thursday evening and stayed with the Mattesons that night. Paul came down to meet us the next morning. It has been cool here since we arrived so the trip up the trail was not very bad. Mrs. Hoover thinks this is a great place so I guess we will get along fine.

We had a little excitement here the other evening. I woke up and heard the chickens making quite a fuss so I went out to see what was wrong. I found a bobcat in the chicken house so I came back to the house to get Paul and a gun. One of us held a flashlight while the other shot him. We skinned it so we will have a souvenir. However, it has killed three chickens so we have been eating chicken all week.

We are getting along fine with the work. Paul had a hard time the few days he was here by himself, but everything is going fine now.

Sincerely,
W. H. Hoover

About the chicken house, Paul admitted, "I had forgotten to lock the small door." He recorded the kill as "three hens and a rooster. Bill and I rushed out in our pajamas with a flash light and rifle. I didn't even put on any slippers, and when I got back began to realize that the traveling had been rough. The cat was out on the roost with the hens. Bill held the flash in his eyes while I put a bullet through his head. He was two feet eight inches long."

Considering the season with its increasing thunderstorm activity in Arizona, observing conditions were generally good for Greeley and Hoover, with good results for their first few weeks. However, the succession of other problems continued to march on.

Mt. Harqua Hala
July 27, 1923

Dear Dr. Abbot:

We had a very severe electric storm last Monday, July 23rd, and also a very heavy rain. It just about filled all our water tanks, but it also caused us considerable trouble. The next day when we tested the deflection we decided that the storm must have changed the magnetic field around the galvanometer. We then changed the position of the control magnet until the deflection and period were about the same as before and ran a test plate to see if the definition was good enough and the scale uniform. The scale was uniform but the definition was not quite the same as before. The results obtained yesterday and today seemed to be OK.

The storm also burned out our radio bulbs although the antenna was not connected to the house but was grounded. I was in the bolometer room at the time and saw a flash.

Sincerely,
W. H. Hoover

In addition, logistics with Wenden seemed doomed because of automobile problems.

Mt. Harqua Hala
Wenden, Arizona
August 22, 1923

Dear Cousin Charles:

We are terribly in need of another auto. Ever since Alfred left Mr. Ellison began to have trouble with it. Finally it got so bad that it didn't have power enough to get into Wenden empty. Dick Bunker towed him in and then worked on it off and on for two weeks, most of the time waiting for parts from Phoenix. In the mean time Bunker made the trips out to the garage costing $6.00 per trip and between 45 and 50 dollars for overhauling it.

It worked fairly well for a trip or two, then started to go wrong again. For the last three Saturdays I have gone to Wenden with Mr. Ellison because he can't make it alone. Always gets stuck in washes and gets back here way after dark, and two weeks ago we didn't get back until the next morning. The cylinders have been rebored twice and over sized rings put on the pistons. It seems foolish of going to that expense again when the engine is a 1911 or 1912 model. There is not much left on it that is Ford now.

It won't start by cranking it when it's cold and if it wasn't for the hill there we would all lose any religion. It is necessary to scrape the soot and oil from the spark plugs several times during one trip. It has very little power even in low. Lately it has developed knocks. Also whistles like a peanut stand. Last trip the steering gear broke in three places up by the throttle. By driving very slow in low most of the way we managed to get to Wenden. The thing needs new tires.

According to my idea, the ideal car for this business would be a Dodge Commercial Car. If you decided to purchase one, thought that I could drive it back when I go out to L.A.[106] Mr. Ellison would be tickled to come out and make the trip back with me.

We have observed 18 days so far this month, and the results look very good.

Sincerely yours,
Paul

---

[106] Greeley was planning to leave Harqua Hala on September 6th for Los Angeles and Catalina Island.

Paul Greeley had a way of getting just what he needed from Charles Abbot. First, Abbot sent him a "folding organ" that Hoover claimed "has been in operation most every day since it arrived." Then, Abbot, who was at Mt. Wilson for the summer, readily arranged to buy a new automobile for the field station. As Abbot explained a few months later to Moore, "I went with Paul to the Dodge place in Los Angeles and got a 1922 delivery auto which functions beautifully. I hope that you will not wish to exchange it for a Ford, although you may be sure that I obtained it with fear and trembling, knowing your preference in that direction."

> Mt. Harqua Hala
> September 26, 1923
>
> Dear Cousin Chas:
>
> Arrived in Wenden the 22nd. The engine didn't miss a stroke and works fine. Mr. Ellison didn't come out to make the trip back. He has been a little under the weather for a week or so.
>
> Twenty-five boxes of Cramer Dry Plates[107] are in Wenden. Mr. Ellison will have to make four extra trips to the landing for them.
>
> The tires for the Dodge are 32x14. No tools came with it either. I bought a pump, tire irons and patches in L.A. but didn't get any jack, or grease gun. Good thing I didn't have any tire trouble on the trip. Left L.A. with $9.40 in my pocket, after saving out enough for gas and oil, and a sack of oranges had to eat coffee and doughnuts. Landed in Wenden with just 38 cents.
>
> Sally has chopped up all of the old boxes back of the shop and wheeled the wood around under the porch with one of Mr. Ellison's wheelbarrows.
>
> Yours truly,
> Paul
>
> P.S. Mr. Matteson is going to write to you about the telegrams. Mr. Ellison says he will give $25 for the Ford, or maybe as high as fifty, but I wouldn't want to be the one to sell it to him for fifty. Nobody in Wenden would take the gift of it, so please let me know what to do with it, or will it be best to let Alfred dispose of it.

---

[107] These were the photographic plates used with the bolograph, supplied by G. Cramer Dry Plate Co., St. Louis, Mo. The price for this shipment was $387.26 for 30 dozen plates.

Beginning about September 15th, the Harqua Hala observers began sending daily solar constant measurements by telegram to Washington. They telephoned these to Matteson's store in Wenden early each morning around eight o'clock. In turn, Matteson would take the report to the telegraph room at the train station, sending them on to Washington.

MATTESON'S MERCHANDISE
J.E. MATTESON, PROPRIETOR

GENERAL MERCHANDISE • MINE MACHINERY • AUTO SUPPLIES

WENDEN, ARIZONA

October 8, 1923

Smithsonian Institution
Washington, D.C.
Gentlemen:
I hereby submit a proposal of ($10.00) ten dollars per month
for receiving telephone reports from Harqua Hala Observation Station
and forwarding same to Washington, D.C. by telegram.
J.E. Matteson

Early in November 1923, Abbot summed up his solar constant work, telling Paul Greeley, "The results from Harqua Hala compare beautifully with those from Montezuma. Since the telegraphic values began to come in, if we make allowance for the definition during the last half of September, it looks as if the mean value between North and South America ought to be accurate to one part in a thousand, or better. The two sets of values go right along, up and down hill, together as prettily as the heart could desire."

November 13, 1923

Dear Cousin Charles:
Am glad to hear that the results are comparing so good. I received the Dodge accessories all O.K. Didn't get any crank however and would like to have one in case the battery goes bad. Have found a way to lock the car and that is take the gear shift lever with you also the revolving commutator inside the little red box where the four contacts go in. So when I go to dances in Wenden have three things to think of, which are: put the commutator in pocket, spare

tire in Matteson's house, and gear shift under the bed. Don't think I'll be careless now unless a whole garage comes along.

Mr. Ellison hasn't felt very well since I went to L.A. Says he has stomach trouble and high blood pressure. The days now are too short for him to make the round trip to Wenden. The nights are pretty cool for him to sleep out on a cot, and he wouldn't stay at Bunkers for a thousand dollars. He wouldn't drive the Dodge alone, says he hasn't got the Ford foot worked out of his head yet. Have been giving the Matteson's some of the vegetables out of the box each week.[108] Sort of helps pay for their kindness to me.

Yours truly,
Paul

William Hoover left Harqua Hala again shortly after Charles Abbot visited the field station on October 8th to work on the apparatus.

---

[108] Every week a Phoenix grocer shipped a box of vegetables to Wenden for the observers.

Chapter 20

The Moores Return

Alfred and Chella Moore returned from Australia arriving in San Francisco November 19th and returning home to Los Angeles the evening of the 21st. However, they needed to delay their return to Arizona: Abbot advised Paul Greeley, "He has to have his eyes attended to, it may be some days before he gets up to Harqua Hala." While in Australia, Moore eyes "gave away due to the strain of making galvanometer needles by electric light." He told Abbot, "I gave them almost complete rest during the voyage home. My oculist here thinks that they should have treatment before fitting new lenses. I'll have to be careful about strain, glare and dust. The trouble manifests itself in the eyes, particularly the left one, being blood shot, and occasional pains shooting through the eyeball."

```
                              Los Angeles, Calif.
                              November 27, 1923
Dear Mr. Abbot:
        When I went to the oculist the next time he said my
eyes were getting better and that it would be fully as
well if not better for me to postpone fitting the lenses
until later. I asked him if it would be all right to wait
possibly three months or so, as I do not expect to be back
in Los Angeles much before that. He said it would. We then
thought we would go back to Wenden today, but we both have
teeth that need attention, and since we may not be back
here until spring thought we should see the dentist about
them. We went to see him yesterday morning and he found
urgent work to do on both of us and is rushing it through
so we can leave here Friday evening. We are both awfully
anxious to get back to the mountain and are sorry for this
extra delay, but when I found how close the nerve came to
being exposed in two of my teeth, I suppose it is well,
```

for he said it would have been a very short time until
they would have ached.

I received a letter from Paul yesterday. He said
things are going fine. He seemed glad of the prospects of
a trip to California for the Christmas holidays.

I am glad that the new short method is working well,
as I'll have more time in which to work at some of the
things that I have stored up for several years.

Yours sincerely,

Alfred

P.S. I took a lesson in running a Dodge from Chella's father a few days ago. Had good luck. A.F.M.

Despite the good tone of his communications with Paul, Moore was desperately
needed back at Harqua Hala to handle problems that Greeley could not. The weather
forecasting test with Clayton using solar constant measurements was well underway,
and, with all the reports of satisfactory results and good correlation between solar constant measurements made in Arizona and Chile, there still seemed to be some fundamental, mysterious problems with the apparatus at Harqua Hala. Abbot wrote to
Moore in Los Angeles.

SMITHSONIAN INSTITUTION
Washington, U.S.A.

November 16, 1923

Dear Alfred:

We found that a very peculiar situation exists at
Harqua Hala, namely, a variation in the excellence of the
definition. I found that in nearly all of the observations from the middle of June to the first of October the
definition was poor. The disturbing thing, however, is
that on some days without any change in definition having
been intentionally made, the definition came up to its
normal value.

I made a trip down there[109] and introduced a new galvanometer needle and refocused the bolometer, so that
you now have some sensitiveness to spare, and a series
resistance has been introduced to bring the conditions

---

[109] Abbot traveled from Mt. Wilson to Harqua Hala on October 8, 1923.

of the bolographs identically with those of South America.

I am at a loss to know why the definition changes from day to day, and I depend upon you to make some experiments to discover this. The most likely thing in my judgment is that changes of temperature introduced by the presence of the refrigerating apparatus near the bolometer alters the focal length of the concave stellite mirror. If this proves to be the cause, it will be necessary for you to move the refrigerating device outside of the building in some manner. In fact, it is very undesirable that any causes of fluctuation of temperature in the observing chamber should be present, and, of course, we have put the observing chambers underground for the sake of minimizing these.

Hoping that you and Chella had a pleasant trip home and are both well, I am,

Very truly yours,

C. G. Abbot

Assistant Secretary

Suddenly, in a flurry of telegrams from Wenden to Los Angeles and Washington, Paul Greeley reported serious problems with the galvanometer. Although Abbot was prepared to make a quick trip from Washington, Alfred Moore left Chella in Los Angeles and expedited his return to Harqua Hala, arriving December 1, 1923. He immediately addressed the problems with the observing apparatus, uncovering more than anticipated.

Mt. Harqua Hala
December 7, 1923

Dear Mr. Abbot:

We have done so much telegraphic communicating the past few days, I'll now write a few lines for Mr. Ellison to mail tomorrow. Paul is going to Wenden with him to give him another lesson in running the Dodge. I managed to run the Dodge to Wenden and return the first of the week when I went down to bring Chella up the mountain. I had no mishap with the car, the only trouble being that I wanted to run it like a Ford, and had to stop and think each time I shifted gears.

Just what caused the trouble with the galvanometer here is still a mystery to me. Paul said it was very windy the night before the trouble began. The next morning he found the needle stuck up against the magnet. He tapped it and it went into place, but when he tried the deflection it was very small. He tried adjusting the control magnet but had no luck.

The above is Paul's story. However, when I tackled it, I found the control magnet "wrong end to." I have had considerable trouble getting all the requisites fulfilled in the adjustment, but I think I about have it now. I ran a test plate to try it out this afternoon, but some surveyors came up, and are spending the night so that I have not had time to read the plate to see how it is. I also found the bolometer out of the focal plane of the concave mirror. This necessitated moving the bolometer toward the concave mirror. The regular bolograph today looked pretty good.

As to the causes in the changes in definition, I am not certain, but I strongly suspect the close proximity of the kitchen to the galvanometer as the chief cause. By actual experiment, I know that moving the stove oven across the room causes a swing on the scale, and moving the wash tub causes even more. The water bucket and the frying pan also. Now if all these things exert enough magnetic force to cause such movements, and since the needle magnet systems are so very closely astaticized, it would not seem impossible to me for the galvanometer to be affected in this way. I cannot agree with you that it is probably that the ice machine affects the definition through temperature changes. In the first place, I noticed these changes in the definition long before we had the Kelvinator. And the motor and coils make very little change in temperature, since the slight cooling in the coils is more than offset by the heating of the motor. And besides the thick paper room intervenes, and paper is a poor conductor of heat.[110] I really think that the cause is likely to be found in the kitchen being located over the galvanometer.

We are getting so very crowded here, both upstairs and downstairs, that it looks as though we will either

---

[110] Walls in the underground observing area of the building were made from roofing paper.

have to build some sort of storeroom or else add a room to
the house. Hence I thought that if another room were to be
built, it might be wise to add a kitchen just east of the
present one. I am not very fond of the idea of more carpenter work to do, but if the kitchen is hurting our observations it would seem to me that the kitchen should be
moved.

As soon as I get straightened around here I must
start on the Australian trip accounts. It will be some
job converting the clumsy English money to our
denomination.

Sincerely yours,

Alfred

Alfred Moore was able to get the observing apparatus "as good now as is possible," at least temporarily, leaving time to work on the other problems at Harqua Hala. For example, Mr. Ellison wanted to fix the road between the garage and the railroad. Moore reported, "The road just below the garage is certainly in a bad fix, and about the only way to repair most of it is to clear off another road for most of the first mile." Abbot replied, "By all means fix it, if necessary, providing the expense is not too onerous. If it runs over $100, let me know."

Moore also needed a means, other than a foot pump, to air the tires on the Dodge. "When the warmer weather starts in, it will be a very strenuous job to pump up those four tires each week. It is very important not to run on soft tires, especially on that rocky road, and I find that the tires lose their air much quicker while standing idle than when in use." Abbot sent out "a power pump to be attached to the Dodge itself to pump up the tires. It sticks in where you crank the engine," he wrote.

But the "good" in the observing apparatus didn't last. Moore wrote, "As I tele-graphed you a few days ago, it seems that one of the pyrheliometers is acting erratic at times. I noticed this shortly after I returned, but was so busy with the galvanometer and bolometer that I did not have time to look into the matter further. When we ran a comparison with the pyranometer and reduced the pyrheliometry, I immediately saw that something was rotten in all of the six successive sets of readings that Paul took. I have looked carefully and can see no cause for it."

SMITHSONIAN INSTITUTION
Washington, U.S.A.

December 19, 1923

Dear Alfred:

The advice about the pyrheliometer disagreement are very disturbing. I see no way but to send out a new pyrheliometer as soon as a box can be made ready. You will be the best judge, after making the comparison, which of your two instruments should be taken out and the new one substituted for it.

I am glad that you were able to get the galvanometer all right again. If now it had to be moved 2 mm to be in the best focus, it proves that something has happened to change the focal length of the concave mirror. That would not be affected by the kitchen, but might be affected by change of temperature in the room. I do not see that it would alter the force of the argument whether the Kelvinator cooled or warmed the room. The real question is, are there changes in the focal length of the concave mirror, and are these produced by controllable changes in the temperature of the room? I wish you would settle that point to your satisfaction and mine.

I agree, however, that the proximity of the kitchen, with iron things, and possibly the proximity of an iron bedstead in the screened porch are bad. You are, as you say, very crowded, and if you think best you are authorized to add another room for the kitchen. Perhaps you can get some local help with the carpentry.

Mrs. Abbot and others here join me in wishing you all a Merry Christmas and Happy New Year.

Yours truly,

C. G. Abbot

Again Moore was able to get the apparatus working smoothly, and Abbot tried to look positively at the observing results from Harqua Hala, justifying the problems. He told Moore, "Queer things seem to happen at your place now and then, but you seem to manage to control them. I think we may be pretty well pleased with the results of the past year, both as to the number of observations and the agreement between the two stations. Harqua Hala results of July and August were almost worthless, I suppose on account of the extensive cirrus which covered the Southwest."

While Abbot encouraged Moore to build a new kitchen, Moore decided against it.

Mt. Harqua Hala
December 21, 1923

Dear Mr. Abbot:

I note what you say about the kitchen. I am not fond
of the idea of having to tackle this job of carpentry unless the injury to the observations make it seem necessary. So I think it might be well to wait a while and see
if the galvanometer continues to behave as well as it has
been doing the past ten days. If so, it may not be necessary to move the kitchen, or we might try getting buckets, dish pans and frying pans, of aluminum, so as to keep
iron away from the galvanometer as much as possible. The
needle is surely behaving most beautifully now as regards drift, in fact, it just naturally does not drift at
all. It gives one a grand feeling when he can lay a
straight-edge on the plate and it passes through the
centers of all the zero positions clear across the plate.

Did you leave instructions to compute the Sunday
observations on Sunday to telegraph them in that day?
Paul does not seem to be sure about it. When I was sending
the telegrams to Clayton in Chile, he used to be quite
satisfied with getting the Sunday values on Monday. It
practically gives us no Sunday at all, when we have to
compute until the middle of the afternoon. On cloudy days
there are always a thousand and one jobs to do around
here, and we have to stay around pretty close for possible changes to observe. Sunday afternoons are about the
only time in the whole week that we can plan hikes. Paul
very often goes to Wenden for dances on Saturday nights,
and I think that it is well that he does. But Chella and I
have practically no time to go places together when the
most of the day is taken up with observing and computing.
The observing of course is absolutely necessary, but I am
wondering if the computing cannot be finished up and
telegraphed in on Monday.

We have had quite a snow the past few days. In fact,
clouds have interfered a good deal since I returned. I
figured out the rainfall for 1922 and thus far this year,
and was quite surprised to find that it practically

equals that of Los Angeles and is distributed over almost every month of the year.

I found more trouble in the radio outfit due to the lightning. The small grid condenser was shot to pieces, and the tuning coils were shot up and some of the turns shorted out. I am ordering others from the Meyberg Co. to repair the trouble. It is almost impossible to tune well the way it is now.

They certainly have the most inconvenient hours at the depot in Wenden. At one time the business hours were from 9 A.M. until 6 P.M. But then the agent could be gotten most any time, provided he was not busy with a poker game, so it was not so bad. But now they have a new set of business hours, from 3 P.M. until 11 P.M. and along with it comes a new agent and he proposes to live up strictly to the rule, which means that we have to ask Mr. Matteson to get our vegetables, freight and express each week and cart them over to his store, for Mr. Ellison cannot wait until 3 P.M. to start from Wenden. The idea was the proud creation of some "efficiency expert" who found that once in a while the evening train from Phoenix was late, and when it was so, the agent chalked up some over time against the company, so he decided to have the agent stay on duty until 11 P.M. So the poor patrons of the railway, and particularly the out of towners like us, are the goats! But I guess nothing can be done about it.

Sincerely yours,

Alfred

Regarding the Sunday calculations, Abbot replied, "We prefer to have the series go on regularly without breaks because Mr. Clayton is sending in his results for every single day. However, I appreciate very well the need of you getting something of a holiday each week. Would it be possible, perhaps, for you and Paul to work up the Sunday values on alternate weeks."

Having just returned to Harqua Hala from their Australian trip, the Moores were obligated to spend Christmas on the mountain

```
                              Mt. Harqua Hala
                              December 28, 1923
Dear Mr. Abbot:
       We have had a most unusual storm here the past three
days, it being very warm so that it was all rain, with a
total precipitation of 3.66 inches for the storm. We had
2.70 inches on Wednesday alone. We have lost the past
five days on account of cloudiness. I think the total
precipitation for 1923 is now well above 20 inches,
pretty good for a dry climate!
       Chella and I spent a quiet Christmas up on the moun-
tain. The Mattesons very kindly invited us down there,
and we had about made our plans to go, but Chella thought
the trip would prove too strenuous for her. She is feel-
ing pretty well, but isn't very strong, and has to take
good care of herself, for she cannot exert herself as
much as formerly. When we found that she and I would not
go to Wenden, we got a Christmas tree, and decorated it up
with twelve miniature electric lights, tin-foil, cotton
for snow, red ribbon, strung cranberries and mistletoe,
so altogether we had a very good looking Christmas tree.
We were very well remembered. Mr. and Mrs. Roebling very
kindly sent the station about ten pounds of nice candies.
Chella's folks were very generous with their gifts, and
my folks sent us a dandy Mah Jong set.
                              Sincerely yours,
                              Alfred
```

Moore also received a "dandy" telegram from the Secretary of the Smithsonian, Charles Walcott.

```
Washington, DC 12-22-23 Congratulating and thanking you
and staff on splendid work of year wish Merry Christmas
and Happy New Year. C.D. Walcott
```

Chapter 21

Moore Versus Greeley

Alfred Moore was the glue that kept the operation going on Mount Harqua Hala and, at the same time, the constant purveyor of bad news and self-appointed critic of the whole solar constant program.

Mt. Harqua Hala
January 1, 1924

Dear Mr. Abbot:

    Happy New Year! We were unfortunate enough last night to lose both our aerial poles through ice forming on the guy wires and breaking some of the strain insulators. I do not think we will try to put them so high again. It is a shame that we lost the poles at this time of year when the radio is the best and when we need it the most in the long winter evenings.

    I have the new pyrheliometer ready to use, but the weather has been too poor thus far for a comparison. I had some trouble in getting the mercury out of the bulb at the upper end.

    A U.S. Coast & Geodetic Survey man came up a few minutes ago to carry on some surveying operations up here for two or three weeks. He will stay with us tonight and tomorrow Mr. Ellison will pack his outfit up from the garage.

Sincerely yours,

Alfred

In with the continuing grind of day-to-day operations on the mountain, the new year brought unexpected news from Moore's assistant, Paul Greeley.

Mt. Harqua Hala
January 7, 1924

Dear Cousin Chas:

Miss Amy Rosco[111] of Wenden and I are engaged. Shortly after my arrival in Wenden we became great pals, so Xmas eve we decided to be partners. There isn't going to be any wedding, however, until I see what I'm going to do here after 1925.

Amy has a fine character and fine disposition. She graduated from the Phoenix High School three years ago. She takes care of Matteson's store when he goes to his meals or when he is away. She is not a Catholic.

I know that you and cousin Lillian and all of the folks will like her very much. Have already written home about it.

I have only had one raise since I have been with the Smithsonian and could use one now right handy. Do you think I could have one?

Sincerely yours,
Paul

Abbot replied, "We were all surprised by your announcement, and wish you and Miss Rosco the greatest of happiness in your proposed venture. As for the increase in salary, financial difficulties stand in the way. You probably know that the government salaries have been subject to a long discussion and reclassification to come into full effect on July 1st. The salary attached to your brother's position has been fixed at $1680 under the reclassification act. You, at present, are getting $1600 from the private funds of the Institution, and we have pleasure in putting you on an equality with him, which is paid from government appropriation. We would call attention, however, to the fact that at the present time your compensation includes not only the $1600, but $200 given by Mr. Roebling for vacation money, and lodging and subsistence amounting to several hundred more, so that our compensation is already of the order of $2300."

Moore immediately saw Paul's engagement as a problem, shifting his attention to activities in Wenden and away from his duties on the mountain. Increasingly, this created friction between the two observers, particularly with their efforts to run the comparisons needed to resolve problems with the pyrheliometers.

---

[111] The surname was actually Orosco.

                                        Mt. Harqua Hala
                                        January 7, 1924
Dear Mr. Abbot:

We have been having quite a siege of some sort of
gripe or mild flu up here. Paul caught a bad cold when in
Wenden Christmas, and later on Chella got it, and a few
days later I fell victim. I was in bed two days, yesterday
and the day before. It settled in my eyes, and I was
scarcely able to see. In addition all three of us had the
most peculiar aches in our scalps, ears, jaws, sides of
our faces, etc.

We have had rather hard luck getting a satisfactory
comparison. In fact, Paul and I never did have much luck
in this line. He seems to get rattled or something when
running a comparison. We got a fairly good one last Friday which indicated that #9 is almost the same as #10, and
that #32[112] is reading erratically at times, but not all
the time. If we do find this to be the case on further
tests, do you want me to return #32 to you? I have just
drawn up a plot of a short comparison that I ran alone
this afternoon with the three pyrheliometers. It makes
me feel pretty much at sea as to just what is the matter.

I have tried hanging a low aerial temporarily, and
find that we can hear the California stations quite well,
and some eastern ones at times, so we will probably not
have to spend much in fixing up the trouble, except to
repair the poles. It is very little trouble to put up 35
or 40 foot poles, and we could erect three of them easier
than two high ones. I think these poles well rodded are
quite a protection against lightning, and the extra one
would help along this line. I have so many things on hand
now with the work that I won't have much time to work on
the radio for several weeks anyway.

                                        Sincerely,

                                        Alfred

Moore was having great difficulty trying to find which of his three pyrheliometer was
most accurate; indeed, his daily dealings with the idiosyncrasies of the instruments
fostered a degree of doubt over the scientific effort. Even back in Washington, despite

---

[112]Pyrheliometer #32 was the instrument that Abbot had just sent from Washington to help resolve the differences that Moore thought he was
seeing with instruments #9 and #10.

the positive feeling he had expressed in previous months, the results were also troubling Abbot. His comments to Moore revealed just how complex, and feeble, the whole effort was. "Mr. Fowle[113] and I are quite a little concerned about the whole proposition, both your work and Mr. Aldrich's, because of the uncertainty we feel in regard to the systematic corrections. In the first place, it is a sad thing to have to make the correction to use the curves you have. It would be really very much more defensible if we should remake the curves to suit the new conditions, but it is such a big job that we have agreed not to go about it at any rate until next summer. In the second place, the variation of the sun, as you easily see, makes it difficult to determine the systematic corrections. If an angel would come and tell us just what the solar constant was for every day, so that we could surely eliminate the solar variation, there would be no trouble. But we have now either to make the assumption that the sun does not vary at all, or that in the mean of each group of function values it does not, in theory, at all, or else we have to correct the values for each day by what we think it has varied before taking these means. In working out your corrections as you now use them, I made the assumption that the solar variation eliminated itself, and in making the systematic corrections for Mr. Aldrich, Mr. Fowle made the assumption that your corrected values were right so that he could allow for the solar variation as determined at Mt. Harqua Hala."

Curiously, Abbot faithfully continued with a sense of accomplishment. Reporting on the weather forecasting work for New York City, he told Moore, "Clayton's own predictions have been on the whole, very good. I have not yet worked out the matter mathematically, but there can be no doubt that he is getting something."

Seeing a crack in Abbot's beliefs about the methodology, once again Moore saw an opportunity to critique the solar constant program and restate his views on the requirement to send data to Clayton on Sundays.

Mt. Harqua Hala
January 11, 1924

Dear Mr. Abbot:

Paul is going to Los Angeles tomorrow. He has had quite a lot of trouble with toothaches and is going to the dentist.

In regard to the systematic error business, it seems to me, too, that we are getting too many such corrections. It may sound startling at first, but I often wonder if this research isn't running with the cart before the horse, as it were! We feel pretty certain now that the sun varies, and it seems to me that too much

---

[113]Mr. Fowle was one of Abbot's assistants at the Smithsonian.

emphasis is being put on making Harqua Hala vary the same
as Montezuma, or vice versa. I think we should first determine whether one station should vary the same as the
other, before so much work and worry is done trying to
make them agree from day to day. If the two stations were
on the same meridian of longitude, and a schedule arranged so that the observations would be exactly simul-
taneous, then I would be more concerned about their
showing the same variation from day to day. On an average
Aldrich takes his observation nearly three hours before
we do, and since we think the sun varies from day to day,
surely we cannot imagine that no change takes place during this three hour interval.

I am still a firm believer in my hypothesis of more
or less rapid solar variation, and I think it is worthy of
a thorough tryout before I would want to take too much
time to make one station agree with the other from day to
day. I think I wrote you along this line a year or two ago,
viz, that it seems very probable to me that there are at
least two kinds of solar variation, one kind having to do
with the gradual stirring up of things on the sun as shown
by sunspots. If this type of variation is prevailing, I
would expect to find Harqua Hala and Montezuma in close
agreement, for three hours does not mean a great deal of
change on the sun. But in the other type, it is my opinion
that there is surely something doing on Old Sol, which we
on the earth can hardly even imagine, and during these
times, with probably great masses of absorbing material
thrown out enormous distances in the course of a few minutes possibly, it would not surprise me if in the course
of the interval between Aldrich's and our observations,
several variations of the "solar constant," as great as
ordinarily we find, take place. And probably in addition
to these two types of variation, in fact the most certain
of all, is the very long period variation having to do
with sunspot maxima and minima.

Since Clayton is sending in results seven days per
week, and Aldrich is cabling his values on Sunday too, I
don't want to throw a monkey wrench into the machine, so
we'll try to arrange it some way. I never was a very big
crank on religion, but I have never been very much stuck
on Sunday work. To do his best, I have always thought that

a person should have one day in the week to rest and let
his mind think other thoughts, for with a perpetual grind
seven days every week, life is a rather monotonous
proposition. In the present experimental stage of this
work, I must confess that I cannot see the necessity for
Clayton sending in his forecast every day.

The General Electric opened up a new 1000 Watt
broadcasting station at Oakland during the past week.
Last night I head Dr. Campbell speak over it. It came in
fine, and he made a very interesting speech.[114]

Sincerely yours,

Alfred

Quickly, the grind of the work and the growing incompatibilities between Moore and
Greeley were coming to a confrontation.

Mt. Harqua Hala
January 18, 1924

Dear Mr. Abbot:

The more that I observe with the old pyrheliometers, the more I am convinced that there is nothing very
serious the matter with them, unless they took a sudden
change for the better just as Paul left for Los Angeles.
My readings this week have looked about as good as they
ever looked. If Paul should be reading them wrong, I
hardly know what to do about it. I would not mind reading
the pyrheliometers regularly if my eyes hold out all
right, but then I am afraid that he will mess up something
in the bolometric apparatus, and with it working as well
as it is now, I'd surely hate for this to happen. Of
course, I am not sure yet that there is nothing wrong with
the pyrheliometers themselves, for he read them very
well indeed when he came up here last June, and in fact
most of the time up to the early part of October.

When we first got back we noticed how very nervous
and fidgety Paul had gotten. Finally, he announced his
engagement to the young lady in Wenden, and since then he
has seemed a little more settled. He told us that he wrote
to you about his engagement just before he went to Los

---

[114]Moore had moved his radio apparatus upstairs into the computing room, adding a couple of shelves, where it was more convenient to use during the evening hours. On January 25th he tried unsuccessfully to hear Paul Greeley "playing" (probably the piano) over KFI from Los Angeles.

Angeles. She is a very nice girl, but neither Chella nor I
are very enthusiastic about an American young fellow
marrying a girl of Mexican parentage. When Paul announced the engagement, he sounded out Chella on the
subject of their coming up on the mountain to live.
Chella was not long in telling him that she considered
this house far too small for two families, so then he said
that they did not intend to marry until after July 1925.
We are hoping that before that time it will blow over, but
Paul is such an impetuous fellow that he isn't given to
much thought in advanced in such matters. Chella and I
have talked it over and we have decided that the best
policy for us to follow is to "saw wood and say nothing."
But I cannot help feeling that this business is apt to be
a very serious handicap to the proper carrying on of the
work up here. What bothers me most is that he will doubtless want to make very frequent trips to Wenden. He has
made quite a number since we have been home, and he always
makes all his plans and then shortly before time to start
informs me that he has a date in Wenden. Now since this
always necessitates losing some of this time from observing and probably computing, it seems it might be a
little better for him to phone or tell me when he is making his dates to see if it is convenient. Thus far I have
said nothing to him about it except that on one occasion,
when we had a pyrheliometer comparison to run, I told him
to get back as early as possible the next morning. He got
back just as I was about through observing, which was
about as early as he could have made it.

Every time that they have a dance down in Wenden,
which is fairly often this time of year, they think that
they simply must have Paul there, and they give the orders and he makes the dates accordingly. Do you wish to
impose some sort of a limit on this business?

From my results this week I think I can carry on the
observing just as accurately alone, and the computing is
not a great hardship, but what bothers me is that I do not
think his loafing around Wenden will serve to give this
place a very good reputation for serious endeavor.

Sincerely yours,

Alfred

Paul returned from Los Angeles on January 24th to what must have been a cold reception.

Chapter 22

Round Two

On the last Thursday evening of January, both Alfred Moore and Paul Greeley sat down, separately, to write to Washington. A recent letter from Abbot to Moore supported Moore's position about Greeley's engagement to Amy Rosco of Wenden; Abbot thought that sending Paul home to New Hampshire for a vacation would get Greeley's parents involved and give the young assistant more time to think about his plans.

                              Mt. Harqua Hala
                              January 31, 1924

Dear Mr. Abbot:

As to Paul's proposed matrimonial venture, I must confess that it is a pretty knotty problem from whatever angle you look at it. From what you wrote, I think your views on the subject about coincide with Chella's and mine. I have found out a few more facts in the case.

Paul got back from Los Angeles a week ago. He brought back a diamond engagement ring for the young lady, for which, he told Chella, he paid $150.

Yesterday he informed Chella that since next Sunday was "his Sunday off" (where he got this idea I do not know) he would go to Wenden Saturday night. I made up my mind that it was about time to call a halt on this business of making dates, taking him away from the observations, without first consulting me.

Yesterday, I found four of the leaves broken on one of the Dodge springs so I do not think any unnecessary trips should be made to Wenden until it is fixed, which will be a week or so, as Bunker will have to send away for the new leaves.

With due consideration beforehand, I picked a time when Chella was in the next room so he would not fly into a

183

tantrum like he once did down in Chile, and also so that
I'd have a witness that I was not asking anything unrea-
sonable of him. As expected he flew off the handle and
said that he supposed that he should hunt another job. I
told him that the Smithsonian is spending a great deal of
money on this research in the hope of getting something
definite by July 1925, and that we should certainly let
nothing stand in the way of the purpose for which we are
up here. I told him if he took exception to doing this I
thought he should hunt another job. Then he flew off on a
tangent about not proposing to put up with the hard
"graft" up here. I promptly squelched this by telling him
that he should have been up here the first two years when
we had to run a lot of long methods and do all the repair
and construction work in addition, and that I thought he
would have a hard time finding a job that would pay him as
well as the one he is on, and with as little work. I then
told him that I did not think it looked well for the
Smithsonian for him to be loafing around Wenden too much.
After this he said he'd go chop some wood! I told him he
could go to Wenden a week from Saturday evening, and that
I would like to know your views on the subject. He said
that he had given out making the trip east this summer. I
did not mention what you said in your letter.

Chella and I have talked the whole matter over together since I got your letter, and we both think that it
will do very little good trying to cure the affect, but
that probably efforts should be put in to cure the cause.
I am sorry to have to admit it, but we feel absolutely
sure that the real cause of this trouble is Mrs.
Matteson. She has been "bugs" over Amy for a long time.
Amy is a likable sort of girl, and I did not blame her for
trying to advance her state in life, but I think it is
carrying it a lot too far when she tries to marry her to an
American. And I do not think she has acted very wisely in
taking Paul away from his work when he was running the
station here alone.

Mr. Ellison volunteered a little information. He
has one of those test phones in his house and the receiver
does not cut out as in a wall phone. The receiver speaks
up very loud and he could not help hearing all the
conversation going on between Harqua Hala and Wenden. He

said it was almost a daily occurrence for Mrs. Matteson
to call up Paul and beg him to go down to Wenden for a card
party or a dance. I do not think it would be at all wise
for me to bring the subject to the Matteson's attention,
but I surely think that in some manner they should find
out that you do not at all approve.

You asked about the young lady's father. I do not
know him for he is away from Wenden a good deal. He raises
a few cattle, and has some horses, and does some truck-
ing. Her mother helps keep the finances up by taking in
washing.

I am surely sorry for all this mix-up, for which we
are in no way to blame, but which is likely to make hard
feelings. I cannot help worrying about it a great deal,
and I can see that it is making Chella nervous at times. I
can't put my mind on the work as I should when something
like this is worrying me.

If Paul continues to fly off the handle and make
life a nightmare up here for Chella and me, I see nothing
to do but let him go and get some young fellow who would
not let the Wenden social whirl turn his head.

As to telling his parents more about the case than
they probably know, I think that you are a better judge of
that than we are. It seems, on general principle, that
they should be informed of it . On the other hand it is a
very delicate subject to handle, and if Paul found out
that you or I was mixing in the matter, he might fly off
the handle and marry right away out of pure spite. Paul
has a very fierce temper, as you likely know. He has a way
of doing things without much thinking before hand.

Sincerely yours,

Alfred

That Thursday evening, as Paul sat in his room also writing to Abbot, the air must have been tensely quite at the field station.

Mt. Harqua Hala
January 31, 1924

Dear Cousin Charles:

Alfred and I had another big argument today, and it is going to be the last one as far as I am concerned. When my February check comes, I'll be through here.

The main trouble was about my trips to Wenden. He seems to think that it doesn't look good for me to spend my time with the bums and loafers in Wenden. Whenever I have been in Wenden my time has been spent mostly with Miss Rosco or at the Mattesons.

He carries his growling too far, and I simply will not stand for it any longer. I have an uncomfortable feeling all the time I'm around him. It seems like about everything I do is wrong. I never had a word with Mr. Aldrich or Mr. Hoover, we just got along fine, but here it's growl for a while which results with a grouch on for the rest of the day.

I have given this a good trial of several months. Not only here, but in Chile, and have come to the conclusion that we cannot work in harmony.

About March 1st I expect to go to the coast. If you would send me some sort of recommendation, I would be pleased, as it might help in anything I attempted to do.

All of this has had to come about sooner or later, and my decision is absolutely final.

Yours truly,
Paul Greeley

The next morning, Alfred found Paul "in better spirits." Not yet knowing about Greeley's resignation, Moore told Abbot in a scribbled postscript to his January 31st letter, "Paul said he wasn't planning on going to Wenden oftener than once every two weeks. Maybe the little lecture did some good. But of course I did not touch on the matrimonial question." Then, once Paul told Alfred and Chella of his resignation, the air between the two observers cleared rather quickly, almost as fast as the run of good skies gave way to clouds.

                                        Mt. Harqua Hala
                                        February 7, 1924
Dear Mr. Abbot:

At last our long run of good skies has been broken
into by clouds. We have lost two days this week and only
got one observation yesterday, and it was rather
unsatisfactory.

Today, we started putting up the new aerial poles.
We got the north one up, and the south one part way, but it
is more difficult, owing to the steep canyon to the west
of us. We are going to put up a third one on the ridge a
little northeast of the house. By pointing the aerial
wire toward the eastern states, we hope to bring in New
York and Chicago clearer. We have extremely sharp points
on the top of each to dissipate the electrical strain in a
silent discharge. These points are well grounded in summer time.

We were quite surprised in a way, and not much surprised either, when Paul informed us last Saturday evening that he had written you his resignation to take
effect March 1st. He did not seem at all "sore" about my
little talk to him, but said that he could not stand this
isolation business any longer. As he expressed it, he
said that his "feet had been itching for sometime."

If he does not change his mind I'll be sorry to see
him leave, for Paul is a likable fellow, but if he is not
contented up here I really do not think it will be good
for the work for him to try to stay on until 1925.

If Paul leaves March 1st as he intends, I suppose
another man will have to be gotten to take his place. I do
not know of anyone who would be suitable.

The day that I was working at the garage, Chella and
Paul were talking about his leaving. From what he told
her, I think he has his mind set on striking out on a new
venture, and I very much doubt if he will consider changing his mind and remaining here longer. I have said very
little to him about the matter of quitting. I thought
that possibly you might come out here during the next few
weeks, when you received Paul's letter, and the letter I
wrote by the same mail.

Chella saw a big fox out near the chicken yard the
day that I was at the garage. He came around for a piece of

meat again last night. Mr. Ellison is going to bring up
one of his big traps and we hope to catch Mr. Fox tomorrow
night.[115]

                              Sincerely yours,

                              Alfred

Once again, the radio was a great comfort to the observers. Shortly after the new aerials were up, Moore described "two treats." "The first a recital by Estella Hart Dryfuss, a noted contralto of Los Angeles, and the other a full grand opera broadcast from Philharmonic Auditorium at Los Angeles by the Los Angeles Examiner. It was Verdi's 'The Force of Destiny' in Italian. It is some contrast from your pioneer days up here, to be able to sit comfortably in your rocker and hear grand opera, isn't it?"

In the days that followed, Paul confided with Chella that he did not blame her nor Alfred in any way, but that he felt that he must get away from this kind of work, that he never did like desk work or computing. Although he stuck to his plan to leave, he seemed willing to ensure a smooth exit.

                              Mt. Harqua Hala
                              February 21, 1924
Dear Mr. Abbot:
        Paul told me about receiving a letter from you,
asking him if he would arrange to remain here a month
longer so as to give you more time to get someone to take
his place. He very kindly consented to remain until April
1st.
        My eyes still bother me some, and since my oculist
told me that he thought I should come back in two or three
months to have new lenses fitted, it seems that I should
go out to Los Angeles and have this done before Paul
leaves. When a new man comes it will likely take some time
to break him in sufficiently to leave all the observing
and computing in his charge. I don't think I should take
too many chances with my eyes, for they have never felt
the same since they gave away in Australia. I try to favor
them as much as I can. They are not inflamed, but at times
sharp pains shoot through them.
        This is getting to be rather a trapper's station.
Chella and I took a walk down to the spring north of the
station last Sunday afternoon and saw some large tracks.
I set a trap night before last, and yesterday morning I

---
[115]Indeed, Mr. Fox fell victim to trap "before 7 o'clock in the evening" and his hide was subsequently "dried in the shop."

found I had a large bobcat. He was sure some mad, and had
chewed up almost everything in reach, but I managed to
end all his seven lives with one shot from my revolver. We
skinned him and gave the meat to the chickens. This wild
meat seems to be a great thing to provide egg material. We
fed them the fox, and have been getting eight and nine
eggs per day from eleven hens.

Since none of the hens have had time to sit, I bought
a little 50 egg incubator a few weeks ago. The chicks are
supposed to hatch today, but last Monday night the temperature got too high and then too low, and I am afraid
that this hatch will be a fizzle. I made a little brooder
for the chicks (counting the chickens before they
hatched!) so last night Chella used the brooder to raise
some sponge for light bread. Some new use for a brooder.

We have had it quite warm, and there have been a good
many clouds of late, but we usually manage to get some
observations. When Chella and I were over at the north
spring last Sunday we were surprised to find some snow
still there in patches, though we have had no snow since
January 1st. Paul and I went down and brought up a couple
of buckets of it, and we had some ice cream a couple of
days ago.

The new aerial favoring the eastern stations seems
to help out a good deal in that regard. Tonight we had
Kansas City on the loud speaker so that we could hear it
all over the house.

Sincerely yours,

Alfred

P.S. The "Little Brown Hen" (incubator) has managed to
hatch out about seven chicks so it isn't entirely a fizzle.

Moore planned to start for Los Angeles by the end of February. Before he left, Abbot
wrote, "Mr. Clayton has just written me a letter in which he points out that his predictions of the temperature of New York City have been completely verified for the
months of November, December and January, in 78 per cent of the cases. His detailed
forecasts three days in advance give 48 percent correlation coefficient, four days in
advance 25 percent, and five days in advanced 10 per cent. I am writing to the heads
of meteorological bureaus in this country, Canada and England, to inquire what

degree of correlation they could expect from the synoptic data alone. I believe that Mr. Clayton's success has been very notable. Of course, this is confidential."

Mt. Harqua Hala
February 26, 1924

Dear Mr. Abbot:

I was very much interested in what you wrote about Mr. Clayton's results. Of course I'll keep this confidential.

We certainly have had a very remarkable run of days for this time of year. We have lost but three days in February this far, making but four days lost since December 28th.

I am glad that it was possible to arrange to go before Paul's departure, for my eyes have been troubling me quite a bit the past few days, and I think I should not delay having them looked after. I have had an eye headache most of today, so it is likely that I should have new lenses. Besides, the drops that he gave me in November are just about gone.

Paul said that he did not think he would go to Wenden while we were away. He said he would be on the job every day so as not to miss any observations.

We expect to return to Wenden on the night of March 14th.

Sincerely yours,

Alfred

Chapter 23

Between Assistants

Alfred and Chella Moore returned from Los Angeles without a delay this time, arriving in Wenden on Saturday morning, March 15th; they "came up the trail that day." Within a few days, Moore's letters to Washington brought Charles Abbot up to date on operations at Harqua Hala.

```
                              Mt. Harqua Hala
                              March 19, 1924
Dear Mr. Abbot:
      We had a very pleasant trip to Los Angeles, but we
were kept very much on the go. I had my eyes looked after
and had new glasses fitted. The oculist gave my eyes a
thorough examination and prescribed other drops.
      While in Los Angeles we got some things to repair
and fix up the house up here. When we got back from Aus-
tralia, we found things pretty badly broken up, espe-
cially the dishes. Also, the interior of the house looked
far different from the way we left it, due to rain having
beaten in last summer. The ceilings and floors will have
to be gone over, and I got some paint for this purpose.
      When I got back I was glad to find that Paul had suc-
ceeded in observing every day while I was gone, continu-
ing the long run of days. We lost yesterday, as the sun
did not shine at all, which was the thirty-ninth day
since we had lost a day. This is a record for Harqua Hala,
I think. We had rain, snow, hail and sleet yesterday, the
first precipitation more than a trace that we have had in
1924. We got busy and shoveled snow yesterday, so that we
now have about 1400 gallons of rain water on hand.
```

We got considerable practice at Mah Jong while in Orange.[116] We get a good deal of pleasure up here out of
playing the game too.

                              Sincerely yours,

                              Alfred

P.S. Paul informed Chella yesterday that he intended to
leave on the 29th, going with Mr. Ellison that day, instead of staying until his month was up on the 31st. I
thought he might have discussed the matter with me, but
since he didn't, and since this involves the loss of
three days' time, I thought that I should write to you. He
may argue that he is entitled to this much time in the way
of vacation, but he has had every other Sunday entirely
off since his last vacation, with the exception of one
when I was in Los Angeles. I will say that I don't take
very much to his always entirely ignoring me in making
such plans, but since he is soon to go I don't intend to
say anything to him about it. A.F.M.

In Washington, Abbot was having trouble finding a replacement for Paul Greeley. He
asked Moore if Paul would extend his stay again, but Moore advised, "I think it is wise
not to interfere with Paul's plans for it will likely do no good and might cause hard
feelings. I can run the station alone for a while. I have a lot of painting to do, and having a vacant room at such times is quite a convenience, when we are so crowded for
room."

As for Paul's replacement, several times Moore suggested to Abbot that "a man
from this part of the country might be more satisfied up here than one from the east,
since he can go out among his friends every few months." Paul Greeley left Harqua
Hala on schedule.

                              Mt. Harqua Hala
                              April 3, 1924
Dear Mr. Abbot:
      April does not seem to be starting out very fine,
for although I have lost no days since Paul's departure,
there has been considerable cloudiness, and the skies
have been far from good.
      Paul left as per (his) schedule last Saturday morn-
ing. We have not heard a word from him since he left, but

---

[116]Chella's home town in Southern California.

he is still in Wenden. Yesterday, Mrs. Matteson called
Chella and said that Paul had accepted their invitation
to remain over until next Sunday, and accompany them to
Yuma, where he would take the train. Things are getting
along fine up here. Even with the rather poor skies, the
results on the whole have looked better than when there
were two observers.

    I am enameling the inside of the refrigerator as it
will then be easier for it to be kept clean. Paul seemed
to think that the ice-plant dynamo did not work well after
they let the field coils get loose last summer and took
off quite a lot of the windings. I wrote to Los Angeles
about rewinding the field coils, but they say a small dynamo like that isn't worth re-winding. I tried it out a
few weeks ago, and it seems to work all right.

    I am going down to the garage this afternoon to
change tires around on the car to save having a blow-out.
We have two new ones which never have been used, and I am
going to put them on. Mr. Ellison has greatly improved
the road and trail.

                             Sincerely yours,

                          Alfred

*P.S. Paul just called up and seemed in very good spirits.
AFM.*

With only one observer at Harqua Hala and the pending training of a new one, it was
hardly the time to start a new project. But Clayton had asked Abbot if his stations
could record sunspot activity each day. Abbot wrote to Moore, "Clayton deplores the
lack of visual observations of the sun's appearance which, if he had them, he thinks
would aid him to make forecasts to twelve days in advance. He employed such data in
South America. I told him that you had a six-inch telescope, and that if we could arrange a suitable code perhaps you could take a look at the sun each day and add to the
daily telegram something about its appearance."

    The initial idea was for Moore to make a drawing of sunspots, tracing an image
projected through the observatory's six-inch telescope. The first problem was that
Moore had not yet gotten the telescope to work well, except for entertaining guests
and looking at Wenden. Moore told Abbot, "On my waiting list of things to do, I have
it down to try to rig up means of photographing the sun each day. The main drawback
is that the mounting that I fixed up is a pretty poor excuse for an instrument of such

power, for the tremor makes it very hard to see anything, especially if the wind is blowing, and it usually is. It would probably be necessary to arrange some sort of covering for the instrument for it is quite a task to carry it back and forth each day. I haven't any sun screen[117] for the eyepieces, so I do not know just how the solar image would look. If you think a smaller glass would answer the purpose better, I see a pretty good one listed in Sears-Roebuck & Co. catalogue."[118]

Despite the problem with the telescope and the other work at the field station, Moore did find time to run a few experiments.

Mt. Harqua Hala
April 10, 1924

Dear Mr. Abbot:
There was a thin cirrus over the sky today until late this afternoon, so this morning I tried out the six-inch telescope. It seems to me that it would be much better to fix it so that we can photograph the sun each day rather than try to draw the sunspots, which would doubtless be pretty difficult to do with the rather flimsy mounting. Since the solar image is so bright, it would probably be necessary to insert a fairly rapid camera shutter.

It seems that most of the tremor in the mounting is in the revolving part, for the legs are really quite sturdy being firmly set in concrete and well braced. I don't think I could make a much better arrangement with the material that I have here, but if you'd care to go to the trouble, it seems to me that castings could easily be made, and then the thing would be solid enough to do something with it. I have measured up the arrangement and drawn up a rough sketch which is enclosed.

It seems to me that if we use the photographic method, I could mail him prints each week.

Sincerely yours,
Alfred

---

[117] A filter to reduce the bright image of the sun.
[118] Moore sent an ad clipped from the Sears-Roebuck catalog, showing "Extra High Grade Telescope, $34.00."

Along with the work on the mountain, and a spurt of ailments, Moore also managed to keep up with the whereabouts of Paul Greeley after he arrived in California.

```
                              Mt. Harqua Hala
                              May 2, 1924
Dear Mr. Abbot:
     I am ordering a canvas cover to go over the tele-
scope. It is supposed to be water-proof.
     We have not heard directly from Paul since his de-
parture, but I heard indirectly through Edgar. He wrote:
"Paul has been around two or three times. I think he has
gotten into the right place now. He is a moving-picture
actor out at Hollywood. While waiting for his Goodyear
Rubber Co. job to turn to, he took a night job at one of
the Hollywood studios."
     Getting back to the telescope, it would be very much
better to make a concrete pier for it, and it would not be
very much trouble, or cost very much. I may try the pre-
sent arrangement first, though.
     The Kelvinator motor pulley was eccentric and a
little too large, so I got a piece of oak up here and made
another one on the lathe. And I came very near taking the
end off my left little finger. I got it caught between the
chuck and tool rest, and mashed it so that I am losing the
nail.
     In some unknown way I sprained my right arm near the
elbow, so that I have been rather crippled the past week.
At first I thought the latter was due to rheumatism, but
later decided it was a sprain. I am troubled some at times
with rheumatism up here, and wonder if it could be due to
Mr. Ellison's spring water since it contains so much
mineral matter. I wonder if it might not be well to have a
sample of it tested. We have never been able to get the
cistern water so it tasted good enough to drink.
                         Sincerely yours,
                         Alfred
```

Throughout May 1924, Moore wrote a steady stream of letters to Abbot. He was waiting for a shipment of parts for the telescope. In addition, Moore was anxious to hear about a "Mr. Worthing," who Abbot had hired to replace Greeley. And, Moore hoped that Abbot would visit Harqua Hala again on his way to Mt. Wilson for summer research.

The new assistant, Arthur B. Worthing, was 24 years old, a graduate of Ripon College in Wisconsin and had done post graduate work at the University of Wisconsin. Working through various recommendations, Abbot found him "in electrical construction work and an inspector with the Western Electric Company." Abbot wrote, "He would like the position and the only thing which may interfere is that the settlement of his father's estate is going on, and he will not be able to report before May 15th, and it is just possible that something might interfere in connection with these matters. If Paul would only have stayed until the close of the schools, we could much more readily have obtained someone." Later Abbot wired to Moore, "Worthing expecting leave Chicago May 20."

                              Mt. Harqua Hala
                              May 9, 1924
Dear Mr. Abbot:
     We are still engaged in the spring cleaning, al-
though, I am glad to say, we are nearly through with the
job.
     I want to be able to get on that telescope job as
soon as the things arrive. I notice a rather large clus-
ter of spots on the sun these days. We observed the transit of Mercury last Wednesday, by throwing the sun's
image on a white screen.[119]
     I have ordered thirty day-old chicks from near
Phoenix.[120] We have had such poor luck at hatching chickens that I have about decided that our eggs aren't good,
so I think we need a new stock. A good many of our hens are
getting old, and ought to be killed off.
     I haven't heard anything more from you in regard to
Mr. Worthing, but suppose that he probably will be with
us shortly.
     Please tell Mrs. Abbot that with George, and Mr.
Ellison's horse "Blink," we can get her up the trail more
comfortably than in 1922, so we hope you both can visit us
enroute to California.
                              Sincerely yours,
                              Alfred

---

[119] In rare occurrences, Mercury passes between the earth and the sun in just the right circumstances to be silhouetted against the sun.
[120] From a chicken farm in Gilbert.

Once again, the periodic problem with the pyrheliometers, and even the pyranometer, plagued Abbot and both field stations.

                              Mt. Harqua Hala
                              May 16, 1924
Dear Mr. Abbot:
        I was sorry to learn of the trouble that Aldrich has
had with the pyrheliometers. I can hardly believe that it
is as much as ten percent. I quite often find discrepan-
cies in the pyrheliometers here, which as yet I have not
been able to explain. I am strongly of the opinion that
these changes are due to some error, possibly fundamental, in the cooling corrections.
        I note what you write about the pyranometer being
affected by wind, making it read as much as ten percent
too low. I knew that the wind sometimes makes the reading
of the instrument almost impossible, due to the constant
moving of the needle. I have noticed of late another
"mystery" in connection with the pyranometer, and that
is that the first reading of a series during a bolograph
almost always is too high, compared with the others that
follow.
        The day old chicks that I ordered have failed to put
in their appearance yet. Maybe they thought the weather
was too hot, for we have had it very warm yesterday and
today. Chella and I went to town last night to get them,
but they failed to arrive. She used George and I use Mr.
Ellison's horse. Going down we saw a big rattlesnake, but
he got under a rock before I could hit him with a rock, and
there was no stick available. We got back at 1:20 A.M.
        Early this morning I heard the most outlandish
noise outside. I couldn't imagine what was causing it, so
I went out to investigate. When I got alongside the little chicken house, I found the cause. It was one of the
two-and-a-half month old roosters trying to crow. There
are four of the crowd of little chicks hatched in the incubator. They hatched out a day or two late, but believe
me, they have been making up for the delay ever since when
it comes to being progressive! They started roosting on
the high perches when they were six weeks old.
                              Sincerely yours,
                              Alfred

The month ended with Worthing arriving in Wenden on May 23rd and the day old chicks on May 30th. For both arrivals, Moore made a trip to town, in the latter case starting out "at daybreak, making it to Wenden in two hours and one minute, and the round trip in five hours and fifteen minutes."

And there was more news from California: Moore wrote to Abbot, "From what Mr. Matteson told us, I guess Paul and his Wenden girl have played quits. They did not take to his movie aspirations very much down in Wenden, and they found out that he was blowing in his money pretty freely out in California. He told Edgar that he had signed a three months' contract to play in the movie play called "Ambition." He has rented a piano for his apartment, and also has a motorcycle."

Abbot replied, "I was glad to hear that there is a good chance of Paul having broken off with his friend in Wenden, and not much surprised to hear that he had gone into the movie business. He is a very engaging character from all angles. He will make a good hero for a novel by and by."

Chapter 24

Worthing Spits!

At first Alfred Moore reported that Worthing "seems a very agreeable fellow. I think he will soon get a good grasp of the subject. He seems to want to read up on the various matters, which is a very good sign." However, by the end of Worthing's first week at Harqua Hala, Moore's opinion had changed dramatically.

Mt. Harqua Hala
May 30, 1924

Dear Mr. Abbot:

We are observing Decoration Day[121] by not observing since it has been cloudy all day today, and while I am writing this we are having an electrical storm and some rain. Rather early for thunderstorms. I have been so busy with the new man, and with some trouble that has appeared in the pyrheliometers, that I haven't had time to work on the telescope this week, but hope to get at it next week.

The pyrheliometer trouble is proving quite a mystery. At times the two instruments read very consistently. At other times there is too much difference between the readings, and at still others, there is too little difference. I am sure that these conditions are not usually due to accidental errors of reading, for they continue for several successive readings. I am hoping that you will be out here before long to look into this matter, and perhaps take the instruments apart, if such becomes necessary.

I now have something to write that has caused me quite a little worry the past few days. This is in regard to the new man. He seems quick at catching on to the operations of observing and computing, but there are other

---

[121]Today, more commonly called Memorial Day.

things that make me greatly fear that he is not the man
for the place. I am practically certain that he has tuberculosis. When he arrived here he was as pale as a
sheet. He is hollow-chested, has a slight cough, and has
to go out to spit very often. He seems to spit a sort of
phlegm. These are pretty strong indications, and what is
more, he seems to have practically no pep. He spends a
large share of his spare time lying on his bed. I thought
he should do as the other boys have done, also attend to
his own room. Thus far he has shown very little attempt at
extra work. I haven't a doubt in the world but that he
would deny having TB and most likely would be insulted at
the mention of it.

I am sure you would not expect us to live in such
close contact with a person having this trouble. Although this climate doubtless is good for such persons,
we certainly do not want to run a sanitarium up here.
Chella isn't very strong, and I often wonder if I am doing
the right thing to continue up here where the extra man
causes her a good deal of extra work. It would not be so
bad if we had a pleasant young fellow up here with a lot of
pep, but I am sure that the present fellow is going to
prove too great a care for us to have him with us very
long. I think his expectorating around outside and then
its drying up is a real menace to us.

I suppose that doubtless you will be out here before
many weeks. My suggestion would be that you size him up
for yourself, and then try to get a western man, perhaps a
graduate of Pomona College or of the University of California. It seems to me that this place is so very different from the east, that you will find it very difficult to
get an eastern man who will readily adapt himself to such
changed conditions of living. On the other hand the
western fellow is more or less brought up in an environment not so very different from this, and most likely
will like it better up here.

We are taking every precaution against getting TB
from Mr. Worthing such as sterilizing his dishes in hot
water, but even so this thing is a source of considerable
worry to us.

Sincerely,

Alfred

Moore now added his preoccupation with Worthing's health to his lists of problems with the pyrheliometers and setting up the telescope for photographing the sun.

```
                              Mt. Harqua Hala
                              June 13, 1924
Dear Mr. Abbot:
     I have rigged up a good camera for the telescope and
made it very rigid. But thus far I have not been able to
get a very satisfactory solar photograph. There was
quite a group of spots when I completed the camera about a
week ago. They showed up fine and clean on the ground
glass, but I couldn't get sharp images at all on the pho-
tographic plates. To focus more clearly, I set on the
crescent moon one night and focused on the craters. With
the same settings I took a shot at the sun the next morn-
ing, but the spots did not show up clear.
     I cannot see any improvement in the new man as re-
gards pep. I have succeeded by keeping at it, in getting
him to do some of the chores around here, but from what I
have seen of him thus far, I would hate to trust the place
entirely in his care if we should go to the coast. And
what is worse, we have about despaired of ever getting
him to be at all companionable. We have invited him sev-
eral times to take part in our games, but he declines, and
goes and lies on his bed and reads. Never once has he
shown the least appreciation of the many nice dishes
Chella has prepared.
     Altogether, his behavior has had a most depressing
effect on both Chella and me. His behavior is probably
largely due to his state of health. He has spoken on sev-
eral occasions about health resorts, and asked about
their location, so we firmly believe that he came out
here primarily for his health. He has taken on consider-
able color since he came up here, but certainly the Har-
qua Hala climate has had no effect on his pep thus far.
The three weeks that he has been here seem much longer to
us than the nearly two months that we were alone.
     The Kelvinator is certainly a grand thing this time
of year. We have installed an arrangement to turn the ice
cream freezer by means of the gas engine, which saves a
lot of hard cranking on a warm day.
```

The little chicks are getting along fine. The other
day when I was coming up the trail I caught a little baby
quail, and brought him up here. He now resides with his
cousins the chicks, and they get along very well together. He is so small that he crawls under one of the
chicks when he goes to sleep.

Sincerely yours,

Alfred

The problems at Harqua Hala were serious enough that Abbot made plans to stop at
the Arizona field station on his way to California for more research at Mt. Wilson.
Moore was elated and immediately confirmed arrival plans: "We note with much
pleasure that you will visit us in a few weeks, and we are happy that Mrs. Abbot will
accompany you. If we make the trip up the trail at night, I am sure that the heat will
not be oppressive. She can ride our faithful steed George, and we can use Mr. Ellison's
horse. With the probability that Mr. Worthing has tuberculosis, we do not think it wise
to put either of you in his room, but Mrs. Abbot can go in with Chella, and you and I
can use the extra bed and cot that we have here."

Mt. Harqua Hala
June 17, 1924

Dear Mr. Abbot:

Under separate cover I am sending three solar photo
prints. Two were taken on one day and one on another. Of
the two, one is printed much darker than the other, and
although not so artistic, I am not sure but that the dark
one brings out what we want to see better than the lighter
one. I found great difficulty in not hopelessly over-
exposing the plates, even with a very narrow slit in the
shutter. I also need very weak developer to try to control the development, but this did not help much either.
It occurred to me to try using an orange glass to pass the
light through to cut down the intensity, and this is the
method I used with the accompanying photos. However, I
think it might be much better to not use this screen, as
it probably tends to distort the image somewhat.

I have ordered some copper sulphate from Phoenix
and will get it tomorrow, and try the Eastman Company's
scheme. I have also ordered some hydroquinone developing
powders, as this gives much more contrast in negatives
than the metolquinol developers that we have here, and

which are intended primarily for photo paper. With these improvements I am hoping to get better results than the accompanying prints show. When you come out here I suppose we can remedy some of these numerous ills.

I am not certain that you will receive this letter before you and Mrs. Abbot leave Washington, but I will have a copy of it here in case you do not. We will be very glad to see you both, and hope that the weather will be fine while you are here. I suppose you will let me know by telegram or letter, when I'll meet you in Wenden. Chella says tell Mrs. Abbot she is looking forward to her visit on Harqua Hala with much pleasure, and is very anxious for her to see the many improvements up here, since her visit of two years ago.

Sincerely yours,

Alfred

Abbot and his wife Lillian arrived in Wenden on July 5th. While he immediately made the trip to the field station on Harqua Hala, it is not clear whether Lillian Abbot also ascended the mountain, stayed in Wenden or traveled on to California ahead of her husband.

Chapter 25

Changes in the Wind

Abbot's trip west the summer of 1924 to Harqua Hala and on to California brought solutions to some of Moore's problems at the Arizona field station and a hope that his fondest wish could come true. Worthing was dismissed,[122] and Abbot revealed thoughts about moving the Smithsonian's U.S. based solar constant station to the more accessible Table Mountain in Southern California.

Once in California for research at Mt. Wilson, Abbot began interviewing "western" candidates to replace Worthing; before the end of the summer he hired Hugh B. Freeman of Glendale.[123] Freeman agreed to report to Harqua Hala on the first of September to train and serve as the "bolometric assistant." Long range plans were for Freeman to transfer "about May 1925" to the station in Montezuma, Chile becoming the director there for three years, succeeding Loyal Aldrich.[124]

Without an assistant through July and August, the Harqua Hala field station was unmanned while the Moore's took a few weeks off for their annual summer break in California away from the heat of Arizona.

> 753 S. Carondelet St.
> Los Angeles
> August 18, 1924
>
> Dear Charles:
> Chella and I have just returned from Orange where we went Saturday afternoon to visit her folks. We expect to leave for Wenden tomorrow afternoon at 5 P.M.
> Yesterday Chella's father took Chella, her sister and me up to Big Pines and we went up on Table Mt. The sky

---

[122]Letters in the Smithsonian Archives do not detail exactly what happened to Worthing, except to say that he would be reimbursed for travel back to Chicago; there is no mention of him following Abbot's visit to Harqua Hala in July 1924.

[123]Freeman lived at 417 W. Doran St., Glendale, Calif.

[124]Freeman's salary began at $135 per month plus subsistence with the potential of rising to $250 per month after 12 months.

was very poor indeed as far as San Bernardino, but when
we reached Big Pines it was fine except for a small patch
of cirrus distant from the sun. I got in touch with the L.A.
County Park Superintendent, Mr. F.E. Wadsworth, and he
seemed very anxious indeed for us to locate there. He says
it cost about $1500 to build a five or six room wooden
house. He said water can be found in all the canyons on
the north side. Since it gets so cold in winter, about zero,
I think it would be quite necessary to have indoor baths
and toilets.[125] They are working on an electric light plant
at present and will have a telephone in there before long.
He is now working on a road to do away with the heavy
grade just before entering Swarout Valley.

 We came back through Glendale to call on the Freemans, but no one was at home. We hope to get out to see
them again before we leave tomorrow evening.

 Sorry we had to cut our Mt. Wilson visit so short,
but we had a fine time there.

Sincerely yours,
Alfred

The Moores returned to Harqua Hala on August 20th. Then, right on schedule, Hugh
Freeman arrived in Wenden on September 1, 1924.

Mt. Harqua Hala
September 3, 1924

Dear Charles:

 I met Mr. Freeman Monday morning, and we got up here
about noon. We are more than pleased with him although
the weather has been so poor ever since he came that I
have not had a chance to try him out much on the work. He
is always pleasant, is good company, and what is most

---

[125] Curiously, neither Moore nor any of the others who lived on Harqua Hala ever mentioned the toilet facilities at the Arizona field station. It is assumed they used an "out house," but none of the photographs show its location.

important, seems full of pep. He is a husky fellow, so we
will not have to run a sanitarium with him around.

     He said, when I asked him how he left Mrs. Freeman,
that she was well, but that she sure hated to see him
leave, since they had not been separated since they were
married. Chella and I talked it over and we think that it
might be best to arrange for her to come up here. There
are very few couples that we would consider this with,
but we feel that they will be better satisfied if she is
up here, and we think we can make out all right, even
though it will be rather crowded. She probably will not
come for a few weeks. I hope that when he gets broken into
the work I can report just as favorably.

                                    Sincerely yours,

                                    Alfred

Now, the Harqua Hala field station was hampered with another difficulty: Santa Fe
closed the Wenden telegraph office. This required a plan to transfer the daily reports
phoned down to Matteson's store, on to Salome via the Santa Fe telephone line at
some cost. Encouraging Abbot to request the railroad to reconsider, Moore wrote, "I
really feel that this matter should be pressed a good deal by the Institution since it is
very likely that the next step will be to close the Wenden depot altogether. This has already been done at Vicksburg, just west of Salome, where they have even removed the
depot building. There has been much fear in Wenden for sometime that the depot will
be taken away from them before long."

With the field station not fully manned through the summer, cloudy skies, and now
with the greater difficulty of getting daily telegraph reports to Washington, there were
great breaks in the continuity of data needed for Clayton's weather forecasting experiments. Moore also lapsed into his "growling" mood, writing to Abbot who was still at
Mt. Wilson.

                              Mt. Harqua Hala
                              October 5, 1924

Dear Charles:

     I was rather surprised at the content of your letter
since you did not favor paying the amount that the Santa
Fe wanted, in a recent letter to me. In my letter to you, I
expressed an opinion that it might be well to wait a while
and to further try to help Wenden get back the telegraph

office. The waiting would cause no great inconvenience to us since it has been too wet to send corrected values.[126] There were six days the latter part of September that we could have telegraphed, but only one day thus far in October, the others being entirely too wet, and too hazy.

We are certainly having some very poor weather for this time of year, there being a great deal of haze, and streakiness. In fact, since August 20th, there have been just two days when the sky was clear, right up to the sun. The more that I see of this haze business, the more pessimistic I become about getting solar constants of any good accuracy. With the thick haze and the sky bright for several degrees around the sun, I think that task is almost as hopeless as with cirrus clouds.[127]

This business certainly does not have a very good effect on a fellow's morale, as they would say in war times. I certainly hate to have to dive into the monumental amount of computing needed to get a new set of curves for Harqua Hala. You have never mentioned the outcome of the campaign for changing the station to Big Pines, where we have a reasonable chance of getting some clear skies. After having seen Big Pines twice, it has required a lot of urging not to get downright discouraged at the clouds and haze and wind we have had here the past several weeks. Without any exaggeration, I think I am safe in saying that on not more than ten days during the three years that I have been at Harqua Hala, have I seen a sky that equaled the two days that I saw at Big Pines.

Another thing is the condition of my eyes, which have bothered me a good deal the past few weeks. This would be the same either for Harqua Hala or Big Pines, and in getting the larger amount of computing done, I might have to have help in Washington, while getting the new arrangement started.

And last, but not least, is the old and often-discussed question of isolation. If this work is to be kept up indefinitely at Harqua Hala, I can see nothing to do but make a change, unless you can work me in some other place. In any event, I hope you can arrange to come out

[126] There was too much moisture in the atmosphere to accurately determine the solar constant.

[127] The solar constant method used the brightness of the sky around the sun as an index of the atmosphere's ability to adsorb solar radiation; good measurements could only be made when the sky appeared clear right up to the sun.

here before going to Washington, so we can better discuss
this and several other matters.

                              Sincerely yours,

                              Alfred

Moore's letters of early October 1924 clearly indicated that, once again, the work at
the Arizona mountain field station was wearing on him. But with the hope of eventually moving the station to California, he continued on.

                              Mt. Harqua Hala
                              October 17, 1924

Dear Charles:

        I suppose the first thing is to congratulate you on
the Senators' victory in the World Series![128] I know it
must have greatly pleased you, and I only wished that you
could have been there to see them do it.

        I have been pretty busy this week, for we have had
several very good days, more like October should be, and
I have taken advantage of them by doing some extra observations, as well as the regular run. In addition, I have
gotten the telescope ready to give it another trial,
which I expect to do tomorrow morning. There is a big
group of spots on the sun, and it ought to be a good time
to try it out.

        Hugh is learning to run bolographs now, in fact, he
ran one of today's set. I think he will soon be able to
observe alone, at least short methods. He expects Mrs.
Freeman to come out next Friday. Chella and I hope to go
to the Canyon a few days soon after the election. This
will give him a chance to keep the thing going alone for
several days. I think I can see some improvement in his
speed the past few days too. This seems to be his greatest
handicap.

        We had some more fried chicken tonight. Last Sunday
we had fried rabbit for a change.

                              Sincerely yours,

                              Alfred

---

[128] Washington defeated New York in game seven, to capture baseball's world championship.

The Moore's friendship with the Matteson's in Wenden was often the best method of breaking up the routine at Harqua Hala. In mid-October Chella stayed a few days with Mrs. Matteson; Alfred accompanied her down the mountain and stayed over one night, joining them for Sunday dinner, before getting back to the work on the mountain.

> Mt. Harqua Hala
> October 21, 1924
>
> Dear Charles:
>
> I am not certain whether this will reach you before you leave California or not, but will send it there anyway.
>
> Enclosed you will find three sun photos. Do you think photos such as these will answer at all? I very much doubt that I can get them much better with the arrangement that we have, for we have to enlarge too much to give very good definition and sharpness and detail. Of course the large spot shows up pretty well, but do you see anything that looks like faculae?[129] I do not feel very much pleased with the result, but I am not a good enough judge of just how the thing should look.
>
> Hugh got along all right at observing alone yesterday. I don't think it will be long before he can handle everything in the regular observing and computing. Then I'll have to break him in on how to repair troubles that may arise.
>
> Our long methods are showing very good agreement with the short method values gotten on the same day. The last two times, one of which was today, they were almost identical, and the other times of late the variation has been very small. This seems to indicate that when we have good skies we get values that are practically the same. On days that are hazy we rarely get anything like such good agreement between the long and short methods.
>
> It seems to me that the new corrections for our station will have to be gotten out before we can telegraph many of the days, even if we had the telegraph, for either the days are too wet or on clear days the functions are too low.

---

[129]Bright patches that form shortly before sunspots.

        I am going to Wenden tomorrow afternoon to bring
Chella up. Mrs. Freeman is due to arrive here Friday
morning.

                              Sincerely yours,

                              Alfred

P.S. I received your letter when I reached Wenden this afternoon. Mr. Matteson and I went up to Salome and saw
the Santa Fe agent there Mr. Hades. He will get proper
authorization and in the meantime, beginning tomorrow
probably, Mr. Matteson will mail our daily reports by
Santa Fe trainmen and Mr. Hades will send the telegram
the same night. As soon as proper authority can be gotten,
he thinks we can temporariily use the Santa Fe dispatch-
ing phone.[130] Then we will have to repair the old phone
line to Salome that Matteson used to use. AFM

Commenting on the photographs of the sun, Abbot replied, "It seems to me that the definition of your telescope is really quite high class. I note quite a lot of detail. There is not only the large spot group, but another one, almost equally as far on the other side of the sun's equator, of very small spots surrounded by faculae, also a considerable showing of faculae along the advancing limb[131]."

        Although Moore hoped that Abbot would stop again in Wenden on his return to Washington, Abbot went directly to the east coast. Mrs. Freeman arrived in Wenden on Friday, October 24th. Moore told Abbot, "She seems a very nice girl, and is quite full of pep, and is very interested in learning about everything." To help make room for the two couples, Alfred and Hugh changed the screen porch into an enclosed room for computing. Not missing an opportunity to plug the proposed California site, Moore told Abbot, "I think this wooden room will give us a pretty good idea on the use of wooden buildings in cold weather, should we move to Big Pines."[132] Indeed, by the end of October Moore was again lobbying for the move to California, finding fault with virtually everything on or about Harqua Hala.

---

[130]This authorization was received and the Smithsonian agreed to pay $30 a year for use of the Santa Fe.phone line.
[131]The edge of the sun's image.
[132]Later, describing the construction of the computing room, Moore said, "I used one inch tongue and groove boards to line the inside, and under these have two thicknesses of black building paper. The floor also has two thicknesses of building paper under it."

Mt. Harqua Hala
October 31, 1924

Dear Mr. Abbot:

I received your letter, written in Kansas, the other day when I went to town to start arrangements for the phone to Salome. I have ordered the equipment necessary, and will probably get it going the coming week.

Early yesterday morning Chella was awakened with a sever pain in the region of the appendix, though not as acute as it was last year. I got the ice bottle, and put some ice in it, and she remained in bed all day, and did not eat solid food. She felt better in the afternoon, and today was up, but felt weak. We certainly hope she will never have a reoccurrence of the siege she had last year.

We have been suspicious that the Ellison spring water is not having a very good effect on the kidneys. Chella always boils the drinking water, but of course this only kills the "animals" not affecting the chemicals that the water contains in solution. Under separate cover I am sending a small bottle of the water as it comes from the spring, to have an analysis made of it.[133]

As to Hugh, I am still "on the fence" as to his suitability to run the Chilean station. He does what he is told to do as well as he can, but I am awfully much afraid that he is very much lacking in initiative, which is pretty essential for taking charge of the station down there. I will keep you posted on his progress, and if you think best, possibly it might not be amiss for you to write him a letter to see if it will wake him up a little. It seems to Chella and me that his wife has to keep prodding him along a good deal, for she seems to have a lot of pep, but of course she is not the one who is to be in charge and keep the apparatus in order down there.

Sincerely yours,

Alfred

---

[133]Later, Moore sent, with a little concern, a larger sample: "Four quart bottles packed in saw dust. Perhaps they might be taken for bootleg whisky."

Chapter 26

Pushing for California

During the final two months of 1924 operations at Harqua Hala again fell into the routine of slight progress mixed with new projects and solving one problem after another. With each problem, Alfred Moore could only think of the possibility of moving to Table Mountain in California.

> Mt. Harqua Hala
> November 9, 1924
>
> Dear Mr. Abbot:
>
> I have been so busy with the Salome phone and the new computing room, besides the regular observing and computing, that I haven't had time to try the experiments on the telescope
>
> I got the phone to Salome working last Tuesday. I went to Wenden early Monday morning, stayed with the Mattesons that night and finished it Tuesday afternoon. I had Mr. Cerf help me on it the two days. I received a letter from Mr. Bassett of the Santa Fe a few days ago, asking to let him know when it was finished, so that a regular three party agreement could be drawn up. [134]
>
> Chella and I are going to start tomorrow on a trip of a few days to the Grand Canyon. She has never been there. It will also give Hugh a chance to see how he can get along keeping things going alone.
>
> We were certainly greatly pleased with the report that you got from the Weather Bureau as regards the precipitation on Table Mountain, [135] as compared with Mt. Wilson. I am more convinced every day of the superiority

---

[134] Eventually Santa Fe decided to charge the nominal rental of $1 per year for the use of their poles from Wenden to Salome.

[135] Data provided by the Weather Bureau showed that several stations within ten miles of Table Mountain reported, "Precipitation there is much less than at Mt. Wilson."

of Table Mountain over Harqua Hala from practically
every point of view.

                              Sincerely yours,
                              Alfred

The Grand Canyon trip was a good break for the Moore's, and seemingly as good for
Hugh Freeman.

                              Wenden
                              November 16, 1924

Dear Charles:
        Chella and I returned from our trip to the Grand
Canyon last evening. We had a fine time. It was somewhat cool but not stormy. The air was very clear and the
sun shone brightly the two days that we were there. Chella
didn't feel equal to taking the mule-back trips into the
Canyon, but we took an auto trip along the rim and several hikes. I called up Hugh when we got back. He said everything was going OK on the mountain.
                              Sincerely yours,
                              Alfred

Despite Freeman's success in running the Arizona station alone, Moore still doubted
the new assistant's suitability. He wrote to Abbot, "Although he is still rather slow, he
is showing some improvement in his work. He reads the pyrheliometer better than he
did, but not extra well yet. There are some things outside of the work proper that cause
me still to wonder if they are the right ones to send down to take charge of the Chile
station. It is hard to explain every thing in letters. I have written three letters along this
line lately and torn them up." Once again there seemed to be personality conflict eating at Alfred Moore.

                              Mt. Harqua Hala
                              November 24, 1924

Dear Mr. Abbot:
        You said when you were here that nearly every letter
from Chile and Harqua Hala had some bad news in it.

Tonight Mr. Ellison called me up on the phone and said that his spring is getting so low that he thought it would be necessary for me to water George up here, since he drinks so much water. We only have about 350 gallons on hand in the cistern, so it will be necessary for Hugh and me to take George down to the spring on the trail. With the Mexican watering ten head of burros at that spring, I doubt if it will hold out very long unless we get some rain or snow soon. If Ellison's spring and the trail spring both go dry, there will be no water nearer than Wenden. With practically no snow last winter, if we get no rain or snow soon, the springs will be pretty apt to all go dry.

I intend to make some more experiments with the telescope unless I have to economize on the water so much that I cannot develop the solar plates and prints.

I wrote you something in regard to not being sure about Hugh. With his three months probation period nearly over, it all causes me quite a bit of worry. I acquiesced in Hugh's wish to have his wife here with him, but I cannot conceal the fact that I have been very much disappointed in Hugh ever since she has been up here. He has been glum and at times rather sulky and does not seem to take the same interest in the work that he did before she came. He is the "spooniest" fellow that I ever saw, and I must say that we get rather tired of this hugging her and petting her before us at about every opportunity. She is only a girl of 19, but he is 28 and ought to have sense enough to make sure of a job to support her, I'd think.

Another thing that makes me dubious is the way she handles all the financial affairs. When his paycheck comes she opens the letter, tells him to sign the check and sends it off to her mother. When he came here they were practically broke, having lived with their relatives ever since they were married. Yet she is planning to give him a $60 Hamilton watch for Christmas.

Perhaps it will be necessary to send them down there, and if you so decide I'll do all in my power to get him in shape to make good at it. I really don't know just how much he knows about the work. Ruth told Chella that Hugh always understood more than he appeared to. The idea

struck me that it might be well to spring a written
examination on him, to see if he has absorbed anything
from the books he has been supposed to be studying.

                              Sincerely yours,

                              Alfred

Finally, Moore got the hoped for positive indication from Abbot about Table Mountain. Abbot wrote, "I saw Mr. Roebling. He takes a great interest in the project of removal, but he considers it very desirable to have some observations made at Table Mountain before committing ourselves in that direction, and he has made an appropriation of $250 to be placed in your hands for that purpose. Our idea is that you should go up there several times during this winter and stay a day or two, so as to see how formidable that cold and snow will be for living. Also, you should arrange with some local man for the measurement of precipitation and especially for observing regularly the cloudiness."

Part of the reasoning behind the move to California and getting a station located under better skies came from continued favorable reports from Clayton, this time tying his forecasts into visual observations of the sun's surface. Abbot reported, "He has made eye observations on nearly every day since April and has been forwarding forecasts of what the solar constant will be five days in advance to us since June. I have reduced these forecasts and find that he is hitting it off pretty well. I spoke to Mr. Clayton and showed him the photographs which you sent lately. He says it would be just as satisfactory if the photographs were on a smaller scale.[136] Clayton has made great strides in the discussion of the effect of solar variation on weather conditions of the United States and Canada, and is gathering his material for a publication by the Smithsonian Institution which doubtless will go forward in a few months, and which I think, will be epoch making."

                              Mt. Harqua Hala
                              December 1, 1924

Dear Mr. Abbot:
     I am pleased to hear that Mr. Clayton is getting
along well with the weather forecasting data, and hope
that we may improve the accuracy of our solar values until he is even more successful.
     I wrote to Mr. Wadsworth the superintendent of the
Los Angeles County Park, nearly two weeks ago, but as yet
have heard nothing from him. I asked him if there is any

---

[136]Moore had finally refined the photographic technique with the telescope to produce a 10 mm solar image printing it on what he called a soft grade paper. Now he planned to make daily images of the sun when possible.

place up near Table Mountain where I could arrange to
stay over night, a few times this winter. Also if he could
recommend someone up there who we might arrange with to
keep tab on the weather for a few months. Possibly he is
away, or possibly he has not had time to write, as he is
doubtless a pretty busy man. He seemed so very cordial
when I met him up there last summer that I cannot think
there is any hitch in the proceedings as far as he is
concerned.

I have looked at the map of the region that I have up
here, and see that there are two other possible locations
not far away where we might find conditions favorable.
One is over 7250 feet, and about two miles east of Table
Mountain. The other is about two miles northwest, and
while the altitude is a little less (6680 ft), it is
nearer the desert, and is to one side of the draw over the
ridge to the south from the San Gabriel Canyon. I know it
is Edgar's idea that before definitely locating a site
for a permanent station, we should pretty thoroughly go
over the region, and try if possible to get the very best.
It would be my idea that if Edgar can go there with me for
a day, that we leave Los Angeles very early so as to have
the full day, and hike all over the region around Table
Mountain, to see where the very best location can be
found. I would look for sky conditions, accessibility,
water nearby and ease of making a road to the place from
the main road.

We have had considerable cloudiness and rather poor
skies of late, but no rain. We are taking George down the
trail to the spring every second day. We bring up enough
water on him to last the intervening day, so as not to
have him drinking our cistern supply.

Mr. Ellison is blasting a shaft back of his water
tunnel to see if he can increase the flow of his spring.
It has been very cloudy all day today with the bolograph
very low, so I am hoping that we may get some rain or snow
soon to bolster up the water supply.

As I rather expected he would, the Santa Fe
electrician objected to our using their cable crossing
over the spur track at Salome, so I went up to Salome to
fix it. I got a man in Wenden who does line work to do the

climbing of the poles. It only took about two hours to change it over.

A skunk got into the chicken house the other night. Chella heard a hen cackle, and I got my revolver and a flashlight and started out to investigate. I found the hen on the floor with the skunk hanging onto her. I shot twice and missed. The shots did not scare him in the least for which I was thankful. The third shot killed him. He had not hurt the hen. This is the first skunk of this variety that I have seen up here. They are small and spotted, while the other kind are striped.

The Freemans are going to Phoenix next Sunday morning to be gone until Thursday. They want to do some Christmas shopping before Chella and I go to California.

Sincerely yours,
Alfred

Finally, Moore heard back from Wadsworth at Table Mountain. He told Moore, "Am very glad you are still considering this site. I will be very glad to keep the data you wish as I am here the year around. I have made arrangements with the Wrights Ranch to take care of you on the 20th of December. We have had a very clear fall with only one small storm and very mild temperatures." Moore wrote to Abbot, "This all looks pretty good for a starter, doesn't it."

With such good news, Moore added a post script on his letter to Abbot. "Hugh has been acting more agreeable the last week or so. He seems to be showing improvement in his work too. If things keep on as they are now I think it will probably be best to keep him." But Abbot had already sent written tests to both Hugh and Ruth Freeman.

Wenden
December 16, 1924

Dear Mr. Abbot:
I am leaving tonight for Los Angeles. Enclosed in separate sealed envelopes you will find Mr. and Mrs. Freeman's answers to the examination questions. As requested I gave them the examination in separate rooms,

and they sealed their answers in the envelopes on completion. I think your plan was a very good one.

The Santa Fe has closed the Wenden depot, altogether. They notified the town yesterday morning that it would be closed last night. Not much notice, I'll say.

Sincerely yours,

Alfred

This time the Moores boarded the train to Los Angeles at the Salome depot.

Chapter 27

Good-by Harqua Hala

Certainly no one in Washington expected that Alfred Moore would find anything wrong with Table Mountain in California; he had been lobbying to move there from Harqua Hala for over three years. Indeed, Moore returned to Arizona with a good report on all aspects of the new location. Everything was finally falling into place as he had wished. Once again Abbot's field stations were on the verge of major changes.

SMITHSONIAN INSTITUTION
Washington U.S.A.

December 24, 1924

Dear Alfred:

    I looked over the examination papers of the Freemans and was very much pleased indeed. Mrs. Freeman shows a fine spirit in connection with the work, and he also is strong for it and shows that he has learned a very great deal about the adjustments of the apparatus. I am glad that you feel disposed, now, to recommend sending them. I feel a great deal of confidence that things will go just as well as they can make them after they go to Chile.

    Mr. Aldrich seems to be somewhat depressed in mind and health since his family returned to the United States, and he intimates that he would like to be relieved somewhat earlier than we had proposed. Will you talk it over with the Freemans and let me know at once what would be the earliest date on which they would be available to start for Chile to relieve Mr. Aldrich? Will you wish to have steps taken to get a successor to Mr. Freeman as soon as possible, or would you prefer to wait a while.

               Very truly yours,

               C. G. Abbot

Immediately, the Freemans made plans to leave Harqua Hala and transfer to Chile after a brief stay at their home in California; they left the mountain around January 15, 1925. And Abbot hired E. E. Smith to replace Hugh Freeman at the Arizona site; Smith arrived on the mountain February 9th.[137] While Moore and Smith kept the Harqua Hala station running, Moore was preoccupied with plans for Table Mountain.[138]

The end of 1924 also brought some preliminary conclusions from Clayton about his efforts to forecast the weather in New York City from the measurements made in Arizona and Chile between December 1923 and November 1924. On December 18, 1924, he provided a lengthy report to Abbot, saying, "The forecasts were based on plots of the solar radiation values furnished by you, together with plots of the observed maximum temperatures for the same day at Williston, North Dakota, Chicago, and New York. Forecasts of the departure of the temperature from the mean were made Friday for the week beginning the following Sunday. For 31 weeks when temperatures above normal were forecasted the temperature averaged 0.9 degrees above normal, and for 20 weeks when temperatures below normal were forecasted the temperature averaged 1.8 degrees below normal."

Almost indecipherably, Clayton continued, "These forecasts were based mainly on the view that with low mean values of solar radiation the mean temperature tends to be above normal in the eastern states in winter and below in summer, but partly also on the prevailing conditions. The correlations are all plus, but so small in the summer half-year that they can hardly be called successful. In the winter half-year the correlation values were nearly five times the probable error for the three days in advance, nearly three times as large for four days, and only slightly larger for five days. The most successful forecasts were made in mid-winter, when the correlations for 62 days rose as high as 0.44 for three days in advance. The least successful were in mid-summer."

Clayton summarized to Abbot, "These results are not so favorable as I hoped they might be when I began, but it seems to me they are encouraging of future possibilities when the solar observations are more continuous and more accurate. These are, I think, the first definite qualitative forecasts ever made for more than one day in advance whose accuracy was definitely ascertained to be better than chance guessing."

While Abbot pointed out some errors in Clayton's data and reasoning, his interpretation resulted in a more positive conclusion.

---

[137]There are no details in the Smithsonian Archives on Smith, his qualifications or his home town.
[138]Beginning in 1925, there was a great break in the letters to and from Harqua Hala. Most likely Moore was often away from the mountain making arrangements for the new station in California.

SMITHSONIAN INSTITUTION
Washington U.S.A.

January 31, 1924

Dear Mr. Clayton:

I am returning herewith your data on the verification of forecasts and our own which is practically independent of it. I checked your sheet of mean monthly maximum temperatures and then found that the observed departures which you took from the maps differed greatly from these given in Climatological Data. From this point our reductions diverge. We recomputed the verifications for the three-day and four-day forecasts and, as you see, results agree essentially with yours in proving that you have had prevision of the event. I have not gone over them carefully enough perhaps, to express an opinion, but it seems to me that reductions with the Climatological Data make a better case for you than your own with the erroneous map data.

I worked out the verifications of the weekly and monthly forecasts, and have introduced some modifications in pencil on your sheets. My results show a decidedly better case for you than your own. I have also worked up the verification of solar predictions and have added several sheets from other angles. For example, I find that the march of the observed solar values when compared to your predicted values of five days in advance indicates a very decided prevision on your part.

On the whole, therefore, I find a clear case of prevision of temperatures in New York on your part three and four days in advance, and seeing that the results agree substantially with yours I have no doubt that yours are approximately true. I find that you have distinct prevision of the march of the solar constant values five days in advance.

Very truly yours,

C. G. Abbot

With these conclusions, and more support from Roebling, Abbot was determined to continue his pursuit of a useful solar constant method, the vision he had inherited from Samuel Langley back in the early 1900s. But now data would come from Chile and the new United States based field station on Table Mountain. The Harqua Hala field station was abandoned the summer of 1925.[139] In late spring, Abbot wrote to Bunker in Wenden, "Whatever we do not take away will doubtless revert to the people of Wenden who can make their own arrangements in regard to it."

The ultimate destiny of the Smithsonian's effort to equate daily solar constant measurements to weather forecasting should have been apparent by late 1925, after Abbot attended a symposium on climate and weather in England.

On the Mediterranean
November 24, 1925

Dear Mr. Roebling and Mr. Clayton:

I have had time to meditate on rather disturbing experiences in England. I talked there with the foremost meteorologists and physicists. It appears that until recently they were little disposed to admit the day to day variability of the sun, though convinced of longer period changes. Some of them now admit the probability of day to day ones also. They express profound confidence and admiration for the solar radiation measurements, and great satisfaction in the prospect of a new station. Thus, as far as my work is concerned, they are in a very receptive mood.

But I regret to report quite the contrary regarding Mr. Clayton's. I had a tremendous discussion with two of the most eminent meteorologists who seemed to be representing the attitude of all the best ones. I will not mention names, for I feel sure they are practically all on one mind about it.

They think Mr. Clayton's researches are abundantly worthwhile, but they are far from convinced that he has proved any valuable connection between weather and solar variation as yet. Contrary to Marvin's[140] attitude, they are intensely interested and hopeful. They have studied Mr. Clayton's publications with great care. But they do not believe his conclusions, though accepting without questions the accuracy of his figures. As one expressed it, "I believe if Mr. Clayton had taken, instead of high

---

[139] Because fewer letters where written from Harqua Hala in 1925, the exact date of departure is unknown. Likely it took several months for Moore and Smith to transfer all the equipment.
[140] Chief of the U.S. Weather Bureau.

and low groups of solar constant values, dates of birthdays of emperors in one group and dates of birthdays of
presidents in another, he would have gotten out a similar
set of temperature relations for the succeeding ten days
march. I shall not believe his curves have any meteorological significance until I see them approximately du-
plicated by similar curves covering independent periods
of time."

When I pointed out that there was a lot of work required to do that, they replied that with their little
means they could not do it themselves. If Mr. Clayton
wants them to believe, they say, it is up to him. They
would like to believe, but must have more proof.

They are entirely unconvinced by the forecasting
for Buenos Aires and New York. They think as good could be
made without the sun, but admit they have not proved
that. They will be entirely unconvinced by any commercial success. "What," say they, "does public approval
amount to?"

In other words, if we are to get that scientific approval indispensable to make our work live after us, we
cannot stop where we are. Two more years of scientific
study by Clayton, with fullest consultations, before
publishing, with eminent foreign meteorologists, seem
to me absolutely necessary. It means the expenditure of
$15,000 to $20,000. With that, our position would be won.
Without it, I fear we may go down to oblivion.

Very sincerely yours,

C. G. Abbot

In the 1925 annual report of the Smithsonian Institution, Abbot outlined the work that
remained. He said, "The investigations hitherto made having indicated that a higher
degree of accuracy in our solar measurements is needed to supply proper data for forecasting purposes, we shall be obliged to regard sources of error which formerly we
supposed would always be negligible. This has led to the designing and construction
of new apparatus for use in pyrheliometry, which eliminates the employment of the observer's watch altogether. It has also required the investigation of the infra-red and ultraviolet portions of the solar spectrum, beyond the usual limits of our daily spectrum
observations. Still more important, it has led to a complete revision of the methods of
measuring and reducing solar energy spectra."[141]

[141]*Annual Report of the Board of Regents of The Smithsonian Institution, 1925,* pp. 103-104.

Abbot added a postscript on the close of his Arizona field station, seemingly taking his remarks right from the mouth of Alfred Moore. He wrote, "The station at Mount Harqua Hala, Arizona, first occupied in 1920, proves to be too far to the east, so that the summer months there are unsuitable for observing because of the severe thunderstorms of Arizona. Very few days of June, July and August have been suitable for our exacting work, and even some of the spring months have been marred by long-continued haziness. Had weather conditions there been first-rate, the observers would gladly have suffered the excessive isolation of the place, which is almost wholly cut off from relaxations, but to make such a sacrifice fruitlessly is indeed very depressing."[142]

Once again Dr. Charles Greeley Abbot began with the belief that his new field station, this time in California, would finally help him achieve the scientific goal he sought. He reported, "Investigations have been made which have fixed on a better site, both as regards weather conditions and comfort. This is chosen on Table Mountain, within the bound of the Los Angeles County Park, about 30 miles northeast[143] of Mount Wilson. Lying on the edge of the Mojave Desert, at 7500 feet elevation, weather observations indicate very decided improvement over Harqua Hala for our purpose. Add to this the convenience of access and pleasant surroundings, and we have combined there great advantages. Mr. John Roebling has added to his already great gifts sufficient means to enable necessary buildings to be erected on Table Mountain, and to remove the observing outfit thence from Harqua Hala. The supervisors of the Los Angeles County Park have cordially assisted in the transfer, giving rights of occupancy, and extending the auto road quite to the door of the proposed observatory, without expense to the Smithsonian Institution. It is expected to occupy Table Mountain beginning about October 1, 1925. Mr. Moore's energetic efforts in the preliminary arrangements and the preparation of buildings deserve high praise."[144]

---

[142]*Ibid.*, pp. 104.

[143]The Table Mountain site was actually southeast of Mt. Wilson in what is today the Angeles National Forest. The facilities built for solar constant measurement back in 1925 no longer stand, having been replaced by the modern Table Mountain Observatory operated by the Jet Propulsion Laboratory of California Institute of Technology.

[144]*Annual Report, 1925*, p. 105.

Chapter 28

Epilogue

Despite the tentative success at Harqua Hala and the looming questions of scientific validity, in 1925 the APO's solar constant program was just beginning 30 more years of work. The new station at Table Mountain remained in operation until 1962, the station in Chile until 1955. In addition, there were several attempts to establish a third station: Mount Brukkaros near Keetmanshoop, South West Africa from December 1926 to June 1932;[145] Mount Saint Katherine in the Sinai, Egypt from January 1934 to November 1937; Burro Mountain near Tyrone, New Mexico from January 1939 to February 1946; and Miami, Florida from May 1947 to August 1949.

Today, remains of the Harqua Hala field station in Arizona are the only vestige of this lengthy, worldwide search for the solar constant and attempt to predict weather; it is the only APO solar constant field station still standing. Indeed, the building is a valuable historic site on the National Register of Historic Places. In 1979 the Bureau of Land Management documented the condition of the building and contracted an architect to stabilize the remains of the Harqua Hala field station. Considering the adobe construction and the early problems with stability, it is amazing that the structure survived the elements for over 50 years before it was protected as a reminder of the work of Dr.Charles Abbot and others.

After closing his Harqua Hala field station, Charles Abbot continued on as the director of the Astrophysical Observatory and solar constant program. In addition he was elected the fifth secretary of the Smithsonian Institution in 1928. He served both these roles until he retired in 1944 at the age of 72. However, even after retirement, Abbot maintained an office at the Smithsonian and continued to pursue a conclusion to his lifetime of solar constant work. Writing to Fred Greeley in later years, he said, "A number of people have become interested in me because I have an office on the 11th

---

[145]Financed by The National Geographic Society.

floor of the 150 foot tower of the Smithsonian and because I'm approaching 95 and still working." Abbot never gave up the vision of Samuel Langley.

November 27, 1965

Dear Fred and Olive,

On the day before Thanksgiving I finished the draught of text, figure and table that will prove the sun's variation, and the response of precipitation in identical periods, to the family of harmonics exactly related to 273 months. The expert meteorologists cannot longer deny it if, as I hope, the Smithsonian will have the finished paper within two weeks, and publish it this winter. Mrs. Roebling and Mrs. Aldrich will be glad to know that their husbands' life-long trust in us is now justified. I am advising you and the Alfred Moores, as the only ones of the team now living, who gave their full life time work to the research.

We are well, busy and happy here. Best wishes!

Charles G. Abbot.

In his later years, Abbot was driven by the thought that he needed to salvage some lasting scientific results from his research; from the mid-1960s he pursued one final publication, keeping Fred Greeley informed. In one letter he said, "I think the meteorologists will be obliged at last to admit that our work has discovered means to forecast precipitation and temperature many years in advance with useful accuracy."

In another letter to Greeley, Abbot showed that his belief in the potential of his work never wavered in his life time. He wrote, "Meteorologists are loath to accept these findings because they cannot understand from theory how changes in solar radiation so small in percentage can affect weather appreciably. I tell those who address me that way that if the sun annoys them they can forget him altogether. For it makes no difference how the 20 periodic weather changes over 22 years were discovered. They exist! This, I think, is the greatest discovery for metrology made in my time. It will enable maps of future weather to be made covering the whole U.S. From such maps farmers and others will be greatly benefited. This results crowns our sacrificial lives in deserts and distant lands. Fortunately the ruin of atmospheric conditions by atom blasts did not occur until we had 30 years of day-to-day solar constant observing. The future forecast maps may be made with no more solar observing at all. Yet, as not over one-half of the days of those 30 years gave satisfactory solar constants, we would like very much to go on if suitable locations can be found. *If we had enough first rate solar stations to give good solar constants every day, meteorologists could give detailed day-to-day forecasts 10 days in advance."*[146]

Abbot published his final paper in the December 1966 issue of the *Proceedings of the National Academy of Sciences.*[147] Seemingly the paper was accepted more as a tribute to Abbot's lifetime effort than to the scientific significance of his work. Dr. Charles Greeley Abbot died in 1973 at 101 years.

Reports in scientific literature show that observers at the various worldwide APO sites made 37,353 solar constant measurements through 1954; these data were used to support Charles Abbot's conclusion that he was measuring a significant variation in the energy that the sun sent earthward. Today, however, Abbot's effort is history not science. Since 1980, modern satellite observations, beginning with the Solar Maximum Mission spacecraft, have detected no variability in solar radiation greater than 0.2%.

Even before scientists obtained data from satellites, Douglas V. Hoyt of the National Oceanic and Atmospheric Administration in Boulder, Colorado, performed a rigorous mathematical evaluation of the 37,353 measurements and came to a dramatically different conclusion than Abbot. Using Abbot's data, Hoyt failed to detect any change in the solar constant greater than a few tenths of a percent. Hoyt surmised, "Perhaps the major failing of the APO solar constant program was the fact that it reached numerous incorrect conclusions about the behavior of the sun. There are some 200 publications, predominantly by Abbot, purporting to show that the sun is variable and that these variations influence weather and climate on earth." Hoyt concluded that although researchers external to the APO criticized Abbot's conclusions, no one within the APO made a detailed critical analysis prior to any publication. "The dedication of the observers and staff not withstanding, because of this lack of critical judgment, most of the publications present conclusions that are simply wrong," reported Hoyt.[148]

Hoyt's analysis and our state-of-the-art knowledge today are certainly not conclusions that Dr. Charles Abbot's efforts were in vain, rather an indication that technology of his day could not fully support his vision. Through the days of the Harqua Hala field station, and beyond, science had not yet been blessed with the array of electronic instrumentation that exists today, not even blessed with the rigors of modern statistical analysis manually calculated. In addition, with our exposure to the

[146] Emphasis has been added by the author; this statement in the 1960s sounds just like Abbot's argument for establishing the Harqua Hala field station back in 1920.

[147] C.G. Abbot, "Solar Variation, A Weather Element," *Proceedings of the National Academy of Sciences*, December 1966, Vol. 56, No. 6, pp. 1627-1634 .

[148] D.V. Hoyt, "The Smithsonian Astrophysical Observatory Solar Constant Program," *Reviews of Geophysics and Space Physics*, Vol. 17, No. 3, May 1979, pp. 427-458.

sophistication of science today and its direct influence over our lives, we tend to lose sight of how far and fast scientific capabilities have come, particularly our understanding of earth's environment, in a relatively short period. Indeed, sometimes we tend to conclude that all scientific work is practially fruitful; in reality, however, many scientists spend their lifetimes providing the rudimentary but nonconclusive foundations that others eventually stand on. Also, let's not forget that even with an accurate measure of the solar constant, scientists are still trying to predict weather and understand our climate in a way that will be beneficial to mankind. The work of Dr. Charles Abbot in the 1920s, and many before him, was the beginning of work that continues.

Today, the story of the Harqua Hala field station is a five-year snapshot of the Smithsonian's effort to find the solar constant as well as a snapshot of how scientific field work was done in the 1920s. The story provides a glimpse of life in the desert West and Arizona, which was just out of being a territory, contrasted to more progressive California. Finally, this story is a proper tribute to the individuals who served and helped on Harqua Hala Mountain from 1920 through 1925.

Loyal Aldrich was always at Abbot's side. When Abbot retired in 1944, Aldrich became director of the APO until he retired in 1955, when the directorship passed to Fred Whipple and the direction of the observatory changed from solar research to space. Aldrich died in 1969.

Alfred Moore served as field station director at Table Mountain until March 1931, again from 1933 to 1936, and finally from 1945 to September 1948, when he retired from the APO. Moore also worked again in Chile from 1941 to 1943 and was instrumental in starting and directing the sites in Egypt and New Mexico. Chella Moore began working with her husband, as a station assistant, in 1943. Letters between Abbot and Fred Greeley showed that the Moores were living in a rest home in San Bernadino, California, in 1966. The dates of their deaths are uncertain.

Fred Greeley also made a career with the APO and served at all the field stations except New Mexico; he served in Chile until 1926, again from 1942 through 1946 and finally from 1951 through 1955 when the station was closed. He served in South West Africa from 1926 through 1929, at Table Mountain from 1930 through 1933, 1936 through 1941, 1948 through 1951, and 1955 through 1956, in Egypt from 1933 through 1936, and in Miami from 1947 through 1948. His duties from 1943 where as station director. Greeley retired from the APO in December 1956 with over 36 years of service. Then he lived in Redlands and Laguna Hills, California until his death in

1980, at 84 years. During his first tour at Table Mountain he met and married, in Riverside, California, Olive Adelia Troup.[149]

Hugh Freeman served at Mount Montezuma in Chile, transferred several times between Chile and Table Mountain, and then left the APO in 1941.

No records have been found of Paul Greeley's movie career. He died in March 1967 while being cared for by his brother Fred, in Redlands.

It is uncertain what became of William Ellison and the several residents of Wenden who befriended the Harqua Hala field station observers back in the 1920s.

---

[149] Olive was born in Maxwell Iowa, June 10, 1901, and died in Laguna Hills, Calif. in 1982.

Chapter 29

Period Photographs

"I reached here Monday afternoon June 21 at about four o'clock. There are not more than thirty houses in Wenden and three general stores. The mountain is a good way from Wenden, but can be reached by auto in about an hour or less." -- Charles Abbot writing to Smithsonian Secretary Charles Walcott on June 24, 1920 (page 10). Photograph is annotated, "Business section of Wenden, arrow indicates position of observatory and "x" the saddle [where the trail ascends]. This is Harqua Hala. Does it look 15 miles away?" (Smithsonian Institution Photo)

"A week ago Monday I went down leaving at 2 p.m. and got back at 11 a.m. on Wednesday, having in the intervening 45 hours visited our station on the Harqua Hala and taken there the picture I enclose. Now we are beginning to pack up for Arizona. Probably we shall be there by Sept. 20." -- Charles Abbot writing from Mt. Wilson, California, to Washington, D.C. (page 15). Photograph shows the almost completed Harqua Hala field station on about August 26, 1920. (Smithsonian Institution Photo)

"Our equipment is all up today and in fine shape. It has been a dangerous job but fortunately there were no accidents, though one close escape. The work takes much out of the animals and is a nerve racking job for the men." – Charles Abbot writing to Smithsonian Institution on September 30, 1920 (page 17). In the photograph, Charles Abbot adjusts the load on a pack mule carrying the coelostat, while Wenden builder, Tom Banks, waits on horseback. (Smithsonian Institution Photo)

Charles Abbot's "camp rustler," Fred Greeley, was a valuable addition to the field station. Abbot told Smithsonian executives (page 19), "Greeley is getting better every day. He observes with the pyrheliometer about as well as I can and takes hold of plotting observations and reading off from plots. He is perfection as a companion in this isolated place." Photograph shows Fred Greeley (right) and Abbot's assistant, Loyal Aldrich, in late February 1921. (Smithsonian Institution Photo)

On Harqua Hala, the observers aimed a variety of instruments toward the sun: they had a theodolite for measuring the sun's altitude above the horizon, and two silver-disk pyrheliometers and a pyranometer for measuring the energy of the sun. Keg Greeley told his mother (page 26), "Everything is timed right on the second." Photograph shows the solar observing equipment readied for an observing session at the Harqua Hala field station. (Smithsonian Institution Photo)

Early in December 1920, the four month old Harqua Hala field station began showing serious structural problems. Abbot wrote to Secretary Walcott (page 33), "Building showing a fault in wall. Going up today to see what can be done to repair building. Devil appears to have claimed everything. Have to exorcise him." Photograph shows damaged south wall with tie rod braces that were used to pull wall straight again; Keg Greeley, on ladder, continues with the constant repair work. (Smithsonian Institution Photo)

By January 1921, Charles Abbot left his Arizona field station in the hands of his assistants. He reported to Secretary Walcott (page 36), "I am leaving in a blaze of glory. We have observed thus far on 11 days in January. We caught 150 gallons of water, took fine bathes and washed our hair in the rain water. The building stood the rain and furious wind. I've found an absolute cure for chilblains. I shall bring a photograph of the patient." The photograph shows that he wrapped his feet in wool socks and canvas. (Smithsonian Institution Photo)

William Ellison's presence on Harqua Hala was invaluable to the field station observers. Writing in February 1921, Aldrich told Abbot (page 42), "Every few days we take our empty water cans down to Ellison's in the evening. He tells us yarns about hunting, mining. We always get something - some chocolate cake, a side of venison , some oyster plant from his garden, sour dough starter for griddle cakes, etc. I don't know what we'd do without Ellison. He is the leaven that lightens our stay here ." The photograph shows Ellison's mining camp on Harqua Hala Mountain. (Smithsonian Institution Photo)

Chella Moore arrived at Harqua Hala May 20, 1921, riding up the trail the first time on one of miner Ellison's mules. By letter, Alfred told Abbot (page 64), "I am glad to report that Chella finds this place much more livable than she anticipated." For the next few years, however, Alfred's negative opinions of the place were constantly at the forefront of his letters to Washington. Photograph shows Chella Moore standing by William Ellison's garden on Harqua Hala. (Smithsonian Institution Photo)

Isolation on remote Harqua Hala Mountain was a constant problem for the observers; Alfred Moore added several facilities for their entertainment. He wrote to Abbot (page 83), "I don't know whether I wrote you about the croquet set or not. We have leveled off a place between the house and the peak, where we get a lot of enjoyment out of it every evening after supper." As the photograph shows, this was a croquet court without grass on the dry mountain top. (Smithsonian Institution Photo)

When Alfred Moore arrived at the Harqua Hala field station, he brought a Ford truck from Los Angeles and built a garage at the foot of the trail; this helped the observers get to Wenden. About the garage, Moore wrote to Abbot (page 63), "We will have a carpenter from Wenden help us, and I think we will get it up in two days. It will be of corrugated iron, as this will be more thief and fire proof." The photograph shows the Moore's at the garage after it was completed. (Smithsonian Institution Photo)

Alfred Moore tried in vain to establish a wireless radio-telephone link from the top of Harqua Hala Mountain to Wenden. As it turned out, the equipment he ordered from Los Angeles was faulty. However, he did manage to salvage the receiver and set it up so the observers, for their entertainment, could listen to broadcasts from across the country. Erecting the necessary aerials was a difficult task. He wrote to Abbot (page 82), "We are now working on the aerials, and I wish we had them up, for it is no fun getting them thirty-five feet above the ground." The photograph shows the task in progress. (Smithsonian Institution Photo)

In June 1921 Charles Abbot and his wife Lillian visited the Harqua Hala field station on their way to Mt. Wilson in California. Moore wrote to Abbot (page 114), "We hope to see you up here soon and we do hope you can bring Mrs. Abbot with you. Chella seems so anxious for her to come, and for her sake too, I hope she will come with you. Chella is writing her by this mail." The photograph shows, left to right, Lillian Abbot, Chella Moore, Alfred Moore and Fred Greeley, on about June 18, 1922. (Smithsonian Institution Photo)

Occasional visitors to the mountain field station included surveyors, sheep herders and cattlemen looking for water, and various residents from Wenden and other nearby towns. On one occasion, Moore wrote to Abbot (page 126), "Mr. Ellison is still dickering [over selling his claims] with Mr. Stokes, the cow man of Aguila. While we were away, eleven people from Aguila came up and camped for about two weeks down near Mr. Ellison's." The photograph shows the eleven campers from Aguila. (Smithsonian Institution Photo)

Alfred Moore purchased a horse in Wenden to help the observers ascend the trail to the mountain top. Initially, Ellison didn't care for horses because he thought they were difficult to handle on the trail. But his attitude changed. Moore told Abbot (page 137), "We have built a small horse shed down below the garden. We will also have to build a similar structure down at Mr. Ellison's for George spends a good deal of his time down there." That's Ellison and George in the photograph. (Smithsonian Institution Photo)

Although the Harqua Hala station's primary instruments were not telescopes, Alfred Moore did try to set up a six-inch refracting telescope to photograph the sun daily and record sunspots. In June 1924 he reported to Abbot (page 201), "I have rigged up a good camera for the telescope and made it very rigid. But thus far I have not been able to get a very satisfactory solar photograph." Eventually, Moore achieved marginal results. Shown is the makeshift telescope. (Smithsonian Institution Photo)

The Harqua Hala field station required constant repair. In addition, Alfred Moore was the consummate planner and builder, constantly adding porches, storage space and other enhancements. This photograph taken circa June 1924 shows the building with its west facing porch, the croquet court, radio aerial, telescope and general surroundings. (Smithsonian Institution Photo)

The Harqua Hala field station with all of its enhancements and facilities, in the latter half of 1924 at the height of its development. This station was closed the year following this photograph. Today, it is only a shell of its stature in 1924. (Smithsonian Institution Photo)